OECD Insurance Statistics 2019

2011-2018

OECD
BETTER POLICIES FOR BETTER LIVES

Please cite this publication as:
OECD (2020), *OECD Insurance Statistics 2019*, OECD Publishing, Paris,
https://doi.org/10.1787/g2g9fade-en.

ISBN 978-92-64-31313-2 (print)
ISBN 978-92-64-31314-9 (pdf)

OECD Insurance Statistics
ISSN 2307-8421 (print)
ISSN 2307-843X (online)

Corrigenda to publications may be found on line at: *www.oecd.org/about/publishing/corrigenda.htm.*

Table of contents

Conventional signs and abbreviations

Signs and abbreviations

c	Confidential data
..	Not available
.	Decimal point
|	Break in series

ISO country codes and abbreviations for currency

	ISO code	Currency	Abbreviation
Australia	AUS	dollar	AUD
Austria	AUT	euro	EUR
Belgium	BEL	euro	EUR
Canada	CAN	dollar	CAD
Chile	CHL	peso	CLP
Czech Republic	CZE	koruna	CZK
Denmark	DNK	krone	DKK
Estonia	EST	euro	EUR
Finland	FIN	euro	EUR
France	FRA	euro	EUR
Germany	DEU	euro	EUR
Greece	GRC	euro	EUR
Hungary	HUN	forint	HUF
Iceland	ISL	króna	ISK
Ireland	IRL	euro	EUR
Israel	ISR	sheqel	ILS
Italy	ITA	euro	EUR
Japan	JPN	yen	JPY
Korea	KOR	won	KRW
Latvia	LVA	euro	EUR
Lithuania	LTU	euro	EUR
Luxembourg	LUX	euro	EUR
Mexico	MEX	peso	MXN
Netherlands	NLD	euro	EUR
New Zealand	NZL	dollar	NZD
Norway	NOR	krone	NOK
Poland	POL	zloty	PLN
Portugal	PRT	euro	EUR
Slovak Republic	SVK	euro	EUR
Slovenia	SVN	euro	EUR
Spain	ESP	euro	EUR
Sweden	SWE	krona	SEK
Switzerland	CHE	franc	CHF
Turkey	TUR	lira	TRY
United Kingdom	GBR	pound	GBP
United States	USA	dollar	USD

Common definitions and notes

Notes on data sources

All the data in the statistical tables of each country have been reported by the relevant national insurance authorities. Regarding comparative tables of indicators, the data are mainly drawn from the tables by country. Data on exchange rates are taken from the IMF International Financial Statistics database. Data on population are taken from the IMF publication *World Economic Outlook*. Data on GDP come from the OECD Annual National Accounts database for OECD countries and from the IMF publication *World Economic Outlook* for all the other countries.

To achieve greater clarity, the number of variables selected and displayed in this publication has been limited. Data have been extracted from the Global Insurance Statistics database. The complete database can be accessed online at the following link:

OECD Insurance Statistics, *http://dx.doi.org/10.1787/ins-data-en*.

A significant effort has been made to achieve comparability among countries. Definitions, classifications, calculation methods, and units have been standardised as far as possible.

General notes

a) Life and non-life categories follow the definitions used in national law. However, the premiums for accident and sickness insurance underwritten by life companies should be included in non-life figures.

b) Up until 2008, the insurance business is broken down between life and non-life business. As of 2009, the insurance business is broken down between the business of pure life, pure non-life and composite undertakings. The insurance business of composite undertakings is further broken down between life and non-life components. Some countries do not allow for insurance undertakings to be active in both life and non-life insurance business and therefore composite insurance undertakings do not exist in these countries. In other countries (e.g., Austria, Hungary, Mexico, Spain) however, composite insurance undertakings account for more than 25% of all insurance undertakings operating in these countries. Therefore, to have comparable data across years for life business data (respectively non-life), one has to sum up the life (respectively non-life) business of pure life (respectively non-life) undertakings and the life (respectively non-life) business of composite undertakings as of 2009.

c) Figures provided for the number of companies and for insurance premiums should include all insurance companies licensed or authorised in the reporting country, *including* professional reinsurers, whether or not these are controlled, but *excluding* any statutory system of social security administered by the State.

d) *Domestic companies* means those companies incorporated under national law, together with those companies in the reporting country which are unincorporated, but excluding the branches and agencies of foreign companies.

e) *Foreign-controlled companies* means those domestic companies controlled by foreign interests, such "control" being defined according to national law (see the definition of foreign controlled companies in notes by country). The data of *foreign-controlled companies* are part of those of *Domestic companies*.

f) *Foreign companies* means companies incorporated outside the reporting country.

In 2016, a new supervisory framework for insurance and reinsurance companies was implemented in the European Union (EU) and the European Economic Area (EEA). This framework includes harmonised reporting requirements across EU/EEA countries. These requirements led to changes in national data collection, which may hamper the data comparability with the ones collected before 2016 for some countries which only collect data with the Solvency II framework.

International Comparisons:

Detailed metadata at: *http://metalinks.oecd.org/ins/20190221/0f8b*.

Country tables

In this part, the main insurance statistics are presented through separate tables for each OECD member country. Figures refer to the calendar year. The premiums and other amounts are described in millions of the national currency unit.

International comparisons

Table 1. Balance sheet and income, direct insurance (All insurance companies)

2018

Million US dollars

	Gross claims payments	Gross operating expenses	Commissions	Outstanding claims provision (changes)	Total assets	Gross technical provisions	Gross technical provisions unit-linked	Shareholders' equity	Net income
Argentina	9 516	4 084	2 528	2 941	20 846	5 674	..	4 578	1 864
Australia	55 957	10 685	3 143	..	221 170	53 615	..	29 114	3 000
Austria	17 146	1 081	3 792	487	144 798	105 110	20 367	11 820	..
Belgium	28 963	3 246	3 121	128	326 815	278 930	41 208	15 100	2 829
Bolivia	283	212	49	..	1 063	487	..	1 567	36
Brazil	12 973	13 569	6 168	631	282 620	198 348	167 796	21 777	5 317
Canada	41 762	19 101	10 705	1 916	1 181 358	462 098	..	92 124	10 280
Chile	8 622	2 042	1 125	2 191	67 002	57 887	5 685	6 402	790
Colombia	283	212	49	..	1 063	487	..	1 567	36
Costa Rica	676	285	219	-33	3 951	1 440	0	1 667	125
Cuba	..	..	..	..	..	..	..	..	..
Czech Republic	4 173	2 203	399	99	21 883	14 699	3 926	3 940	641
Denmark	27 732	2 603	315	8 093	497 500	407 749	171 435	29 202	-227
Dominican Republic	607	375	127	..	1 431	..	..	400	81
Ecuador	784	..	..	..	..	..	..	..	..
Egypt	838	..	..	..	..	..	..	..	..
El Salvador	321	128	85	94	893	223	..	397	38
Estonia	509	222	..	..	2 179	1 310	546	528	97
Finland	8 467	1 305	319	52	80 464	71 846	41 527	6 401	1 083
France	279 259	54 245	..	-18 307	3 102 905	2 473 624	389 067	..	..
Germany	187 607	18 058	22 540	7 898	1 851 278	1 682 893	118 451	68 630	3 197
Greece	2 322	1 290	..	..	19 534	14 417	2 758	3 767	..
Guatemala	507	290	152	..	1 376	629	..	502	118
Honduras	176	63	60	87	554	214	..	132	921
Hong Kong, China	2 854	640	871	..	..	..	..	..	..
Hungary	2 236	945	582	66	9 666	7 956	4 081	1 080	267
India	..	..	..	..	..	..	..	..	..
Indonesia	..	..	..	..	..	..	..	..	..
Iceland	492	124	..	..	1 322	727	53	473	61
Ireland	33 994	1 238	3 652	0	346 296	301 836	237 079	27 971	..
Israel[1]	10 797	3 906	2 214	624	144 525	126 563	86 248	7 065	381
Italy	114 227	16 285	12 838	-383	993 100	857 424	155 646	74 889	4 931
Japan	313 425	72 428	11 921	18 518	3 774 580	2 972 432	..	141 537	21 723
Korea	102 708	48 406	..	..	1 021 484	730 449	90 415	97 578	6 455
Latvia	479	146	77	120	949	690	64	185	15
Lithuania	381	201	14	-22	1 770	1 277	556	360	53
Luxembourg	18 297	2 790	1 621	716	225 900	212 166	142 873	6 645	421
Malaysia	9 490	2 559	1 393	63	71 332	58 685	11 093	8 399	1 665
Mexico	14 222	1 807	3 922	5 771	78 140	60 316	..	10 831	2 531
Morocco	..	..	..	..	..	..	..	..	..
Netherlands	87 392	9 535	..	-384	533 928	428 165	98 051	67 644	4 880
New Zealand	..	..	..	..	..	..	..	..	..
Nicaragua	98	25	20	33	372	157	..	135	33
Norway	14 016	2 975	487	-183	204 096	171 863	36 363	20 749	1 856
Panama	..	..	..	..	..	..	..	..	..
Paraguay	..	..	..	..	..	..	..	..	..
Peru	2 110	1 115	580	128	14 484	10 759	..	2 134	320
Poland	11 743	5 474	548	2 408	51 021	28 163	11 460	17 537	1 828
Portugal	11 718	1 907	828	65	60 633	32 859	13 610	4 833	473
Puerto Rico	..	..	..	..	..	..	..	..	..
Russia	8 337	6 842	4 435	4 263	42 016	26 358	..	9 749	2 630
Singapore	..	..	..	..	..	..	..	..	..
Slovak Republic	..	..	..	..	..	..	..	..	..
Slovenia	1 790	557	133	-51	8 128	5 616	1 236	1 608	157
South Africa	..	..	..	..	..	..	..	..	..
Spain	53 724	11 086	6 715	527	353 958	255 380	17 519	46 156	5 242
Sri Lanka	561	340	116	87	3 286	773	10	1 009	314
Sweden	17 798	3 836	1 085	32 841	516 908	209 870	153 340	120 183	1 155
Switzerland	56 924	4 800	5 090	-507	483 050	355 456	..	52 147	7 460
Thailand	..	..	..	..	..	..	..	..	..
Tunisia	445	..	..	..	..	..	..	..	..
Turkey	5 546	2 008	1 572	953	33 144	13 337	..	4 084	1 121
United Kingdom	448 352	52 134	..	30 713	2 917 083	2 468 099	1 515 378	205 847	..
United States	1 434 074	414 609	140 970	67 309	6 603 672	1 175 367	..	1 382 623	131 833
Uruguay	..	..	..	..	..	..	..	..	..

.. Not available

Note: Detailed metadata at: *http://metalinks.oecd.org/ins/20200312/6f03.*

1. Information on data for Israel: *http://oe.cd/israel-disclaimer.*

Source: Balance sheet and income, OECD Insurance Statistics (database)

Table 2. Balance sheet and income, direct insurance (Life insurance companies)

2018

Million US dollars

	Gross claims payments	Gross operating expenses	Commissions	Outstanding claims provision (changes)	Total assets	Gross technical provisions	Gross technical provisions unit-linked	Shareholders' equity	Net income
Argentina	304	153	27	5	3 182	2 636	..	356	214
Australia	32 005	5 038	1 795	..	143 235	..	..	12 766	780
Austria	1 101	44	87	0	12 076	10 194	3 670	427	..
Belgium	863	72	76	8	13 643	11 654	1 282	993	47
Bolivia	125	93	22	..	659	408	..	618	13
Brazil	622	1 863	468	-2	144 965	110 969	108 295	3 066	610
Canada	4	27	0	0	2 553	397	..	64	2
Chile	6 388	1 210	562	2 197	60 413	53 019	5 685	5 170	644
Colombia	125	93	22	..	659	408	..	618	13
Costa Rica	..	..	..	..	..	..	..	..	..
Cuba	..	..	..	..	..	..	..	..	..
Czech Republic	270	103	2	0	2 070	1 892	893	98	33
Denmark	20 404	814	64	7 645	471 391	393 149	171 435	21 238	-1 101
Dominican Republic	64	45	2	..	..	..	..	..	..
Ecuador	89	..	..	..	..	..	..	..	..
Egypt	431	..	..	..	..	..	..	..	..
El Salvador	154	57	35	55	312	107	..	100	12
Estonia	.. c	.. c	..	..	.. c	.. c	.. c	.. c	.. c
Finland	5 470	424	137	109	64 812	60 803	41 527	2 726	781
France	158 174	19 338	..	-19 454	488 097	421 297	73 131	..	..
Germany	83 696	4 607	5 938	434	1 240 773	1 162 439	118 400	19 695	1 067
Greece	195	46	..	..	3 425	3 001	140	326	..
Guatemala	..	..	..	..	..	..	..	..	..
Honduras	..	3	1	4	15	73	..	3	55
Hong Kong, China	..	..	..	..	..	..	..	..	..
Hungary	581	121	56	-6	2 993	2 671	1 178	223	25
India	..	..	..	..	..	..	..	..	..
Indonesia	..	..	..	..	..	..	..	..	..
Iceland	16	13	..	..	159	65	53	56	15
Ireland	27 403	495	2 002	..	293 871	270 292	237 079	14 540	..
Israel[1]	..	..	..	..	..	..	..	..	..
Italy	24 919	1 090	705	297	261 504	246 975	85 608	8 631	-11
Japan	257 147	43 587	..	18 219	3 496 164	2 972 432	..	106 203	15 601
Korea	71 391	33 921	..	..	766 656	542 070	90 415	66 181	3 664
Latvia	0	0	0	0	0	0	..	..	..
Lithuania	39	19	0	0	320	282	240	34	13
Luxembourg	15 703	1 482	798	80	209 041	201 278	142 873	3 629	256
Malaysia	6 701	1 487	1 062	..	62 154	53 731	11 093	3 432	962
Mexico	949	77	100	77	17 487	15 750	..	1 479	263
Morocco	..	..	..	..	..	..	..	..	..
Netherlands	23 771	2 172	..	-477	456 702	383 280	98 051	40 888	3 874
New Zealand	..	..	..	..	..	..	..	..	..
Nicaragua	..	..	..	..	..	..	..	..	..
Norway	7 278	977	91	..	177 324	158 611	36 363	12 200	1 119
Panama	..	..	..	..	..	..	..	..	..
Paraguay	..	..	..	..	..	..	..	..	..
Peru	286	116	31	15	1 807	1 397	..	277	22
Poland	5 925	1 577	37	2 406	25 226	16 340	11 460	7 216	678
Portugal	3 904	330	105	39	32 236	16 116	13 459	1 474	75
Puerto Rico	..	..	..	..	..	..	..	..	..
Russia	1 226	1 776	1 452	27	15 071	13 110	..	1 245	482
Singapore	..	..	..	..	..	..	..	..	..
Slovak Republic	..	..	..	..	..	..	..	..	..
Slovenia	..	..	..	..	..	..	..	..	..
South Africa	..	..	..	..	..	..	..	..	..
Spain	3 656	572	345	49	31 166	24 404	3 951	2 815	414
Sri Lanka	120	144	58	1	1 525	358	10	412	239
Sweden	8 908	1 737	405	4 243	446 450	173 856	153 340	105 441	297
Switzerland	33 602	1 145	849	-107	333 795	289 506	..	14 807	1 378
Thailand	..	..	..	..	..	..	..	..	..
Tunisia	33	..	..	..	..	..	..	..	..
Turkey	748	613	414	31	21 601	2 028	..	1 426	569
United Kingdom	351 870	11 978	..	25 090	2 090 532	1 834 313	1 375 357	83 804	..
United States	385 960	74 099	51 212	43 085	4 328 971	18 139	..	448 858	43 784
Uruguay	..	..	..	..	..	..	..	..	..

.. Not available; c Confidential data

Note: Detailed metadata at: *http://metalinks.oecd.org/ins/20200312/6f03.*

1. Information on data for Israel: *http://oe.cd/israel-disclaimer.*

Source: Balance sheet and income, OECD Insurance Statistics (database)

Table 3. Balance sheet and income, direct insurance (Non-life insurance companies)

2018

Million US dollars

	Gross claims payments	Gross operating expenses	Commissions	Outstanding claims provision (changes)	Total assets	Gross technical provisions	Gross technical provisions unit-linked	Shareholders' equity	Net income
Argentina	4 391	1 050	561	1 481	6 434	522	..	1 213	356
Australia	23 952	5 647	1 348	..	77 935	53 615	..	16 348	2 220
Austria	2 227	162	894	165	16 263	4 668	0	5 056	..
Belgium	1 756	451	473	-19	13 346	8 117	..	2 608	226
Bolivia	158	120	27	..	404	79	..	949	22
Brazil	2 291	1 596	799	81	7 134	4 438	0	1 409	181
Canada	27 816	4 050	6 590	1 459	106 787	20 493	..	18 066	1 625
Chile	2 235	832	563	-6	6 589	4 867	..	1 232	147
Colombia	158	120	27	..	404	79	..	949	22
Costa Rica	31	14	12	3	89	51	0	26	-1
Cuba	..	..	..	..	..	..	..	..	..
Czech Republic	185	202	34	14	635	308	..	192	30
Denmark	7 328	1 789	252	448	26 109	14 601	0	7 964	874
Dominican Republic	544	330	126	..	..	..	..	..	..
Ecuador	144	..	..	..	..	..	..	..	..
Egypt	407	..	..	..	..	..	..	..	..
El Salvador	52	30	20	13	212	37	..	118	5
Estonia	372	181	..	..	958	434	0	416	65
Finland	2 997	881	182	-57	15 652	11 044	0	3 674	302
France	121 086	34 907	..	1 148	337 544	152 782	..	..	..
Germany	103 911	13 451	16 602	7 464	610 504	520 455	52	48 936	2 130
Greece	314	286	..	..	1 992	1 074	0	716	..
Guatemala	6	15	5	..	148	31	..	79	14
Honduras	..	3	2	10	22	2	..	4	30
Hong Kong, China	2 854	640	871	..	..	..	..	..	..
Hungary	126	71	54	18	424	186	0	164	28
India	..	..	..	..	..	..	..	..	..
Indonesia	..	..	..	..	..	..	..	..	..
Iceland	476	111	..	..	1 162	662	0	416	46
Ireland	5 879	743	1 488	..	52 425	31 544	0	13 431	..
Israel[1]	610	9	100	121	4 229	3 093	0	510	67
Italy	6 483	3 304	2 598	-22	26 282	16 262	0	6 960	533
Japan	56 278	28 841	11 921	299	278 416	..	..	35 334	6 122
Korea	31 317	14 485	..	..	254 828	188 378	..	31 397	2 791
Latvia	372	140	76	120	730	494	..	162	19
Lithuania	283	155	13	-23	749	426	0	205	31
Luxembourg	2 594	1 308	824	636	16 859	10 888	0	3 016	165
Malaysia	2 789	1 073	332	63	9 177	4 954	..	4 967	702
Mexico	1 707	429	574	1 506	8 005	4 714	..	1 781	260
Morocco	..	..	..	..	..	..	..	..	..
Netherlands	63 620	7 363	..	93	77 227	44 885	..	26 756	1 006
New Zealand	..	..	..	..	..	..	..	..	..
Nicaragua	..	..	..	..	..	..	..	..	..
Norway	6 738	1 998	396	-183	26 772	13 251	..	8 550	737
Panama	..	..	..	..	..	..	..	..	..
Paraguay	..	..	..	..	..	..	..	..	..
Peru	298	216	103	5	1 179	499	..	314	36
Poland	5 817	3 896	511	2	25 795	11 823	0	10 321	1 150
Portugal	1 807	606	306	26	4 055	1 302	0	294	4
Puerto Rico	..	..	..	..	..	..	..	..	..
Russia	6 394	4 650	2 748	4 043	24 525	12 322	..	7 472	1 848
Singapore	..	..	..	..	..	..	..	..	..
Slovak Republic	..	..	..	..	..	..	..	..	..
Slovenia	473	63	10	3	314	103	0	168	3
South Africa	..	..	..	..	..	..	..	..	..
Spain	11 458	3 620	1 856	103	29 258	14 096	0	9 122	1 118
Sri Lanka	318	135	39	30	642	306	..	256	39
Sweden	8 890	2 100	680	28 598	70 457	36 014	..	14 742	859
Switzerland	23 322	3 655	4 241	-400	149 255	65 950	..	37 340	6 082
Thailand	..	..	..	..	..	..	..	..	..
Tunisia	84	..	..	..	..	..	..	..	..
Turkey	4 799	1 394	1 157	923	11 544	11 309	..	2 658	552
United Kingdom	30 035	17 412	..	167	140 474	84 682	..	34 918	..
United States	1 048 114	340 510	89 758	24 224	2 274 701	1 157 228	..	933 765	88 049
Uruguay	..	..	..	..	..	..	..	..	..

.. Not available

Note: Detailed metadata at: *http://metalinks.oecd.org/ins/20200312/6f03*.

1. Information on data for Israel: *http://oe.cd/israel-disclaimer*.

Source: Balance sheet and income, OECD Insurance Statistics (database)

Table 4. Portfolio allocation, direct insurance (All insurance companies)

2018

Million US dollars

	Cash and deposits	Land and buildings	Equity	Bills and bonds	Loans	Collective investment schemes	Private equity funds	Hedge funds	Structured products	Assets for unit-linked contracts	Total investments
Argentina	264	229	1 021	8 602	47	4 064	0	0	0	0	16 330
Australia	7 324	3 489	5 973	47 020	2 115	7 527	..	..	..	95 979	169 914
Austria	4 711	9 727	16 546	56 339	4 654	24 005	108	..	1 386	21 017	138 560
Belgium	8 277	10 033	17 822	217 402	35 738	13 354	983	..	1 427	40 981	346 637
Bolivia	18	132	9	408	27	0	46	0	0	0	655
Brazil	317	337	672	19 878	112	21 124	6 413	392	0	205 343	254 631
Canada	18 274	17 531	34 389	378 283	63 625	16 949	..	..	..	..	566 231
Chile	1 949	8 867	681	33 022	7 528	3 855	0	0	0	5 720	61 530
Colombia	18	132	9	408	27	0	46	0	0	0	655
Costa Rica	96	54	139	2 439	358	58	0	0	0	0	3 145
Cuba	..	..	..	..	..	..	..	..	..	..	..
Czech Republic	..	..	..	..	..	..	..	..	..	..	..
Denmark	13 490	1 857	129 010	114 985	5 509	22 611	..	..	..	177 673	497 500
Dominican Republic	461	93	12	99	1	..	..	..	..	..	695
Ecuador	..	..	..	..	..	..	..	..	..	..	..
Egypt	..	..	..	..	..	..	..	..	..	..	..
El Salvador	79	7	52	361	36	..	..	..	..	..	674
Estonia	323	0	2	1 021	9	85	0	0	6	616	2 064
Finland	3 608	1 442	3 545	17 897	2 005	6 073	..	..	..	41 506	77 842
France	62 020	39 161	225 245	1 609 764	..	443 183	..	..	..	399 401	2 886 616
Germany	14 290	33 722	138 388	878 742	108 106	616 816	4 360	..	..	117 576	1 934 263
Greece	1 036	700	143	11 359	139	1 383	0	0	1	2 677	17 858
Guatemala	222	45	17	536	6	..	..	..	..	..	933
Honduras	32	6	..	172	24	..	..	..	..	..	234
Hong Kong, China	..	..	..	..	..	..	..	..	..	..	..
Hungary	235	92	60	4 350	23	387	..	..	..	4 108	9 449
India	..	..	..	..	..	..	..	..	..	..	..
Indonesia	4 358	1 139	3 041	7 367	14	7 176	..	..	..	17 082	40 362
Iceland	56	15	292	468	24	203	..	..	..	52	1 110
Ireland	..	..	..	..	..	..	..	..	..	..	..
Israel[1]	3 444	1 818	1 424	27 219	5 299	1 984	1 491	135	129	86 006	131 065
Italy	10 184	6 312	70 197	554 851	6 772	..	..	..	..	155 930	924 288
Japan	..	..	..	..	..	..	..	..	..	..	..
Korea	20 177	16 652	34 211	378 040	184 476	..	..	..	..	91 407	974 882
Latvia	94	15	8	502	8	75	0	2	0	66	773
Lithuania	70	7	12	728	11	108	0	0	6	556	1 521
Luxembourg	19 016	217	19 523	43 026	98	50 739	..	..	..	32 380	220 590
Malaysia	4 473	1 225	10 698	35 723	2 983	..	..	..	..	11 879	71 255
Mexico	325	891	905	47 273	1 545	7 976	0	..	..	..	62 955
Morocco	..	..	..	..	..	..	..	..	..	..	..
Netherlands	14 782	7 460	10 934	193 673	93 804	26 501	..	..	8 708	87 086	475 194
New Zealand	..	..	..	..	..	..	..	..	..	..	..
Nicaragua	124	9	3	96	10	..	..	..	..	..	259
Norway	1 719	14 162	10 092	76 514	16 729	35 646	..	..	..	36 592	193 921
Panama	..	..	..	..	..	..	..	..	..	..	..
Paraguay	..	..	..	..	..	..	..	..	..	..	..
Peru	513	838	490	7 857	4	221	5	0	0	1 444	12 120
Poland	1 639	499	7 180	20 822	954	4 452	26	7	12	12 485	48 001
Portugal	3 643	521	3 029	31 962	87	2 224	109	23	215	13 665	55 525
Puerto Rico	..	..	..	..	..	..	..	..	..	..	..
Russia	11 790	1 090	2 993	19 885	258	163	..	..	..	..	47 795
Singapore	..	..	..	..	..	..	..	..	..	..	..
Slovak Republic	..	..	..	..	..	..	..	..	..	..	..
Slovenia	214	277	673	4 298	94	341	..	..	15	1 704	7 623
South Africa	..	..	..	..	..	..	..	..	..	..	..
Spain	22 473	12 724	16 650	242 326	3 141	12 794	593	447	6 015	20 163	330 231
Sri Lanka	274	78	779	993	133	9	..	..	..	..	2 417
Sweden	10 764	11 892	128 831	144 111	10 377	59 286	..	..	..	128 388	511 935
Switzerland	25 198	50 754	19 512	204 402	55 904	20 004	3 049	3 611	260	18 305	457 035
Thailand	..	..	..	..	..	..	..	..	..	..	..
Tunisia	..	..	..	..	..	..	..	..	..	..	..
Turkey	7 182	94	424	3 387	40	177	..	..	..	872	12 175
United Kingdom	338 090	22 563	88 368	1 447 584	231 233	187 101	1 681	6 587	674	5 944 610	9 987 138
United States	..	..	..	..	..	..	..	..	..	..	..
Uruguay	..	..	..	..	..	..	..	..	..	..	..

.. Not available

Note: Detailed metadata at: *http://metalinks.oecd.org/ins/20200312/2fa8.*

1. Information on data for Israel: *http://oe.cd/israel-disclaimer.*

Source: Outstanding investment by direct insurance companies, OECD Insurance Statistics (database)

Table 5. Portfolio allocation, direct insurance (Life insurance companies)

2018

Million US dollars

	Cash and deposits	Land and buildings	Equity	Bills and bonds	Loans	Collective investment schemes	Private equity funds	Hedge funds	Structured products	Assets for unit-linked contracts	Total investments
Argentina	7	32	20	2 024	5	726	0	0	0	0	3 082
Australia	4 225	3 415	4 930	18 947	564	..	..	..	..	95 979	128 232
Austria	74	10	93	3 190	189	4 560	5	..	67	3 695	11 883
Belgium	745	301	540	6 753	2 241	1 650	16	..	415	1 284	14 165
Bolivia	11	105	5	284	27	0	36	0	0	0	479
Brazil	75	27	12	4 458	76	5 686	127	184	0	131 545	142 190
Canada	26	0	11	493	1	..	..	..	..	..	531
Chile	1 410	8 806	672	31 641	7 518	3 742	0	0	0	5 720	59 360
Colombia	11	105	5	284	27	0	36	0	0	0	479
Costa Rica	..	..	..	..	..	..	..	..	..	..	..
Cuba	..	..	..	..	..	..	..	..	..	..	..
Czech Republic	..	..	..	..	..	..	..	..	..	..	..
Denmark	10 478	1 506	124 452	100 313	5 052	21 183	..	..	..	177 673	471 391
Dominican Republic	..	..	..	..	..	..	..	..	..	..	..
Ecuador	..	..	..	..	..	..	..	..	..	..	..
Egypt	..	..	..	..	..	..	..	..	..	..	..
El Salvador	29	6	0	150	4	..	..	..	..	..	290
Estonia	.. c	..	.. c	.. c	.. c	.. c	..	..	..	.. c	.. c
Finland	2 156	808	1 903	13 437	1 150	3 079	..	..	..	41 506	64 113
France	8 867	8 489	28 869	266 419	..	59 465	..	..	..	74 553	463 377
Germany	5 545	21 789	55 871	560 979	90 611	427 372	2 360	..	..	117 525	1 298 893
Greece	162	1	55	2 920	0	8	0	0	0	139	3 367
Guatemala	..	..	..	..	..	..	..	..	..	..	..
Honduras	..	..	..	..	..	..	..	..	..	..	..
Hong Kong, China	..	..	..	..	..	..	..	..	..	..	..
Hungary	64	6	14	1 576	4	132	..	..	..	1 191	3 006
India	..	..	..	..	..	..	..	..	..	..	..
Indonesia	2 175	1 071	2 288	6 082	11	6 026	..	..	..	17 082	34 888
Iceland	6	0	3	66	0	13	..	..	..	52	140
Ireland	..	..	..	..	..	..	..	..	..	..	..
Israel[1]	..	..	..	..	..	..	..	..	..	..	..
Italy	1 875	311	5 491	139 321	64	..	..	..	..	85 708	250 687
Japan	81 094	54 058	242 957	2 399 703	287 402	..	..	..	..	..	3 428 786
Korea	13 995	11 462	28 897	300 119	123 261	..	..	..	..	91 407	743 126
Latvia	..	..	..	..	..	..	..	..	..	..	..
Lithuania	13	0	0	59	0	2	0	0	0	240	315
Luxembourg	17 864	56	19 052	37 195	98	50 193	..	..	..	32 380	207 585
Malaysia	2 253	1 091	7 916	33 062	2 972	..	..	..	..	11 879	62 154
Mexico	12	18	6	16 437	193	46	0	..	..	..	17 244
Morocco	..	..	..	..	..	..	..	..	..	..	..
Netherlands	10 856	6 925	7 801	164 922	90 286	15 869	..	..	8 089	87 086	418 334
New Zealand	..	..	..	..	..	..	..	..	..	..	..
Nicaragua	..	..	..	..	..	..	..	..	..	..	..
Norway	909	13 606	8 053	66 346	16 344	32 187	..	..	..	36 592	176 181
Panama	..	..	..	..	..	..	..	..	..	..	..
Paraguay	..	..	..	..	..	..	..	..	..	..	..
Peru	55	151	71	1 054	1	26	0	0	0	198	1 578
Poland	622	108	587	8 776	335	1 937	0	0	6	12 485	24 853
Portugal	604	167	151	15 537	42	966	27	0	48	13 547	31 088
Puerto Rico	..	..	..	..	..	..	..	..	..	..	..
Russia	3 318	116	196	12 478	6	25	..	..	..	..	17 121
Singapore	..	..	..	..	..	..	..	..	..	..	..
Slovak Republic	..	..	..	..	..	..	..	..	..	..	..
Slovenia	..	..	..	..	..	..	..	..	..	..	..
South Africa	..	..	..	..	..	..	..	..	..	..	..
Spain	1 337	310	504	20 938	432	668	122	25	1 038	3 929	29 331
Sri Lanka	190	65	773	743	131	9	..	..	..	19	2 036
Sweden	8 561	9 265	111 589	121 450	8 390	49 719	..	..	..	125 491	450 427
Switzerland	14 788	43 038	14 273	161 510	43 902	10 937	2 052	2 278	202	18 295	323 847
Thailand	..	..	..	..	..	..	..	..	..	..	..
Tunisia	..	..	..	..	..	..	..	..	..	..	..
Turkey	1 761	47	37	1 050	40	29	..	..	..	872	3 836
United Kingdom	14 315	4 310	35 249	641 491	188 139	92 522	553	3 238	605	5 537 745	7 286 689
United States	94 740	20 649	147 900	3 012 831	649 544	..	..	24 395	2 796	..	4 161 392
Uruguay	..	..	..	..	..	..	..	..	..	..	..

.. Not available; c Confidential data

Note: Detailed metadata at: *http://metalinks.oecd.org/ins/20200312/2fa8.*

1. Information on data for Israel: *http://oe.cd/israel-disclaimer.*

Source: Outstanding investment by direct insurance companies, OECD Insurance Statistics (database)

Table 6. Portfolio allocation, direct insurance (Non-life insurance companies)
2018

Million US dollars

	Cash and deposits	Land and buildings	Equity	Bills and bonds	Loans	Collective investment schemes	Private equity funds	Hedge funds	Structured products	Assets for unit-linked contracts	Total investments
Argentina	80	55	102	2 710	3	1 457	0	0	0	0	5 299
Australia	3 099	74	1 043	28 073	1 551	7 527	..	..	..	..	41 681
Austria	1 561	729	8 729	1 543	266	2 188	0	..	5	0	15 020
Belgium	828	326	1 281	6 287	312	1 085	1	..	47	..	10 198
Bolivia	8	27	4	124	0	0	10	0	0	0	176
Brazil	66	6	15	1 920	0	1 273	2	29	0	0	3 312
Canada	2 782	221	4 783	40 628	464	16 949	..	..	..	..	68 571
Chile	540	61	9	1 382	10	113	0	0	0	0	2 170
Colombia	8	27	4	124	0	0	10	0	0	0	176
Costa Rica	15	0	0	33	17	0	0	0	0	0	65
Cuba	..	..	..	..	..	..	..	..	..	..	..
Czech Republic	..	..	..	..	..	..	..	..	..	..	..
Denmark	3 012	350	4 558	14 672	457	1 428	..	..	..	0	26 109
Dominican Republic	..	..	..	..	..	..	..	..	..	..	..
Ecuador	..	..	..	..	..	..	..	..	..	..	..
Egypt	..	..	..	..	..	..	..	..	..	..	..
El Salvador	18	0	52	52	0	..	..	..	..	..	160
Estonia	254	0	1	561	2	24	0	0	6	0	851
Finland	1 452	633	1 642	4 461	855	2 994	..	..	..	..	13 729
France	15 746	7 140	72 901	123 142	..	50 339	..	..	..	0	279 250
Germany	8 745	11 933	82 518	317 763	17 495	189 444	2 000	..	..	52	635 369
Greece	220	164	26	1 048	1	228	0	0	0	0	1 732
Guatemala	38	3	0	68	3	0	0	0	0	0	130
Honduras	..	..	..	..	..	..	..	..	..	..	..
Hong Kong, China	..	..	..	..	..	..	..	..	..	..	..
Hungary	38	3	0	293	0	12	..	..	..	0	360
India	..	..	..	..	..	..	..	..	..	..	..
Indonesia	2 183	69	753	1 284	3	1 150	..	..	..	..	5 474
Iceland	50	15	289	402	24	190	..	..	..	0	970
Ireland	..	..	..	..	..	..	..	..	..	..	..
Israel[1]	358	54	87	1 608	199	805	51	8	6	0	3 200
Italy	798	561	2 164	14 276	27	..	..	..	..	0	19 786
Japan	17 835	7 723	59 071	67 377	12 943	..	..	..	..	..	248 906
Korea	6 181	5 190	5 314	77 921	61 215	..	..	..	..	0	231 756
Latvia	87	15	8	411	8	22	0	0	0	0	553
Lithuania	37	7	4	389	4	61	0	0	0	0	523
Luxembourg	1 152	160	471	5 831	0	546	..	..	..	0	13 005
Malaysia	2 220	133	2 783	2 661	11	..	..	..	..	..	9 101
Mexico	106	190	102	2 812	31	244	0	..	..	..	3 876
Morocco	..	..	..	..	..	..	..	..	..	..	..
Netherlands	3 926	535	3 133	28 751	3 519	10 632	..	..	618	..	56 861
New Zealand	..	..	..	..	..	..	..	..	..	..	..
Nicaragua	..	..	..	..	..	..	..	..	..	..	..
Norway	810	556	2 039	10 167	384	3 459	..	..	..	..	17 740
Panama	..	..	..	..	..	..	..	..	..	..	..
Paraguay	..	..	..	..	..	..	..	..	..	..	..
Peru	78	65	101	187	0	28	0	0	0	0	619
Poland	1 017	391	6 593	12 046	619	2 515	26	7	7	0	23 148
Portugal	222	109	44	2 479	7	214	2	20	18	0	3 115
Puerto Rico	..	..	..	..	..	..	..	..	..	..	..
Russia	7 263	882	2 247	5 577	194	38	..	..	..	..	25 833
Singapore	..	..	..	..	..	..	..	..	..	..	..
Slovak Republic	..	..	..	..	..	..	..	..	..	..	..
Slovenia	33	20	1	191	0	5	..	..	0	0	250
South Africa	..	..	..	..	..	..	..	..	..	..	..
Spain	3 031	2 151	2 523	10 508	482	3 049	158	246	112	0	22 373
Sri Lanka	83	13	6	246	2	0	..	..	..	..	376
Sweden	2 204	2 627	17 242	22 661	1 987	9 567	..	..	..	2 897	61 507
Switzerland	10 409	7 715	5 238	42 892	12 003	9 067	996	1 333	58	10	133 188
Thailand	..	..	..	..	..	..	..	..	..	..	..
Tunisia	..	..	..	..	..	..	..	..	..	..	..
Turkey	5 421	47	387	2 337	0	148	..	..	..	0	8 339
United Kingdom	31 418	1 629	26 295	347 203	2 911	62 449	1 128	3 309	..	365	472 270
United States	149 209	19 651	437 944	1 236 457	20 973	..	..	0	-21	..	2 024 693
Uruguay	..	..	..	..	..	..	..	..	..	..	..

.. Not available

Note: Detailed metadata at: *http://metalinks.oecd.org/ins/20200312/2fa8*.

1. Information on data for Israel: *http://oe.cd/israel-disclaimer*.

Source: Outstanding investment by direct insurance companies, OECD Insurance Statistics (database)

Table 7. Total gross premiums (Life and Non-life)

Million US dollars

	2011	2012	2013	2014	2015	2016	2017	2018
Argentina	..	13 983	16 643	18 622	19 376	19 749	18 519	20 137
Australia	84 541	85 880	87 591	97 011	78 796	74 145	72 339	69 991
Austria	..	..	25 084	25 102	21 091	20 647	20 485	21 880
Belgium	40 872	41 936	37 521	38 345	30 746	30 432	30 839	33 703
Bolivia	..	316	..	..	..	468	499	549
Brazil	..	..	..	69 867	55 519	58 914	66 431	57 595
Canada	94 024	97 020	98 512	93 189	83 612	81 909	87 408	87 012
Chile	9 699	11 298	11 776	10 976	11 413	12 401	12 860	14 006
Colombia	..	316	..	..	..	468	499	549
Costa Rica	793	927	1 036	1 157	1 049	1 211	1 319	1 337
Cuba	..	..	..	..	..	..	..	..
Czech Republic	8 764	7 846	7 998	7 608	6 173	6 002	6 402	7 052
Denmark	33 844	32 745	225 775	37 098	31 997	33 498	37 549	40 976
Dominican Republic	..	..	..	..	..	..	..	1 222
Ecuador	..	..	..	..	2 316	2 135	..	..
Egypt	..	..	..	..	..	..	..	..
El Salvador	478	503	546	572	609	619	..	658
Estonia	561	617	774	839	764	815	924	1 092
Finland	10 133	9 352	13 061	14 125	11 917	10 012	10 084	5 156
France	289 082	258 641	275 750	294 033	250 873	314 251	314 319	338 708
Germany	255 708	302 739	333 713	338 764	293 086	294 660	311 208	335 669
Greece	6 893	5 781	5 407	5 056	3 964	3 908	4 213	4 485
Guatemala	..	611	683	749	804	856	953	964
Honduras	..	..	368	379	398	..	..	631
Hong Kong, China	29 268	33 191	37 856	43 121	47 901	59 301	64 310	69 089
Hungary	4 054	3 377	3 582	3 584	2 991	3 146	3 484	3 767
India	71 625	..	..	..	70 878	..	100 841	..
Indonesia	..	16 249	15 782	14 325	14 629	17 290	19 483	18 967
Iceland	415	404	419	444	420	487	611	652
Ireland	44 591	45 586	45 314	52 557	48 802	54 182	49 821	48 129
Israel[1]	12 665	12 471	13 941	14 366	14 117	15 142	17 427	18 560
Italy	156 982	138 232	161 161	193 455	165 854	151 423	150 732	163 781
Japan	590 342	475 139	349 905	347 080	313 822	434 737	390 096	402 773
Korea	137 828	163 065	169 186	187 068	183 642	185 646	189 587	192 810
Latvia	555	574	626	687	589	589	730	893
Lithuania	686	665	753	798	716	786	895	1 037
Luxembourg	19 176	25 168	24 705	28 945	21 278	20 289	24 314	24 539
Malaysia	14 878	16 338	16 974	17 588	15 346	15 100	15 156	16 716
Mexico	22 683	23 596	27 184	27 349	24 929	24 150	26 569	28 250
Morocco	..	..	..	..	..	..	..	..
Netherlands	58 654	51 267	51 142	48 603	37 399	77 358	80 465	86 997
New Zealand	..	4 590	5 139	5 359	4 657	4 753	5 144	..
Nicaragua	..	138	157	178	191	204	..	224
Norway	23 794	25 748	25 536	26 461	20 647	20 210	20 407	21 993
Panama	..	1 159	1 316	..	..	..	..	..
Paraguay	..	226	363	..	428	368	390	..
Peru	2 660	3 041	3 392	3 602	3 709	3 354	3 500	3 938
Poland	19 289	19 231	18 307	17 412	14 539	14 213	16 495	17 211
Portugal	15 642	13 559	17 003	18 667	13 945	12 079	12 941	14 868
Puerto Rico	..	..	9 610	9 108	11 145	13 470	..	..
Russia	23 718	..	..	26 658	17 299	18 218	22 517	24 301
Singapore	23 470	24 947	27 186	30 379	30 331	33 160	36 830	..
Slovak Republic	2 998	2 772	2 959	2 986	2 400	..	5 047	..
Slovenia	3 039	2 816	2 808	2 783	2 386	2 416	2 596	2 863
South Africa	56 005	51 452	54 268	51 527	47 054	42 473	..	..
Spain	86 378	72 880	77 177	76 604	65 514	73 655	74 242	78 578
Sri Lanka	..	..	..	746	931	..	1 128	1 147
Sweden	28 062	24 669	27 203	49 890	40 254	39 107	44 382	49 044
Switzerland	71 482	70 214	74 264	74 480	70 367	67 483	67 772	69 456
Thailand	15 644	..	..	..	..	..	..	..
Tunisia	..	..	..	..	..	864	909	..
Turkey	10 247	11 399	13 212	12 314	11 775	13 718	13 074	11 333
United Kingdom	339 365	368 525	340 385	365 688	336 743	403 794	394 114	469 120
United States	2 154 851	2 279 817	2 289 921	2 431 323	2 621 083	2 703 793	2 836 293	2 632 284
Uruguay	..	1 062	1 208	1 303	1 277	..	1 576	..
OECD Total	4 637 901	4 689 617	4 864 790	4 951 051	4 843 302	5 205 837	5 335 868	5 298 667

.. Not available

Note: Detailed metadata at: *http://metalinks.oecd.org/ins/20200312/1e50.*

1. Information on data for Israel: *http://oe.cd/israel-disclaimer.*

Source: Insurance activity indicators, OECD Insurance Statistics (database)

Table 8. Total gross premiums (Life)

Million US dollars

	2011	2012	2013	2014	2015	2016	2017	2018
Argentina	..	2 891	2 969	3 076	2 966	3 158	2 724	2 886
Australia	47 949	46 069	48 122	59 315	46 633	41 066	37 668	34 664
Austria	..	..	8 556	8 901	7 440	6 701	6 493	6 543
Belgium	25 829	27 140	21 651	21 664	17 045	16 560	16 547	18 437
Bolivia	..	69	..	..	..	157	202	238
Brazil	..	..	..	42 061	34 819	38 935	44 172	37 052
Canada	32 014	31 143	32 379	26 712	24 001	23 795	25 754	26 213
Chile	6 067	7 400	7 830	7 224	7 795	8 726	8 930	9 633
Colombia	..	69	..	..	..	157	202	238
Costa Rica	84	110	139	142	133	186	194	216
Cuba	..	..	..	..	..	..	..	..
Czech Republic	4 069	3 680	3 657	3 429	2 537	2 435	2 451	2 583
Denmark	23 069	22 489	215 331	25 124	22 055	23 001	25 945	28 664
Dominican Republic	..	..	..	..	..	..	..	196
Ecuador	..	..	..	..	453	471	..	..
Egypt	..	..	..	..	..	..	..	..
El Salvador	99	114	146	147	156	153	..	165
Estonia	223	209	227	254	238	245	252	275
Finland	5 185	4 786	7 423	8 108	6 943	5 063	5 115	5 156
France	184 602	160 618	172 187	188 634	160 946	182 414	173 606	186 967
Germany	116 788	107 425	120 293	121 746	99 628	97 651	99 769	106 802
Greece	3 012	2 497	2 238	2 500	2 000	1 846	2 125	2 220
Guatemala	..	124	136	156	156	170	196	197
Honduras	..	..	114	134	145	..	..	210
Hong Kong, China	24 808	28 123	32 425	37 459	41 972	53 421	58 134	62 257
Hungary	2 212	1 790	1 951	1 965	1 529	1 559	1 679	1 742
India	61 214	..	..	..	55 415	..	71 312	..
Indonesia	..	11 465	10 720	9 490	10 093	12 560	14 530	13 832
Iceland	30	29	33	36	35	43	54	54
Ireland	35 321	36 584	36 525	43 221	38 853	37 127	39 617	36 272
Israel[1]	6 682	6 602	7 374	7 426	7 568	7 986	9 368	10 016
Italy	105 316	91 858	115 147	148 645	129 077	114 779	112 984	122 310
Japan	476 138	475 139	349 905	347 080	313 822	328 210	293 005	302 966
Korea	79 314	96 195	100 261	106 188	104 801	104 560	102 273	102 507
Latvia	102	101	118	142	128	137	164	171
Lithuania	226	213	241	286	262	273	261	293
Luxembourg	17 331	23 497	22 711	27 166	19 641	18 568	22 318	22 523
Malaysia	8 976	9 907	10 200	10 594	9 306	9 317	9 603	10 709
Mexico	10 143	10 900	12 523	12 812	11 530	11 266	11 421	12 672
Morocco	..	..	..	..	..	..	..	..
Netherlands	30 172	24 392	24 263	23 202	16 307	15 198	14 654	14 136
New Zealand	..	..	..	..	..	..	..	..
Nicaragua	..	22	27	32	33	38	..	46
Norway	12 771	14 051	13 838	14 629	11 383	11 202	11 313	12 291
Panama	..	447	523	..	..	..	..	..
Paraguay	..	..	44	..	57	1	54	..
Peru	1 276	1 435	1 587	1 768	1 794	1 519	1 644	1 909
Poland	10 749	11 170	9 892	9 087	7 302	6 051	6 499	6 009
Portugal	10 043	8 582	11 984	13 617	9 411	7 200	7 581	9 188
Puerto Rico	..	..	411	570	542	1 279	..	..
Russia	1 777	..	..	3 353	2 408	3 721	6 171	7 784
Singapore	15 723	16 402	18 449	20 808	21 033	23 739	27 593	..
Slovak Republic	1 594	1 493	1 642	1 621	1 229	..	3 712	..
Slovenia	670	623	629	637	552	545	582	621
South Africa	43 695	40 746	42 679	41 476	37 576	33 870	..	..
Spain	40 552	33 821	34 397	33 612	28 532	34 695	33 262	34 263
Sri Lanka	..	..	..	265	395	..	467	474
Sweden	13 923	13 311	14 190	34 734	29 507	29 302	33 761	37 087
Switzerland	34 589	33 598	35 791	36 140	34 407	31 672	30 486	30 835
Thailand	10 794	..	..	..	..	..	..	..
Tunisia	..	..	..	..	..	175	179	..
Turkey	1 880	1 758	2 072	1 510	1 390	2 048	2 268	1 801
United Kingdom	249 303	277 966	246 475	268 267	246 702	277 703	269 267	336 122
United States	864 830	919 547	881 541	880 040	973 634	970 503	1 009 291	1 139 513
Uruguay	..	280	347	384	427	..	665	..
OECD Total	2 452 699	2 496 676	2 563 397	2 485 677	2 384 864	2 420 127	2 420 477	2 661 550

.. Not available

Note: Detailed metadata at: *http://metalinks.oecd.org/ins/20200312/1e50.*

1. Information on data for Israel: *http://oe.cd/israel-disclaimer.*

Source: Insurance activity indicators, OECD Insurance Statistics (database)

Table 9. Total gross premiums (Non-life)

Million US dollars

	2011	2012	2013	2014	2015	2016	2017	2018
Argentina	..	11 092	13 673	15 546	16 410	16 591	15 795	17 251
Australia	36 592	39 812	39 469	37 695	32 163	33 079	34 671	35 328
Austria	..	..	16 527	16 201	13 651	13 946	13 992	15 337
Belgium	15 043	14 796	15 870	16 681	13 701	13 871	14 292	15 266
Bolivia	..	248	..	..	..	312	297	311
Brazil	..	..	..	27 806	20 699	19 979	22 258	20 543
Canada	62 010	65 877	66 133	66 477	59 610	58 115	61 654	60 799
Chile	3 633	3 898	3 946	3 751	3 619	3 676	3 930	4 373
Colombia	..	248	..	..	..	312	297	311
Costa Rica	709	816	897	1 014	916	1 024	1 125	1 121
Cuba	..	..	..	..	..	..	..	..
Czech Republic	4 695	4 165	4 341	4 179	3 636	3 566	3 951	4 469
Denmark	10 775	10 256	10 445	11 974	9 943	10 497	11 604	12 312
Dominican Republic	..	..	..	..	..	..	..	1 026
Ecuador	..	..	..	..	1 864	1 665	..	..
Egypt	..	..	..	..	..	..	..	..
El Salvador	379	389	400	412	437	446	..	493
Estonia	338	408	547	584	526	570	672	817
Finland	4 947	4 566	5 638	6 017	4 974	4 949	4 968	..
France	104 480	98 023	103 563	105 399	89 928	131 837	140 713	151 741
Germany	138 920	195 315	213 420	217 018	193 459	197 010	211 439	228 866
Greece	3 881	3 284	3 169	2 556	1 964	2 063	2 088	2 265
Guatemala	..	487	547	593	648	685	757	767
Honduras	..	..	254	246	253	..	..	421
Hong Kong, China	4 460	5 068	5 431	5 661	5 929	5 880	6 177	6 832
Hungary	1 842	1 587	1 631	1 619	1 462	1 588	1 804	2 025
India	10 411	..	..	..	15 463	..	29 529	..
Indonesia	..	4 784	5 062	4 835	4 537	4 730	4 954	5 136
Iceland	385	374	385	408	384	444	556	598
Ireland	9 270	9 002	8 789	9 335	9 949	17 055	9 625	10 006
Israel[1]	5 983	5 868	6 567	6 940	6 548	7 156	8 059	8 544
Italy	51 665	46 374	46 013	44 811	36 777	36 645	37 748	41 470
Japan	114 204	..	..	..	..	106 527	97 090	99 808
Korea	58 515	66 870	68 925	80 880	78 841	81 086	87 315	90 303
Latvia	453	473	507	546	462	452	566	721
Lithuania	460	452	512	513	454	513	634	744
Luxembourg	1 845	1 671	1 993	1 779	1 637	1 720	1 996	2 016
Malaysia	5 902	6 431	6 773	6 994	6 041	5 782	5 553	6 007
Mexico	12 540	12 696	14 661	14 536	13 399	12 884	15 148	15 578
Morocco	..	..	..	..	..	..	..	..
Netherlands	28 482	26 875	26 878	25 401	21 093	62 160	64 818	71 621
New Zealand	..	4 590	5 139	5 359	4 657	4 753	5 144	..
Nicaragua	..	116	130	146	158	166	..	178
Norway	11 023	11 697	11 697	11 833	9 264	9 008	9 094	9 702
Panama	..	713	793	..	..	..	..	..
Paraguay	..	161	318	..	371	367	335	..
Peru	1 384	1 605	1 805	1 834	1 916	1 835	1 856	2 029
Poland	8 540	8 061	8 416	8 325	7 237	8 162	9 996	11 202
Portugal	5 599	4 977	5 018	5 050	4 534	4 879	5 360	5 680
Puerto Rico	..	..	9 199	8 538	10 603	12 191	..	..
Russia	20 193	..	..	16 937	14 891	14 497	16 346	16 518
Singapore	7 748	8 544	8 737	9 571	9 298	9 421	9 238	..
Slovak Republic	1 404	1 279	1 318	1 366	1 171	..	1 335	..
Slovenia	2 370	2 192	2 179	2 146	1 833	1 871	2 014	2 242
South Africa	12 310	10 706	11 589	10 051	9 478	8 602	..	..
Spain	45 826	39 059	42 780	42 992	36 982	38 959	40 979	44 315
Sri Lanka	..	..	..	481	535	..	661	673
Sweden	14 140	11 357	13 013	15 156	10 746	9 805	10 621	11 957
Switzerland	36 893	36 616	38 474	38 340	35 959	35 811	37 287	38 621
Thailand	4 850	..	..	..	..	..	..	..
Tunisia	..	..	..	..	..	689	730	..
Turkey	8 367	9 641	11 140	10 804	10 386	11 670	10 806	9 532
United Kingdom	90 062	90 559	93 910	97 421	90 041	126 091	124 847	132 998
United States	1 290 021	1 360 270	1 408 380	1 551 283	1 647 449	1 733 290	1 827 002	1 492 771
Uruguay	..	782	862	918	850	..	911	..
OECD Total	2 185 203	2 192 942	2 301 393	2 465 374	2 458 438	2 785 711	2 913 818	2 634 027

.. Not available

Note: Detailed metadata at: *http://metalinks.oecd.org/ins/20200312/1e50.*

1. Information on data for Israel: *http://oe.cd/israel-disclaimer.*

Source: Insurance activity indicators, OECD Insurance Statistics (database)

Table 10. Market share in OECD (Life and Non-life)

Per cent

	2011	2012	2013	2014	2015	2016	2017	2018
Australia	1.8	1.8	1.8	2.0	1.6	1.4	1.4	1.3
Austria	..	..	0.5	0.5	0.4	0.4	0.4	0.4
Belgium	0.9	0.9	0.8	0.8	0.6	0.6	0.6	0.6
Canada	2.0	2.1	2.0	1.9	1.7	1.6	1.6	1.6
Chile	0.2	0.2	0.2	0.2	0.2	0.2	0.2	0.3
Czech Republic	0.2	0.2	0.2	0.2	0.1	0.1	0.1	0.1
Denmark	0.7	0.7	4.6	0.7	0.7	0.6	0.7	0.8
Estonia	0.0	0.0	0.0	0.0	0.0	0.0	0.0	0.0
Finland	0.2	0.2	0.3	0.3	0.2	0.2	0.2	0.1
France	6.2	5.5	5.7	5.9	5.2	6.0	5.9	6.4
Germany	5.5	6.5	6.9	6.8	6.1	5.7	5.8	6.3
Greece	0.1	0.1	0.1	0.1	0.1	0.1	0.1	0.1
Hungary	0.1	0.1	0.1	0.1	0.1	0.1	0.1	0.1
Iceland	0.0	0.0	0.0	0.0	0.0	0.0	0.0	0.0
Ireland	1.0	1.0	0.9	1.1	1.0	1.0	0.9	0.9
Israel	0.3	0.3	0.3	0.3	0.3	0.3	0.3	0.4
Italy	3.4	2.9	3.3	3.9	3.4	2.9	2.8	3.1
Japan	12.7	10.1	7.2	7.0	6.5	8.4	7.3	7.6
Korea	3.0	3.5	3.5	3.8	3.8	3.6	3.6	3.6
Latvia	0.0	0.0	0.0	0.0	0.0	0.0	0.0	0.0
Lithuania	0.0	0.0	0.0	0.0	0.0	0.0	0.0	0.0
Luxembourg	0.4	0.5	0.5	0.6	0.4	0.4	0.5	0.5
Mexico	0.5	0.5	0.6	0.6	0.5	0.5	0.5	0.5
Netherlands	1.3	1.1	1.1	1.0	0.8	1.5	1.5	1.6
New Zealand	..	0.1	0.1	0.1	0.1	0.1	0.1	..
Norway	0.5	0.5	0.5	0.5	0.4	0.4	0.4	0.4
Poland	0.4	0.4	0.4	0.4	0.3	0.3	0.3	0.3
Portugal	0.3	0.3	0.4	0.4	0.3	0.2	0.2	0.3
Slovak Republic	0.1	0.1	0.1	0.1	0.1	..	0.1	..
Slovenia	0.1	0.1	0.1	0.1	0.0	0.0	0.0	0.1
Spain	1.9	1.6	1.6	1.5	1.4	1.4	1.4	1.5
Sweden	0.6	0.5	0.6	1.0	0.8	0.8	0.8	0.9
Switzerland	1.5	1.5	1.5	1.5	1.5	1.3	1.3	1.3
Turkey	0.2	0.2	0.3	0.2	0.2	0.3	0.2	0.2
United Kingdom	7.3	7.9	7.0	7.4	7.0	7.8	7.4	8.9
United States	46.5	48.6	47.1	49.1	54.1	51.9	53.2	49.7
OECD Total	100.0	100.0	100.0	100.0	100.0	100.0	100.0	100.0

.. Not available

Note: Detailed metadata at: *http://metalinks.oecd.org/ins/20200312/1e50.*

Source: Insurance activity indicators, OECD Insurance Statistics (database)

Table 11. Market share in OECD (Life)

Per cent

	2011	2012	2013	2014	2015	2016	2017	2018
Australia	2.0	1.8	1.9	2.4	2.0	1.7	1.6	1.3
Austria	..	..	0.3	0.4	0.3	0.3	0.3	0.2
Belgium	1.1	1.1	0.8	0.9	0.7	0.7	0.7	0.7
Canada	1.3	1.2	1.3	1.1	1.0	1.0	1.1	1.0
Chile	0.2	0.3	0.3	0.3	0.3	0.4	0.4	0.4
Czech Republic	0.2	0.1	0.1	0.1	0.1	0.1	0.1	0.1
Denmark	0.9	0.9	8.4	1.0	0.9	1.0	1.1	1.1
Estonia	0.0	0.0	0.0	0.0	0.0	0.0	0.0	0.0
Finland	0.2	0.2	0.3	0.3	0.3	0.2	0.2	0.2
France	7.5	6.4	6.7	7.6	6.7	7.5	7.2	7.0
Germany	4.8	4.3	4.7	4.9	4.2	4.0	4.1	4.0
Greece	0.1	0.1	0.1	0.1	0.1	0.1	0.1	0.1
Hungary	0.1	0.1	0.1	0.1	0.1	0.1	0.1	0.1
Iceland	0.0	0.0	0.0	0.0	0.0	0.0	0.0	0.0
Ireland	1.4	1.5	1.4	1.7	1.6	1.5	1.6	1.4
Israel	0.3	0.3	0.3	0.3	0.3	0.3	0.4	0.4
Italy	4.3	3.7	4.5	6.0	5.4	4.7	4.7	4.6
Japan	19.4	19.0	13.7	14.0	13.2	13.6	12.1	11.4
Korea	3.2	3.9	3.9	4.3	4.4	4.3	4.2	3.9
Latvia	0.0	0.0	0.0	0.0	0.0	0.0	0.0	0.0
Lithuania	0.0	0.0	0.0	0.0	0.0	0.0	0.0	0.0
Luxembourg	0.7	0.9	0.9	1.1	0.8	0.8	0.9	0.8
Mexico	0.4	0.4	0.5	0.5	0.5	0.5	0.5	0.5
Netherlands	1.2	1.0	0.9	0.9	0.7	0.6	0.6	0.5
New Zealand	..	..	..	..	..	..	..	..
Norway	0.5	0.6	0.5	0.6	0.5	0.5	0.5	0.5
Poland	0.4	0.4	0.4	0.4	0.3	0.3	0.3	0.2
Portugal	0.4	0.3	0.5	0.5	0.4	0.3	0.3	0.3
Slovak Republic	0.1	0.1	0.1	0.1	0.1	..	0.2	..
Slovenia	0.0	0.0	0.0	0.0	0.0	0.0	0.0	0.0
Spain	1.7	1.4	1.3	1.4	1.2	1.4	1.4	1.3
Sweden	0.6	0.5	0.6	1.4	1.2	1.2	1.4	1.4
Switzerland	1.4	1.3	1.4	1.5	1.4	1.3	1.3	1.2
Turkey	0.1	0.1	0.1	0.1	0.1	0.1	0.1	0.1
United Kingdom	10.2	11.1	9.6	10.8	10.3	11.5	11.1	12.6
United States	35.3	36.8	34.4	35.4	40.8	40.1	41.7	42.8
OECD Total	100.0	100.0	100.0	100.0	100.0	100.0	100.0	100.0

.. Not available

Note: Detailed metadata at: *http://metalinks.oecd.org/ins/20200312/1e50.*

Source: *Insurance activity indicators, OECD Insurance Statistics (database)*

Table 12. Market share in OECD (Non-life)

Per cent

	2011	2012	2013	2014	2015	2016	2017	2018
Australia	1.7	1.8	1.7	1.5	1.3	1.2	1.2	1.3
Austria	..	..	0.7	0.7	0.6	0.5	0.5	0.6
Belgium	0.7	0.7	0.7	0.7	0.6	0.5	0.5	0.6
Canada	2.8	3.0	2.9	2.7	2.4	2.1	2.1	2.3
Chile	0.2	0.2	0.2	0.2	0.1	0.1	0.1	0.2
Czech Republic	0.2	0.2	0.2	0.2	0.1	0.1	0.1	0.2
Denmark	0.5	0.5	0.5	0.5	0.4	0.4	0.4	0.5
Estonia	0.0	0.0	0.0	0.0	0.0	0.0	0.0	0.0
Finland	0.2	0.2	0.2	0.2	0.2	0.2	0.2	..
France	4.8	4.5	4.5	4.3	3.7	4.7	4.8	5.8
Germany	6.4	8.9	9.3	8.8	7.9	7.1	7.3	8.7
Greece	0.2	0.2	0.1	0.1	0.1	0.1	0.1	0.1
Hungary	0.1	0.1	0.1	0.1	0.1	0.1	0.1	0.1
Iceland	0.0	0.0	0.0	0.0	0.0	0.0	0.0	0.0
Ireland	0.4	0.4	0.4	0.4	0.4	0.6	0.3	0.4
Israel	0.3	0.3	0.3	0.3	0.3	0.3	0.3	0.3
Italy	2.4	2.1	2.0	1.8	1.5	1.3	1.3	1.6
Japan	5.2	..	..	..	..	3.8	3.3	3.8
Korea	2.7	3.0	3.0	3.3	3.2	2.9	3.0	3.4
Latvia	0.0	0.0	0.0	0.0	0.0	0.0	0.0	0.0
Lithuania	0.0	0.0	0.0	0.0	0.0	0.0	0.0	0.0
Luxembourg	0.1	0.1	0.1	0.1	0.1	0.1	0.1	0.1
Mexico	0.6	0.6	0.6	0.6	0.5	0.5	0.5	0.6
Netherlands	1.3	1.2	1.2	1.0	0.9	2.2	2.2	2.7
New Zealand	..	0.2	0.2	0.2	0.2	0.2	0.2	..
Norway	0.5	0.5	0.5	0.5	0.4	0.3	0.3	0.4
Poland	0.4	0.4	0.4	0.3	0.3	0.3	0.3	0.4
Portugal	0.3	0.2	0.2	0.2	0.2	0.2	0.2	0.2
Slovak Republic	0.1	0.1	0.1	0.1	0.0	..	0.0	..
Slovenia	0.1	0.1	0.1	0.1	0.1	0.1	0.1	0.1
Spain	2.1	1.8	1.9	1.7	1.5	1.4	1.4	1.7
Sweden	0.6	0.5	0.6	0.6	0.4	0.4	0.4	0.5
Switzerland	1.7	1.7	1.7	1.6	1.5	1.3	1.3	1.5
Turkey	0.4	0.4	0.5	0.4	0.4	0.4	0.4	0.4
United Kingdom	4.1	4.1	4.1	4.0	3.7	4.5	4.3	5.0
United States	59.0	62.0	61.2	62.9	67.0	62.2	62.7	56.7
OECD Total	100.0	100.0	100.0	100.0	100.0	100.0	100.0	100.0

.. Not available

Note: Detailed metadata at: *http://metalinks.oecd.org/ins/20200312/1e50.*

Source: *Insurance activity indicators, OECD Insurance Statistics (database)*

Table 13. Density (Life and Non-life)

US dollar per inhabitant

	2011	2012	2013	2014	2015	2016	2017	2018
Argentina	..	333	393	405	418	422	393	427
Australia	3 378	3 328	3 350	3 688	2 926	2 660	2 540	2 383
Austria	2 744	2 492	2 603	2 657	2 227	2 143	2 176	2 284
Belgium	3 601	3 684	3 260	3 308	2 653	2 613	2 653	2 900
Bolivia	..	31	..	..	..	43	43	47
Brazil	319	334	337	346	273	287	321	276
Canada	2 517	2 562	2 538	2 168	1 930	1 919	2 011	2 086
Chile	560	645	665	613	630	675	694	748
Colombia	..	31	..	..	..	43	43	47
Costa Rica	172	198	218	241	216	246	265	265
Cuba	..	35	..	..	..	..	..	..
Czech Republic	822	733	747	712	574	555	590	652
Denmark	6 069	5 823	6 079	6 543	5 610	5 699	6 315	6 842
Dominican Republic	..	..	..	..	..	..	..	119
Ecuador	..	..	..	..	139	127	..	..
Egypt	..	..	..	..	..	..	..	..
El Salvador	..	..	..	..	..	..	..	94
Estonia	422	466	587	638	581	619	702	828
Finland	1 850	1 699	2 371	2 556	2 150	1 797	1 803	933
France	4 186	3 645	3 893	4 110	3 554	4 108	4 248	4 569
Germany	..	2 890	3 112	3 131	2 597	2 602	2 838	3 049
Greece	609	511	480	457	361	359	388	414
Guatemala	41	39	43	46	48	50	55	54
Honduras	..	42	43	43	44	..	..	67
Hong Kong, China	3 917	4 403	5 003	5 658	6 259	7 652	8 266	8 807
Hungary	403	336	357	360	300	317	350	381
India	58	..	..	..	55	63	72	..
Indonesia	60	63	60	55	56	66	73	71
Iceland	1 281	1 232	1 270	1 329	1 245	1 436	1 783	1 840
Ireland	9 575	9 702	9 606	11 052	10 154	11 107	10 207	9 531
Israel[1]	1 631	1 577	1 731	1 749	1 685	1 772	2 001	2 090
Italy	2 553	2 239	2 600	3 125	2 678	2 445	2 437	2 645
Japan	4 416	3 355	2 545	2 580	2 370	3 201	2 893	3 010
Korea	2 612	3 090	3 182	3 502	3 417	3 436	3 478	3 501
Latvia	264	277	309	343	297	299	374	461
Lithuania	226	222	254	272	246	274	317	372
Luxembourg	36 749	47 314	45 569	51 995	37 506	35 103	41 043	40 668
Malaysia	478	514	520	530	454	441	439	481
Mexico	192	198	226	224	203	194	211	223
Morocco	..	..	..	..	..	..	..	..
Netherlands	3 488	3 018	2 998	2 840	2 172	4 519	4 610	4 968
New Zealand	..	1 024	1 141	1 169	964	983	1 006	..
Nicaragua	21	24	26	30	31	33	35	36
Norway	4 785	5 111	5 011	5 132	3 967	3 972	3 858	4 131
Panama	278	286	321	..	..	..	..	..
Paraguay	..	46	54	..	63	53	56	..
Peru	88	99	110	116	118	106	109	122
Poland	502	500	475	453	372	361	420	436
Portugal	1 427	1 237	1 570	1 735	1 293	1 110	1 189	1 369
Puerto Rico	..	..	2 661	2 552	3 182	3 927	..	..
Russia	159	..	..	179	117	123	152	164
Singapore	3 391	3 728	4 047	4 489	4 400	4 631	5 411	..
Slovak Republic	551	508	542	544	434	..	927	..
Slovenia	1 305	1 202	1 209	1 198	1 012	1 028	1 105	1 223
South Africa	1 086	..	998	934	840	742	..	..
Spain	1 737	1 518	1 529	1 521	1 295	1 458	1 471	1 559
Sri Lanka	..	..	..	35	44	..	51	52
Sweden	2 781	2 376	2 644	4 908	3 961	3 796	4 248	4 646
Switzerland	7 969	7 634	7 898	7 892	7 456	7 025	6 904	6 962
Thailand	232	..	..	..	..	..	..	..
Tunisia	..	..	..	..	..	75	75	..
Turkey	133	146	168	151	145	162	152	126
United Kingdom	4 937	5 316	4 793	5 098	4 598	3 950	5 113	5 643
United States	5 493	5 752	5 686	5 970	6 305	6 500	6 717	7 082
Uruguay	268	310	351	377	368	..	451	..
OECD Total	3 297	3 197	3 131	3 294	3 157	3 313	3 424	3 630

.. Not available

Note: Detailed metadata at: *http://metalinks.oecd.org/ins/20200312/1e50.*

1. Information on data for Israel: *http://oe.cd/israel-disclaimer.*

Source: Insurance activity indicators, OECD Insurance Statistics (database)

Table 14. Density (Life)

US dollar per inhabitant

	2011	2012	2013	2014	2015	2016	2017	2018
Argentina	..	68	70	70	67	70	60	63
Australia	1 993	1 856	1 898	2 321	1 781	1 521	1 335	1 180
Austria	1 145	981	1 007	1 039	860	765	735	735
Belgium	2 337	2 445	1 937	1 930	1 512	1 458	1 454	1 611
Bolivia	..	7	..	..	..	14	18	20
Brazil	190	210	204	209	171	190	214	178
Canada	856	820	834	629	555	561	604	625
Chile	351	424	444	406	432	475	482	515
Colombia	..	7	..	..	..	14	18	20
Costa Rica	18	24	29	30	27	38	39	43
Cuba	..	..	..	..	..	..	..	..
Czech Republic	388	350	348	326	241	229	230	242
Denmark	4 147	4 005	4 236	4 443	3 878	4 006	4 495	4 939
Dominican Republic	..	..	..	..	..	..	..	19
Ecuador	..	..	..	..	28	28	..	..
Egypt	..	..	..	..	..	..	..	..
El Salvador	..	..	..	..	..	..	..	24
Estonia	168	158	172	193	181	186	191	209
Finland	963	885	1 366	1 485	1 268	923	929	933
France	2 762	2 305	2 486	2 684	2 344	2 391	2 450	2 641
Germany	..	1 326	1 445	1 456	1 180	1 148	1 197	1 282
Greece	268	225	203	228	184	171	197	207
Guatemala	8	8	9	10	9	10	11	11
Honduras	..	20	21	15	16	..	..	22
Hong Kong, China	3 454	3 882	4 446	5 082	5 644	7 041	7 642	8 152
Hungary	221	180	197	199	155	159	171	178
India	50	..	..	..	43	48	54	..
Indonesia	44	47	43	38	39	49	56	52
Iceland	95	92	103	111	107	128	161	155
Ireland	7 637	7 851	7 803	9 158	8 141	7 729	8 198	7 395
Israel[1]	861	835	915	904	903	935	1 076	1 128
Italy	1 714	1 487	1 866	2 413	2 096	1 864	1 837	1 994
Japan	3 651	3 355	2 545	2 580	2 370	2 496	2 252	2 348
Korea	1 566	1 894	1 966	2 069	2 031	2 015	1 959	1 950
Latvia	49	49	59	71	64	70	84	89
Lithuania	75	71	81	97	90	95	93	105
Luxembourg	33 218	44 173	41 868	48 768	34 604	32 123	37 673	37 331
Malaysia	305	332	333	340	294	290	295	325
Mexico	87	93	105	106	95	92	92	101
Morocco	..	..	..	..	..	..	..	..
Netherlands	1 806	1 455	1 444	1 375	962	892	854	822
New Zealand	..	..	..	..	..	..	..	..
Nicaragua	3	4	5	5	5	6	7	7
Norway	2 568	2 789	2 715	2 837	2 187	2 133	2 139	2 309
Panama	18	112	128	..	..	..	..	..
Paraguay	..	..	7	..	8	0	8	..
Peru	42	47	51	57	57	48	52	59
Poland	282	293	260	239	192	159	171	158
Portugal	951	816	1 146	1 309	908	697	736	893
Puerto Rico	..	..	114	161	156	373	..	..
Russia	12	..	..	23	17	26	43	54
Singapore	2 723	2 725	3 045	3 392	3 404	3 611	4 374	..
Slovak Republic	296	276	303	299	227	..	683	..
Slovenia	327	303	305	309	268	264	282	300
South Africa	847	..	804	769	686	609	..	..
Spain	858	722	729	712	606	737	706	727
Sri Lanka	..	..	..	13	19	..	22	22
Sweden	1 466	1 362	1 469	3 562	2 994	2 931	3 335	3 625
Switzerland	4 372	4 177	4 385	4 378	4 113	3 739	3 573	3 592
Thailand	163	..	..	..	..	..	..	..
Tunisia	..	..	..	..	..	15	15	..
Turkey	25	23	26	19	17	25	27	21
United Kingdom	3 670	4 054	3 488	3 781	3 411	2 508	3 652	4 112
United States	2 518	2 641	2 472	2 475	2 576	2 587	2 641	2 779
Uruguay	65	82	101	111	123	..	190	..
OECD Total	1 906	1 849	1 737	1 824	1 701	1 654	1 706	1 810

.. Not available

Note: Detailed metadata at: *http://metalinks.oecd.org/ins/20200312/1e50.*

1. Information on data for Israel: *http://oe.cd/israel-disclaimer.*

Source: Insurance activity indicators, OECD Insurance Statistics (database)

Table 15. Density (Non-life)

US dollar per inhabitant

	2011	2012	2013	2014	2015	2016	2017	2018
Argentina	..	265	323	335	351	352	333	364
Australia	1 385	1 473	1 453	1 367	1 145	1 139	1 205	1 204
Austria	1 599	1 511	1 596	1 617	1 367	1 377	1 441	1 550
Belgium	1 265	1 239	1 323	1 378	1 142	1 156	1 200	1 289
Bolivia	..	24	..	..	..	28	26	27
Brazil	129	124	133	138	102	97	108	99
Canada	1 660	1 743	1 704	1 539	1 375	1 358	1 407	1 461
Chile	209	221	221	208	198	200	212	233
Colombia	..	24	..	..	..	28	26	27
Costa Rica	154	174	189	211	188	208	226	222
Cuba	..	35	..	..	..	..	..	..
Czech Republic	434	383	399	386	333	325	360	410
Denmark	1 923	1 818	1 843	2 101	1 732	1 692	1 820	1 903
Dominican Republic	..	..	..	..	..	..	..	100
Ecuador	..	..	..	..	112	98	..	..
Egypt	..	..	..	..	..	..	..	..
El Salvador	..	..	..	..	..	..	..	70
Estonia	254	308	415	444	400	433	510	620
Finland	886	814	1 005	1 071	882	875	873	..
France	1 424	1 340	1 407	1 427	1 209	1 717	1 798	1 928
Germany	..	1 564	1 667	1 674	1 417	1 454	1 641	1 767
Greece	341	286	277	229	177	188	190	207
Guatemala	33	31	34	36	39	40	43	43
Honduras	..	22	22	28	28	..	..	45
Hong Kong, China	463	521	557	577	615	611	624	655
Hungary	182	156	160	161	145	158	179	203
India	8	..	..	..	12	15	18	..
Indonesia	16	17	17	18	17	17	18	18
Iceland	1 186	1 140	1 166	1 217	1 138	1 308	1 621	1 685
Ireland	1 938	1 851	1 803	1 894	2 013	3 378	1 890	1 910
Israel[1]	771	742	815	845	782	838	925	962
Italy	840	752	735	712	582	581	600	651
Japan	765	..	..	..	..	705	641	662
Korea	1 046	1 196	1 215	1 433	1 386	1 421	1 519	1 552
Latvia	214	228	250	273	232	230	290	373
Lithuania	152	151	173	175	156	179	224	267
Luxembourg	3 531	3 141	3 700	3 227	2 902	2 980	3 370	3 337
Malaysia	173	182	187	190	160	150	144	156
Mexico	105	105	121	118	108	103	119	122
Morocco	..	..	..	..	..	..	..	..
Netherlands	1 681	1 563	1 554	1 464	1 209	3 627	3 756	4 146
New Zealand	..	1 024	1 141	1 169	964	983	1 006	..
Nicaragua	18	20	22	24	26	27	29	28
Norway	2 217	2 322	2 295	2 295	1 780	1 840	1 719	1 822
Panama	..	174	192	..	..	..	..	..
Paraguay	..	27	48	..	54	53	48	..
Peru	46	53	59	59	61	58	58	62
Poland	220	207	216	214	180	202	249	278
Portugal	476	421	424	426	385	413	454	476
Puerto Rico	..	..	2 546	2 391	3 026	3 554	..	..
Russia	135	..	..	112	100	97	109	110
Singapore	668	1 004	1 001	1 098	996	1 021	1 037	..
Slovak Republic	256	232	238	244	207	..	244	..
Slovenia	978	899	904	889	744	765	823	923
South Africa	239	..	195	165	154	133	..	..
Spain	879	795	800	809	690	721	765	833
Sri Lanka	..	..	..	22	25	..	30	30
Sweden	1 315	1 015	1 175	1 346	967	865	913	1 021
Switzerland	3 597	3 458	3 513	3 514	3 343	3 286	3 331	3 370
Thailand	69	..	..	..	..	..	..	..
Tunisia	..	..	..	..	..	60	59	..
Turkey	108	123	141	131	128	137	125	105
United Kingdom	1 267	1 262	1 306	1 317	1 188	1 441	1 461	1 530
United States	2 975	3 111	3 214	3 495	3 729	3 913	4 076	4 304
Uruguay	203	228	250	266	245	..	261	..
OECD Total	1 392	1 348	1 394	1 471	1 455	1 659	1 717	1 819

.. Not available

Note: Detailed metadata at: *http://metalinks.oecd.org/ins/20200312/1e50.*

1. Information on data for Israel: *http://oe.cd/israel-disclaimer.*

Source: Insurance activity indicators, OECD Insurance Statistics (database)

Table 16. Penetration (Life and Non-life)

Per cent

	2011	2012	2013	2014	2015	2016	2017	2018
Argentina	..	2.3	2.4	2.4	2.6	2.6	2.6	2.3
Australia	4.9	4.8	5.1	6.0	5.6	4.9	4.4	4.1
Austria	5.3	5.1	5.1	5.1	5.0	4.7	4.6	4.5
Belgium	7.6	8.2	7.0	6.9	6.4	6.2	6.0	6.1
Bolivia	..	1.2	..	..	..	1.4	1.3	1.3
Brazil	2.4	2.7	2.7	2.8	3.1	3.3	3.2	3.1
Canada	4.8	4.9	4.8	4.2	4.4	4.5	4.4	4.5
Chile	3.8	4.2	4.2	4.2	4.6	4.9	4.6	4.7
Colombia	..	1.2	..	..	..	1.4	1.3	1.3
Costa Rica	1.9	2.0	2.1	2.3	1.9	2.1	2.3	2.2
Cuba	..	..	..	..	..	..	..	..
Czech Republic	3.8	3.7	3.8	3.6	3.2	3.0	2.9	2.8
Denmark	9.8	9.9	9.9	10.4	10.5	10.4	11.0	11.1
Dominican Republic	..	..	..	..	..	..	..	1.5
Ecuador	..	..	..	..	2.3	2.1	..	..
Egypt	..	..	..	..	..	..	..	..
El Salvador	..	..	..	..	..	..	..	2.4
Estonia	2.4	2.7	3.1	3.1	3.3	3.4	3.4	3.6
Finland	3.6	3.6	4.7	5.1	5.0	4.1	3.9	1.9
France	9.2	8.6	8.8	9.2	9.4	10.7	10.6	10.6
Germany	..	6.6	6.7	6.5	6.3	6.2	6.4	6.4
Greece	2.4	2.3	2.2	2.1	2.0	2.0	2.1	2.0
Guatemala	1.3	1.2	1.2	1.2	1.2	1.2	1.2	1.2
Honduras	..	1.9	2.0	1.9	1.9	..	..	2.6
Hong Kong, China	11.2	12.0	13.1	14.1	14.8	17.6	17.9	18.2
Hungary	2.9	2.6	2.6	2.5	2.4	2.4	2.4	2.4
India	3.8	..	..	..	3.4	3.6	3.6	..
Indonesia	1.6	1.7	1.6	1.6	1.7	1.8	1.9	1.8
Iceland	2.7	2.7	2.6	2.4	2.4	2.3	2.5	2.5
Ireland	18.5	19.9	18.6	19.9	16.4	17.6	14.7	12.2
Israel[1]	4.8	4.8	4.8	4.6	4.7	4.7	4.9	5.0
Italy	6.7	6.5	7.3	8.8	8.9	7.9	7.5	7.7
Japan	8.8	6.8	6.4	6.8	6.8	7.7	7.4	7.8
Korea	10.4	12.1	11.7	12.0	11.9	11.7	11.0	10.5
Latvia	1.9	2.0	2.1	2.2	2.2	2.1	2.4	2.6
Lithuania	1.6	1.6	1.6	1.6	1.7	1.8	1.9	1.9
Luxembourg	31.3	43.8	39.6	43.2	36.6	33.3	37.8	34.5
Malaysia	4.7	4.8	4.9	4.8	4.8	4.7	4.5	4.4
Mexico	1.9	1.9	2.1	2.0	2.1	2.2	2.3	2.3
Morocco	..	..	..	..	..	..	..	..
Netherlands	6.4	6.0	5.7	5.4	4.8	9.8	9.5	9.3
New Zealand	..	2.6	2.7	2.7	2.5	2.5	2.4	..
Nicaragua	1.3	1.3	1.4	1.5	1.5	1.6	1.6	1.7
Norway	4.8	5.1	4.9	5.3	5.4	5.7	5.1	5.1
Panama	3.0	2.7	2.7	..	..	..	..	..
Paraguay	..	0.9	0.9	..	1.0	1.0	1.0	..
Peru	1.5	1.6	1.7	1.8	1.9	1.7	1.6	1.7
Poland	3.6	3.8	3.5	3.2	3.0	2.9	3.0	2.8
Portugal	6.1	6.0	7.2	7.8	6.7	5.6	5.5	5.8
Puerto Rico	..	..	9.3	8.8	10.7	12.9	..	..
Russia	1.1	..	..	1.3	1.2	1.4	1.4	1.4
Singapore	6.4	6.8	7.2	7.8	8.0	8.2	9.0	..
Slovak Republic	3.0	2.9	3.0	2.9	2.7	..	5.3	..
Slovenia	5.2	5.3	5.1	4.9	4.8	4.8	4.7	4.7
South Africa	13.4	..	14.5	14.4	14.5	13.9	..	..
Spain	5.5	5.4	5.3	5.2	5.0	5.5	5.2	5.1
Sri Lanka	..	..	..	0.9	1.1	..	1.3	1.3
Sweden	4.6	4.1	4.4	8.2	7.7	7.4	8.0	8.5
Switzerland	9.0	9.1	9.2	9.1	9.0	8.7	8.5	8.4
Thailand	4.1	..	..	..	..	..	..	..
Tunisia	..	..	..	..	..	2.0	2.2	..
Turkey	1.2	1.3	1.4	1.3	1.3	1.5	1.4	1.3
United Kingdom	11.7	12.5	11.0	10.7	10.2	9.6	12.7	13.1
United States	11.0	11.2	10.7	10.9	11.1	11.2	11.2	11.3
Uruguay	1.9	2.1	2.1	2.3	2.4	..	2.7	..
OECD Total	8.6	8.3	8.1	8.4	8.6	8.8	8.8	8.9

.. Not available

Note: Detailed metadata at: *http://metalinks.oecd.org/ins/20200312/1e50.*

1. Information on data for Israel: *http://oe.cd/israel-disclaimer.*

Source: Insurance activity indicators, OECD Insurance Statistics (database)

Table 17. Penetration (Life)

Per cent

	2011	2012	2013	2014	2015	2016	2017	2018
Argentina	..	0.5	0.4	0.4	0.4	0.4	0.4	0.3
Australia	2.9	2.7	2.9	3.7	3.4	2.8	2.3	2.0
Austria	2.2	2.0	2.0	2.0	1.9	1.7	1.5	1.4
Belgium	4.9	5.5	4.1	4.0	3.7	3.5	3.3	3.4
Bolivia	..	0.3	..	..	..	0.5	0.5	0.6
Brazil	1.4	1.7	1.7	1.7	1.9	2.2	2.2	2.0
Canada	1.6	1.6	1.6	1.2	1.3	1.3	1.3	1.3
Chile	2.4	2.8	2.8	2.8	3.2	3.4	3.2	3.2
Colombia	..	0.3	..	..	..	0.5	0.5	0.6
Costa Rica	0.2	0.2	0.3	0.3	0.2	0.3	0.3	0.4
Cuba	..	..	..	..	..	..	..	..
Czech Republic	1.8	1.8	1.7	1.7	1.4	1.2	1.1	1.0
Denmark	6.7	6.8	6.9	7.1	7.3	7.3	7.8	8.0
Dominican Republic	..	..	..	..	..	..	..	0.2
Ecuador	..	..	..	..	0.5	0.5	..	..
Egypt	..	..	..	..	..	..	..	..
El Salvador	..	..	..	..	..	..	..	0.6
Estonia	1.0	0.9	0.9	0.9	1.0	1.0	0.9	0.9
Finland	1.9	1.9	2.7	2.9	3.0	2.1	2.0	1.9
France	6.1	5.4	5.6	6.0	6.2	6.2	6.1	6.2
Germany	..	3.0	3.1	3.0	2.9	2.7	2.7	2.7
Greece	1.0	1.0	0.9	1.1	1.0	0.9	1.0	1.0
Guatemala	0.2	0.2	0.3	0.3	0.2	0.2	0.3	0.2
Honduras	..	0.9	1.0	0.7	0.7	..	..	0.9
Hong Kong, China	9.9	10.6	11.6	12.6	13.3	16.2	16.6	16.8
Hungary	1.6	1.4	1.4	1.4	1.2	1.2	1.2	1.1
India	3.3	..	..	..	2.7	2.7	2.7	..
Indonesia	1.2	1.2	1.2	1.1	1.2	1.3	1.4	1.3
Iceland	0.2	0.2	0.2	0.2	0.2	0.2	0.2	0.2
Ireland	14.7	16.1	15.1	16.5	13.2	12.3	11.8	9.5
Israel[1]	2.6	2.6	2.5	2.4	2.5	2.5	2.7	2.7
Italy	4.5	4.3	5.3	6.8	6.9	6.0	5.7	5.8
Japan	7.3	6.8	6.4	6.8	6.8	6.0	5.8	6.1
Korea	6.2	7.4	7.2	7.1	7.1	6.9	6.2	5.9
Latvia	0.4	0.4	0.4	0.5	0.5	0.5	0.5	0.5
Lithuania	0.5	0.5	0.5	0.6	0.6	0.6	0.5	0.5
Luxembourg	28.3	40.9	36.4	40.5	33.7	30.5	34.7	31.7
Malaysia	3.0	3.1	3.1	3.1	3.1	3.1	3.0	3.0
Mexico	0.9	0.9	1.0	1.0	1.0	1.0	1.0	1.0
Morocco	..	..	..	..	..	..	..	..
Netherlands	3.3	2.9	2.8	2.6	2.1	1.9	1.8	1.5
New Zealand	..	..	..	..	..	..	..	..
Nicaragua	0.2	0.2	0.2	0.3	0.3	0.3	0.3	0.3
Norway	2.6	2.8	2.6	2.9	3.0	3.0	2.8	2.8
Panama	0.2	1.0	1.1	..	..	..	..	..
Paraguay	..	..	0.1	..	0.1	0.0	0.1	..
Peru	0.7	0.7	0.8	0.9	0.9	0.8	0.8	0.8
Poland	2.0	2.2	1.9	1.7	1.5	1.3	1.2	1.0
Portugal	4.1	4.0	5.3	5.9	4.7	3.5	3.4	3.8
Puerto Rico	..	..	0.4	0.6	0.5	1.2	..	..
Russia	0.1	..	..	0.2	0.2	0.3	0.4	0.5
Singapore	5.1	5.0	5.4	5.9	6.2	6.4	7.3	..
Slovak Republic	1.6	1.6	1.7	1.6	1.4	..	3.9	..
Slovenia	1.3	1.3	1.3	1.3	1.3	1.2	1.2	1.1
South Africa	10.5	..	11.6	11.8	11.8	11.4	..	..
Spain	2.7	2.5	2.5	2.4	2.4	2.8	2.5	2.4
Sri Lanka	..	..	..	0.3	0.5	..	0.5	0.5
Sweden	2.4	2.4	2.4	6.0	5.9	5.7	6.2	6.7
Switzerland	4.9	5.0	5.1	5.0	5.0	4.6	4.4	4.3
Thailand	2.9	..	..	..	..	..	..	..
Tunisia	..	..	..	..	..	0.4	0.4	..
Turkey	0.2	0.2	0.2	0.2	0.2	0.2	0.3	0.2
United Kingdom	8.7	9.5	8.0	8.0	7.6	6.1	9.0	9.6
United States	5.1	5.1	4.7	4.5	4.5	4.5	4.4	4.4
Uruguay	0.5	0.5	0.6	0.7	0.8	..	1.1	..
OECD Total	5.0	4.8	4.5	4.7	4.7	4.4	4.4	4.4

.. Not available

Note: Detailed metadata at: *http://metalinks.oecd.org/ins/20200312/1e50.*

1. Information on data for Israel: *http://oe.cd/israel-disclaimer.*

Source: Insurance activity indicators, OECD Insurance Statistics (database)

Table 18. Penetration (Non-life)

Per cent

	2011	2012	2013	2014	2015	2016	2017	2018
Argentina	..	1.8	2.0	2.0	2.2	2.1	2.2	2.0
Australia	2.0	2.1	2.2	2.2	2.2	2.1	2.1	2.1
Austria	3.1	3.1	3.1	3.1	3.1	3.0	3.0	3.0
Belgium	2.7	2.8	2.8	2.9	2.8	2.7	2.7	2.7
Bolivia	..	0.9	..	..	..	0.9	0.8	0.7
Brazil	1.0	1.0	1.1	1.1	1.1	1.1	1.1	1.1
Canada	3.2	3.3	3.2	3.0	3.2	3.2	3.1	3.1
Chile	1.4	1.4	1.4	1.4	1.5	1.4	1.4	1.5
Colombia	..	0.9	..	..	..	0.9	0.8	0.7
Costa Rica	1.7	1.8	1.8	2.0	1.7	1.8	1.9	1.9
Cuba	..	..	..	..	..	..	..	..
Czech Republic	2.0	1.9	2.0	2.0	1.9	1.8	1.8	1.8
Denmark	3.1	3.1	3.0	3.3	3.2	3.1	3.2	3.1
Dominican Republic	..	..	..	..	..	..	..	1.3
Ecuador	..	..	..	..	1.8	1.6	..	..
Egypt	..	..	..	..	..	..	..	..
El Salvador	..	..	..	..	..	..	..	1.8
Estonia	1.4	1.8	2.2	2.2	2.3	2.4	2.5	2.7
Finland	1.7	1.7	2.0	2.1	2.1	2.0	1.9	..
France	3.1	3.2	3.2	3.2	3.2	4.5	4.5	4.5
Germany	..	3.6	3.6	3.5	3.4	3.5	3.7	3.7
Greece	1.3	1.3	1.3	1.1	1.0	1.0	1.0	1.0
Guatemala	1.0	0.9	1.0	1.0	1.0	1.0	1.0	0.9
Honduras	..	1.0	1.0	1.2	1.2	..	..	1.8
Hong Kong, China	1.3	1.4	1.5	1.4	1.5	1.4	1.4	1.4
Hungary	1.3	1.2	1.2	1.1	1.2	1.2	1.2	1.3
India	0.5	..	..	..	0.7	0.9	0.9	..
Indonesia	0.4	0.4	0.5	0.5	0.5	0.5	0.5	0.5
Iceland	2.5	2.5	2.3	2.2	2.2	2.1	2.2	2.3
Ireland	3.7	3.8	3.5	3.4	3.3	5.4	2.7	2.4
Israel[1]	2.3	2.3	2.2	2.2	2.2	2.2	2.3	2.3
Italy	2.2	2.2	2.1	2.0	1.9	1.9	1.9	1.9
Japan	1.5	..	..	..	..	1.7	1.7	1.7
Korea	4.2	4.7	4.5	4.9	4.8	4.9	4.8	4.7
Latvia	1.6	1.7	1.7	1.7	1.7	1.6	1.9	2.1
Lithuania	1.1	1.1	1.1	1.1	1.1	1.2	1.3	1.4
Luxembourg	3.0	2.9	3.2	2.7	2.8	2.8	3.1	2.8
Malaysia	1.7	1.7	1.7	1.7	1.7	1.6	1.5	1.4
Mexico	1.0	1.0	1.1	1.1	1.1	1.2	1.3	1.2
Morocco	..	..	..	..	..	..	..	..
Netherlands	3.1	3.1	3.0	2.8	2.7	7.9	7.7	7.8
New Zealand	..	2.6	2.7	2.7	2.5	2.5	2.4	..
Nicaragua	1.1	1.1	1.2	1.2	1.3	1.3	1.3	1.3
Norway	2.2	2.3	2.2	2.4	2.4	2.6	2.3	2.2
Panama	..	1.6	1.6	..	..	..	..	..
Paraguay	..	0.5	0.8	..	0.9	1.0	0.9	..
Peru	0.8	0.8	0.9	0.9	1.0	0.9	0.9	0.9
Poland	1.6	1.6	1.6	1.5	1.4	1.6	1.8	1.8
Portugal	2.1	2.0	2.0	1.9	2.0	2.1	2.1	2.0
Puerto Rico	..	..	8.9	8.3	10.2	11.7	..	..
Russia	0.9	..	..	0.8	1.1	1.1	1.0	1.0
Singapore	1.3	1.8	1.8	1.9	1.8	1.8	1.7	..
Slovak Republic	1.4	1.3	1.3	1.3	1.3	..	1.4	..
Slovenia	3.9	4.0	3.8	3.7	3.6	3.5	3.5	3.5
South Africa	3.0	..	2.8	2.5	2.7	2.5	..	..
Spain	2.8	2.8	2.8	2.7	2.7	2.7	2.7	2.7
Sri Lanka	..	..	..	0.6	0.6	..	0.7	0.7
Sweden	2.2	1.8	1.9	2.3	1.9	1.7	1.7	1.9
Switzerland	4.0	4.1	4.1	4.0	4.1	4.1	4.1	4.1
Thailand	1.2	..	..	..	..	..	..	..
Tunisia	..	..	..	..	..	1.6	1.7	..
Turkey	1.0	1.1	1.1	1.1	1.2	1.3	1.2	1.1
United Kingdom	3.0	3.0	3.0	2.8	2.6	3.5	3.6	3.6
United States	6.0	6.0	6.1	6.4	6.6	6.8	6.8	6.8
Uruguay	1.4	1.5	1.5	1.6	1.6	..	1.5	..
OECD Total	3.6	4.0	4.0	4.2	4.4	4.4	4.4	4.5

.. Not available

Note: Detailed metadata at: *http://metalinks.oecd.org/ins/20200312/1e50.*

1. Information on data for Israel: *http://oe.cd/israel-disclaimer.*

Source: Insurance activity indicators, OECD Insurance Statistics (database)

Table 19. Life insurance share
Percentage of total insurance

Per cent

	2011	2012	2013	2014	2015	2016	2017	2018
Argentina	..	20.7	17.8	16.5	15.3	16.0	14.7	14.3
Australia	56.7	53.6	54.9	61.1	59.2	55.4	52.1	49.5
Austria	..	..	34.1	35.5	35.3	32.5	31.7	29.9
Belgium	63.2	64.7	57.7	56.5	55.4	54.4	53.7	54.7
Bolivia	..	21.8	..	..	..	33.5	40.4	43.3
Brazil	..	..	..	60.2	62.7	66.1	66.5	64.3
Canada	34.0	32.1	32.9	28.7	28.7	29.1	29.5	30.1
Chile	62.5	65.5	66.5	65.8	68.3	70.4	69.4	68.8
Colombia	..	21.8	..	..	..	33.5	40.4	43.3
Costa Rica	10.6	11.9	13.4	12.3	12.7	15.4	14.7	16.1
Cuba	..	..	..	..	..	..	..	..
Czech Republic	46.4	46.9	45.7	45.1	41.1	40.6	38.3	36.6
Denmark	68.2	68.7	95.4	67.7	68.9	68.7	69.1	70.0
Dominican Republic	..	..	..	..	..	..	..	16.1
Ecuador	..	..	..	..	19.5	22.0	..	..
Egypt	..	..	..	..	..	..	..	..
El Salvador	20.7	22.7	26.7	25.7	25.6	24.7	..	25.1
Estonia	39.8	33.9	29.3	30.3	31.2	30.0	27.3	25.2
Finland	51.2	51.2	56.8	57.4	58.3	50.6	50.7	100.0
France	63.9	62.1	62.4	64.2	64.2	58.0	55.2	55.2
Germany	45.7	35.5	36.0	35.9	34.0	33.1	32.1	31.8
Greece	43.7	43.2	41.4	49.5	50.5	47.2	50.4	49.5
Guatemala	..	20.3	19.9	20.8	19.4	19.9	20.5	20.5
Honduras	..	..	30.9	35.3	36.4	..	..	33.3
Hong Kong, China	84.8	84.7	85.7	86.9	87.6	90.1	90.4	90.1
Hungary	54.6	53.0	54.5	54.8	51.1	49.5	48.2	46.2
India	85.5	..	..	..	78.2	..	70.7	..
Indonesia	..	70.6	67.9	66.2	69.0	72.6	74.6	72.9
Iceland	7.3	7.3	7.9	8.2	8.4	8.8	8.9	8.3
Ireland	79.2	80.3	80.6	82.2	79.6	68.5	79.5	75.4
Israel[1]	52.8	52.9	52.9	51.7	53.6	52.7	53.8	54.0
Italy	67.1	66.5	71.4	76.8	77.8	75.8	75.0	74.7
Japan	80.7	100.0	100.0	100.0	100.0	75.5	75.1	75.2
Korea	57.5	59.0	59.3	56.8	57.1	56.3	53.9	53.2
Latvia	18.4	17.6	18.9	20.6	21.6	23.2	22.5	19.2
Lithuania	33.0	32.0	32.0	35.8	36.6	34.7	29.2	28.3
Luxembourg	90.4	93.4	91.9	93.9	92.3	91.5	91.8	91.8
Malaysia	60.3	60.6	60.1	60.2	60.6	61.7	63.4	64.1
Mexico	44.7	46.2	46.1	46.8	46.3	46.7	43.0	44.9
Morocco	..	..	..	..	..	..	..	..
Netherlands	51.4	47.6	47.4	47.7	43.6	19.6	18.2	16.2
New Zealand	..	..	..	..	..	..	..	..
Nicaragua	..	15.8	17.2	17.8	17.4	18.6	..	20.4
Norway	53.7	54.6	54.2	55.3	55.1	55.4	55.4	55.9
Panama	..	38.5	39.7	..	..	..	..	..
Paraguay	..	..	12.2	..	13.3	0.2	13.9	..
Peru	48.0	47.2	46.8	49.1	48.4	45.3	47.0	48.5
Poland	55.7	58.1	54.0	52.2	50.2	42.6	39.4	34.9
Portugal	64.2	63.3	70.5	72.9	67.5	59.6	58.6	61.8
Puerto Rico	..	..	4.3	6.3	4.9	9.5	..	..
Russia	7.5	..	..	12.6	13.9	20.4	27.4	32.0
Singapore	67.0	65.8	67.9	68.5	69.3	71.6	74.9	..
Slovak Republic	53.2	53.9	55.5	54.3	51.2	..	73.6	..
Slovenia	22.0	22.1	22.4	22.9	23.1	22.5	22.4	21.7
South Africa	78.0	79.2	78.6	80.5	79.9	79.7	..	..
Spain	46.9	46.4	44.6	43.9	43.6	47.1	44.8	43.6
Sri Lanka	..	..	..	35.5	42.5	..	41.4	41.3
Sweden	49.6	54.0	52.2	69.6	73.3	74.9	76.1	75.6
Switzerland	48.4	47.9	48.2	48.5	48.9	46.9	45.0	44.4
Thailand	69.0	..	..	..	..	..	..	..
Tunisia	..	..	..	..	..	20.3	19.7	..
Turkey	18.3	15.4	15.7	12.3	11.8	14.9	17.3	15.9
United Kingdom	73.5	75.4	72.4	73.4	73.3	68.8	68.3	71.7
United States	40.1	40.3	38.5	36.2	37.1	35.9	35.6	43.3
Uruguay	..	26.4	28.7	29.5	33.4	..	42.2	..
OECD Total	52.9	53.2	52.7	50.2	49.2	46.5	45.4	50.2

.. Not available

Note: Detailed metadata at: *http://metalinks.oecd.org/ins/20200312/1e50.*

1. Information on data for Israel: *http://oe.cd/israel-disclaimer.*

Source: Insurance activity indicators, OECD Insurance Statistics (database)

Table 20. Direct total gross premiums per insurance company employee

US dollars

	2011	2012	2013	2014	2015	2016	2017	2018
Argentina	..	..	289 071	296 157	290 581	..	264 715	291 050
Australia	..	..	..	..	..	..	..	..
Austria	831 859	765 392	795 367	816 717	688 586	660 884	676 184	729 985
Belgium	..	..	..	..	..	..	..	..
Bolivia	..	..	..	..	..	112 942	99 464	101 913
Brazil	..	..	..	..	..	..	..	..
Canada	..	..	..	..	..	..	..	..
Chile	448 189	486 192	493 638	454 677	495 261	510 666	519 672	558 276
Colombia	..	..	..	..	..	112 942	99 464	101 913
Costa Rica	..	..	..	..	..	..	..	..
Cuba	..	..	..	..	..	..	..	..
Czech Republic	..	..	..	..	..	..	..	..
Denmark	2 092 465	2 052 306	2 215 121	2 158 639	1 927 585	2 018 459	2 661 767	3 419 049
Dominican Republic	..	..	..	..	..	..	..	..
Ecuador	..	..	..	..	2 202 989	292 344	..	..
Egypt	..	..	..	..	..	..	..	..
El Salvador	..	..	..	..	..	..	..	195 773
Estonia	209 048	224 236	200 224	221 998	200 416	..	..	..
Finland	1 029 267	949 631	1 363 735	1 514 861	1 311 479	1 088 453	1 237 491	633 977
France	..	..	..	..	..	..	..	..
Germany	..	1 508 895	1 607 786	1 649 160	1 371 091	1 367 654	1 520 578	1 653 171
Greece	..	..	..	..	..	..	..	..
Guatemala	..	137 904	..	159 900	..	181 604	186 479	185 720
Honduras	..	..	267 721	183 148	217 165	..	..	1 497 747
Hong Kong, China	..	..	..	..	..	..	617 084	632 451
Hungary	151 723	143 598	157 425	161 509	147 122	169 626	168 073	197 023
India	..	..	..	..	..	..	32 479	..
Indonesia	..	23 320	..	..	..	..	..	..
Iceland	624 626	..	665 881	731 603	703 782	..	..	..
Ireland	4 527 571	5 145 784	5 005 661	..	..	..	..	..
Israel[1]	..	..	..	..	..	..	..	..
Italy	573 201	516 300	588 605	729 106	622 717	585 098	..	..
Japan	..	..	129 385	130 139	144 659	..	1 060 963	..
Korea	387 679	442 588	466 477	580 301	590 964	611 062	638 558	627 817
Latvia	134 539	144 559	198 764	237 445	301 825	..	..	..
Lithuania	131 719	116 317	128 847	136 520	120 842	130 040	147 705	172 038
Luxembourg	1 410 243	1 776 184	1 556 437	4 328 321	2 997 287	2 886 004	3 019 973	2 823 429
Malaysia	492 814	567 984	651 774	650 745	461 454	465 847	435 343	475 776
Mexico	447 668	457 259	436 528	403 458	330 532	410 335	423 179	..
Morocco	..	..	..	..	..	..	..	..
Netherlands	..	..	..	..	..	..	..	..
New Zealand	..	425 805	473 708	..	..	..	..	..
Nicaragua	..	..	1 704 849	119 312	2 050 664	..	..	..
Norway	..	..	..	..	..	..	..	..
Panama	..	347 935	392 524	..	..	..	..	..
Paraguay	..	104 274	382 149	..	124 344	..	..	..
Peru	257 668	251 417	285 142	301 442	290 594	..	..	295 065
Poland	181 339	198 127	169 341	183 458	167 678	..	..	..
Portugal	414 633	389 138	490 972	551 505	416 277	371 983	413 352	506 932
Puerto Rico	..	..	780 437	704 962	856 812	1 042 984	..	..
Russia	51 053	..	..	73 609	..	61 185	121 961	89 910
Singapore	..	..	..	..	..	..	..	..
Slovak Republic	418 170	378 453	..	403 610	..	..	..	..
Slovenia	..	..	..	..	..	..	..	..
South Africa	..	..	..	..	..	..	..	..
Spain	..	..	424 700	403 450	..	..	..	..
Sri Lanka	..	..	..	24 436	26 631	..	17 383	17 439
Sweden	1 264 886	1 073 328	1 210 867	2 042 276	1 771 433	..	1 686 900	1 927 908
Switzerland	..	..	..	..	..	..	..	..
Thailand	..	..	..	..	..	..	..	..
Tunisia	..	..	..	..	..	173 680	..	..
Turkey	369 673	322 731	379 315	335 385	298 749	233 812	204 510	261 141
United Kingdom	..	..	..	..	..	..	..	..
United States	..	..	..	..	..	..	..	..
Uruguay	..	..	..	..	..	..	..	..
OECD Total	531 467	665 134	318 550	333 066	333 535	719 416	919 764	960 285

.. Not available

Note: Detailed metadata at: *http://metalinks.oecd.org/ins/20200312/1e50.*

1. Information on data for Israel: *http://oe.cd/israel-disclaimer.*

Source: Insurance activity indicators, OECD Insurance Statistics (database)

Table 21. Retention ratio (Life and Non-life)

Per cent

	2011	2012	2013	2014	2015	2016	2017	2018
Argentina	..	88.9	90.6	86.5	87.5	88.4	88.7	89.3
Australia	84.5	84.1	84.5	86.0	83.8	80.4	77.1	77.9
Austria	..	..	81.3	83.6	84.2	81.1	82.7	87.2
Belgium	95.1	92.6	91.2	88.7	88.5	87.2	87.5	87.2
Bolivia	..	50.3	..	..	..	49.8	51.5	54.9
Brazil	..	..	..	95.2	95.4	95.8	95.7	95.3
Canada	75.2	73.3	73.1	73.5	71.4	74.0	72.4	79.1
Chile	80.6	83.1	84.4	84.0	84.8	84.4	83.4	84.1
Colombia	..	50.3	..	..	..	49.8	51.5	54.9
Costa Rica	81.1	80.9	78.6	80.2	77.9	78.9	79.4	77.6
Cuba	..	..	..	..	..	..	..	..
Czech Republic	81.5	81.3	80.6	80.3	79.3	78.9	78.7	79.0
Denmark	95.8	96.3	99.4	97.2	97.1	96.9	96.7	97.2
Dominican Republic	..	..	..	..	..	..	..	69.1
Ecuador	..	..	..	..	72.4	72.3	..	..
Egypt	..	..	..	..	..	..	..	..
El Salvador	61.0	62.0	66.6	66.6	66.5	64.2	..	63.7
Estonia	95.1	..	..	..	..	..	..	..
Finland	96.7	96.7	97.4	97.6	97.7	97.3	97.4	99.5
France	89.9	89.2	89.3	91.0	88.6	84.8	88.0	87.7
Germany	..	90.2	89.7	89.0	87.7	87.9	87.5	86.1
Greece	83.3	88.1	79.8	87.6	87.2	88.8	89.2	88.7
Guatemala	..	68.0	66.3	64.2	64.9	67.8	67.2	65.2
Honduras	..	..	55.7	54.4	53.0	..	..	58.7
Hong Kong, China	86.0	87.6	87.0	87.7	88.3	90.4	90.4	90.7
Hungary	83.9	83.3	86.1	86.1	86.1	86.7	87.4	87.6
India	95.5	..	..	..	95.2	..	91.8	..
Indonesia	..	86.2	85.5	83.8	84.8	86.0	87.3	86.8
Iceland	92.9	93.3	93.9	94.4	94.8	95.4	96.0	95.9
Ireland	86.7	88.4	87.8	89.2	88.0	79.6	..	..
Israel[1]	85.6	85.7	87.3	88.5	88.4	84.9	86.5	85.8
Italy	95.5	95.1	96.2	97.1	97.2	96.4	96.3	96.2
Japan	93.3	94.1	94.9	94.3	94.6	89.5	89.8	88.8
Korea	94.6	95.0	94.7	94.7	94.7	94.7	94.3	94.0
Latvia	94.0	94.2	96.3	96.3	95.9	95.3	93.2	89.8
Lithuania	..	..	..	95.2	95.1	95.0	91.5	90.4
Luxembourg	78.4	68.6	74.9	71.8	84.1	82.2	85.8	76.8
Malaysia	86.5	86.9	87.8	87.8	87.9	88.3	88.6	89.2
Mexico	82.3	83.8	82.6	83.9	83.0	84.4	81.4	83.2
Morocco	..	..	..	..	..	..	..	..
Netherlands	86.2	92.0	92.3	89.4	91.7	98.3	97.6	98.0
New Zealand	..	112.4	107.9	111.2	112.7	107.0	106.8	..
Nicaragua	..	62.0	63.8	63.3	65.7	66.7	..	60.9
Norway	..	93.0	92.9	93.1	92.2	92.7	93.0	93.3
Panama	..	57.4	55.6	..	..	..	..	..
Paraguay	..	102.3	79.1	..	79.6	78.0	77.4	..
Peru	78.0	76.7	76.7	75.5	74.5	73.3	75.0	76.3
Poland	93.3	92.7	92.7	92.4	90.5	87.9	88.4	88.4
Portugal	91.1	89.6	91.1	92.0	90.5	88.9	88.6	89.4
Puerto Rico	..	..	99.6	98.6	92.9	93.9	..	..
Russia	97.7	..	..	86.9	88.6	88.9	91.7	92.4
Singapore	86.9	85.5	85.9	86.8	79.2	77.6	77.0	..
Slovak Republic	85.5	85.6	85.8	85.3	84.5	..	92.2	..
Slovenia	87.2	87.1	87.8	86.9	88.1	87.7	86.5	86.8
South Africa	85.1	90.9	87.6	88.2	89.7	88.9	..	..
Spain	93.0	92.5	90.0	91.3	91.3	91.0	90.6	91.0
Sri Lanka	..	..	..	87.0	86.6	..	85.6	87.9
Sweden	92.9	92.2	92.7	95.6	97.0	97.3	97.2	97.4
Switzerland	93.0	92.5	92.6	92.9	93.1	93.7	92.6	92.6
Thailand	90.2	..	..	..	..	..	..	..
Tunisia	..	..	..	..	..	80.9	100.0	..
Turkey	74.9	77.9	75.6	75.0	74.8	76.1	72.0	70.9
United Kingdom	88.4	87.7	87.4	84.8	89.0	77.0	87.9	80.6
United States	74.0	73.6	71.3	74.9	72.8	72.5	71.4	83.7
Uruguay	..	91.0	91.2	90.8	91.5	..	92.9	..
OECD Total	82.3	82.1	80.7	82.5	80.7	79.4	79.6	85.6

.. Not available

Note: Detailed metadata at: *http://metalinks.oecd.org/ins/20200312/1e50.*

1. Information on data for Israel: *http://oe.cd/israel-disclaimer.*

Source: Insurance activity indicators, OECD Insurance Statistics (database)

Table 22. Retention ratio (Life)

Per cent

	2011	2012	2013	2014	2015	2016	2017	2018
Argentina	..	92.7	96.6	97.1	97.2	96.7	96.8	96.8
Australia	91.9	92.1	92.3	92.5	91.3	89.3	82.5	84.2
Austria	..	..	96.7	97.4	97.6	97.4	97.8	97.8
Belgium	97.6	97.7	97.0	97.6	97.9	96.7	98.0	97.7
Bolivia	..	79.5	..	..	..	64.6	63.7	71.9
Brazil	..	..	..	99.6	99.5	99.6	99.5	99.5
Canada	75.6	73.9	75.2	69.5	67.6	72.1	72.9	75.4
Chile	96.3	97.4	98.0	97.7	97.5	95.0	92.6	93.3
Colombia	..	79.5	..	..	..	64.6	63.7	71.9
Costa Rica	93.3	90.8	84.7	87.4	81.4	82.8	81.4	79.1
Cuba	..	..	..	..	..	..	..	..
Czech Republic	96.1	95.0	93.9	93.0	92.4	92.3	91.7	91.4
Denmark	99.7	99.7	100.0	99.8	99.8	99.8	99.8	99.9
Dominican Republic	..	..	..	..	..	..	..	76.5
Ecuador	..	..	..	..	81.6	99.2	..	..
Egypt	..	..	..	..	..	..	..	..
El Salvador	78.4	81.1	95.0	87.3	81.6	80.8	..	78.2
Estonia	98.9	..	..	..	..	..	..	..
Finland	99.0	99.0	99.4	99.5	99.5	99.3	99.4	99.5
France	93.1	92.9	92.5	94.1	90.7	86.5	93.2	93.9
Germany	..	96.9	96.8	97.0	97.0	96.6	97.0	96.2
Greece	84.8	95.1	94.8	95.6	95.9	96.2	95.0	95.1
Guatemala	..	76.6	75.3	76.6	76.9	80.9	79.9	78.1
Honduras	..	..	61.1	45.4	56.1	..	..	56.0
Hong Kong, China	89.2	91.0	90.0	90.5	91.0	92.8	92.7	93.4
Hungary	93.1	93.6	95.0	96.3	96.8	97.3	98.7	99.1
India	99.8	..	..	..	99.6	..	99.5	..
Indonesia	..	97.3	97.2	96.7	96.8	97.3	97.4	97.1
Iceland	82.0	82.5	83.9	82.3	83.7	85.2	85.9	85.0
Ireland	91.3	94.4	93.7	94.0	94.1	94.9	..	..
Israel[1]	95.0	95.2	95.3	95.2	95.5	95.1	95.2	95.4
Italy	98.2	98.3	98.8	99.0	99.1	99.1	99.1	99.1
Japan	96.4	94.1	94.9	94.3	94.6	93.1	93.6	92.7
Korea	98.5	98.8	98.8	98.8	98.7	98.6	98.4	98.4
Latvia	99.7	99.7	99.8	99.8	99.8	99.8	99.8	99.8
Lithuania	..	..	..	98.5	98.0	98.5	98.3	97.8
Luxembourg	80.0	68.9	76.4	72.1	85.3	83.6	87.4	77.4
Malaysia	96.8	96.7	97.3	96.9	96.7	96.6	95.9	96.0
Mexico	94.6	94.8	95.3	96.6	96.4	96.2	95.4	95.4
Morocco	..	..	..	..	..	..	..	..
Netherlands	94.6	94.9	95.4	89.6	94.0	97.2	96.4	97.7
New Zealand	..	..	..	..	..	..	..	..
Nicaragua	..	63.7	60.3	55.3	59.2	58.2	..	62.4
Norway	..	98.6	98.8	98.9	98.7	98.9	98.9	99.1
Panama	..	80.4	77.7	..	..	..	..	..
Paraguay	..	..	80.7	..	81.7	41.0	83.0	..
Peru	90.8	88.8	89.5	84.4	84.7	82.4	83.7	85.0
Poland	99.1	97.6	98.6	98.5	98.2	98.3	99.4	98.7
Portugal	97.9	96.4	97.0	97.7	97.2	96.5	96.5	96.9
Puerto Rico	..	..	103.3	100.0	56.0	78.0	..	..
Russia	252.8	..	..	98.4	98.6	98.8	99.2	99.3
Singapore	96.3	96.6	95.1	96.1	88.4	84.3	82.3	..
Slovak Republic	98.3	98.4	98.4	98.2	97.9	..	99.0	..
Slovenia	97.6	97.5	97.2	96.9	96.7	96.3	96.4	96.4
South Africa	89.4	94.9	92.5	93.2	95.2	94.6	..	..
Spain	98.0	94.7	93.9	96.4	96.8	97.3	96.2	97.1
Sri Lanka	..	..	..	96.3	96.3	..	96.0	99.5
Sweden	98.0	99.1	98.7	99.6	99.8	99.9	99.7	99.8
Switzerland	99.3	99.4	99.3	99.4	99.4	99.3	99.3	98.8
Thailand	98.4	..	..	..	..	..	..	..
Tunisia	..	..	..	..	..	90.4	100.0	..
Turkey	90.5	95.1	95.7	94.8	95.1	95.8	96.2	95.5
United Kingdom	90.4	89.0	88.9	85.4	91.2	80.3	95.3	84.5
United States	84.3	83.5	77.4	88.3	80.4	80.0	77.8	75.2
Uruguay	..	97.0	97.5	97.6	97.6	..	97.4	..
OECD Total	90.7	89.8	87.6	91.6	88.6	86.7	87.6	84.9

.. Not available

Note: Detailed metadata at: *http://metalinks.oecd.org/ins/20200312/1e50.*

1. Information on data for Israel: *http://oe.cd/israel-disclaimer.*

Source: Insurance activity indicators, OECD Insurance Statistics (database)

Table 23. Retention ratio (Non-life)

Per cent

	2011	2012	2013	2014	2015	2016	2017	2018
Argentina	..	87.9	89.3	84.4	85.7	86.8	87.3	88.0
Australia	74.9	74.9	75.0	75.7	73.0	69.3	71.3	71.8
Austria	..	..	73.2	76.0	77.0	73.3	75.8	82.7
Belgium	87.0	83.2	83.4	77.2	76.8	75.8	75.4	74.5
Bolivia	..	42.2	..	..	..	42.4	43.1	41.9
Brazil	..	..	..	88.5	88.5	88.4	88.3	87.7
Canada	75.0	73.0	72.1	75.2	72.9	74.7	72.2	80.6
Chile	54.4	55.9	57.6	57.7	57.4	59.1	62.7	63.8
Colombia	..	42.2	..	..	..	42.4	43.1	41.9
Costa Rica	79.7	79.5	77.6	79.2	77.3	78.2	79.0	77.3
Cuba	..	..	..	..	..	..	..	..
Czech Republic	68.8	69.2	69.4	69.8	70.2	69.8	70.6	71.9
Denmark	87.3	88.9	88.1	91.7	91.1	90.6	89.9	91.1
Dominican Republic	..	..	..	..	..	..	..	67.7
Ecuador	..	..	..	..	70.1	64.7	..	..
Egypt	..	..	..	..	..	..	..	..
El Salvador	56.4	56.3	56.2	58.4	60.1	57.1	..	58.8
Estonia	92.5	..	..	..	..	..	..	..
Finland	94.3	94.3	94.7	95.0	95.2	95.3	95.4	..
France	84.2	83.2	84.1	85.3	84.8	82.4	81.7	80.1
Germany	..	86.5	85.7	84.6	82.9	83.7	83.0	81.3
Greece	82.2	82.9	69.1	79.8	78.3	82.2	83.3	82.5
Guatemala	..	65.9	64.0	61.0	62.0	64.5	63.9	61.8
Honduras	..	..	53.3	59.3	51.3	..	..	60.1
Hong Kong, China	68.5	68.7	69.3	69.0	69.8	68.9	68.7	65.8
Hungary	72.9	71.6	75.3	73.6	75.0	76.2	76.9	77.7
India	70.4	..	..	..	79.5	..	73.1	..
Indonesia	..	59.4	60.8	58.4	58.3	55.7	57.6	58.9
Iceland	93.7	94.2	94.7	95.5	95.8	96.3	97.0	96.9
Ireland	69.3	64.1	63.1	67.1	64.1	46.3	..	..
Israel[1]	75.1	75.0	78.2	81.2	80.2	73.6	76.4	74.6
Italy	90.0	89.0	89.9	90.5	90.6	87.9	87.8	87.6
Japan	80.2	..	..	..	..	78.4	78.2	76.9
Korea	89.4	89.5	88.6	89.5	89.4	89.8	89.5	88.9
Latvia	92.7	93.0	95.5	95.4	94.8	93.9	91.3	87.4
Lithuania	..	..	..	93.3	93.4	93.0	88.6	87.5
Luxembourg	64.1	64.3	58.5	65.9	68.9	66.7	67.7	69.2
Malaysia	70.9	71.8	73.6	74.0	74.4	74.9	76.0	77.0
Mexico	72.5	74.4	71.7	72.8	71.5	74.0	70.8	73.2
Morocco	..	..	..	..	..	..	..	..
Netherlands	77.2	89.4	89.5	89.2	89.9	98.5	98.1	98.3
New Zealand	..	78.7	77.5	80.0	80.5	73.8	74.4	..
Nicaragua	..	61.7	64.6	65.0	67.0	68.7	..	60.5
Norway	..	86.2	85.9	85.9	84.3	85.0	85.5	86.0
Panama	..	43.0	41.0	..	..	..	..	..
Paraguay	..	71.2	78.9	..	79.3	78.0	76.5	..
Peru	66.1	65.8	65.5	67.0	65.0	65.7	67.3	68.1
Poland	85.9	85.9	85.8	85.8	82.8	80.2	81.3	82.8
Portugal	78.8	77.9	76.9	76.8	76.6	77.7	77.4	77.1
Puerto Rico	..	..	99.5	98.5	94.8	95.5	..	..
Russia	84.3	..	..	82.0	87.0	86.4	88.9	89.2
Singapore	67.9	64.2	66.5	66.5	58.4	60.9	61.0	..
Slovak Republic	71.0	70.7	70.1	69.9	70.4	..	73.3	..
Slovenia	84.3	84.2	85.1	84.0	85.5	85.2	83.6	84.2
South Africa	69.5	75.7	69.8	67.7	68.0	66.8	..	..
Spain	88.5	90.5	86.8	87.3	87.0	85.3	86.0	86.2
Sri Lanka	..	..	..	81.9	79.4	..	78.3	79.8
Sweden	87.9	84.0	86.1	86.5	89.3	89.5	89.1	89.9
Switzerland	87.0	86.1	86.4	86.7	87.0	88.8	87.1	87.5
Thailand	72.1	..	..	..	..	..	..	..
Tunisia	..	..	..	..	..	78.6	100.0	..
Turkey	71.4	74.8	71.9	72.2	72.1	72.7	66.9	66.2
United Kingdom	82.8	83.8	83.4	83.2	82.8	69.5	72.0	70.7
United States	67.1	66.9	67.4	67.3	68.2	68.3	67.9	90.1
Uruguay	..	88.9	88.7	87.9	88.4	..	89.7	..
OECD Total	72.7	73.3	73.5	73.4	73.0	73.0	72.9	86.3

.. Not available

Note: Detailed metadata at: *http://metalinks.oecd.org/ins/20200312/1e50.*

1. Information on data for Israel: *http://oe.cd/israel-disclaimer.*

Source: Insurance activity indicators, OECD Insurance Statistics (database)

Table 24. Ratio of reinsurance accepted (Life and Non-life)

Per cent

	2011	2012	2013	2014	2015	2016	2017	2018
Argentina	..	0.5	0.3	7.2	7.0	6.7	6.6	5.5
Australia	10.0	11.1	10.9	10.1	10.9	12.5	13.0	14.3
Austria	..	..	12.0	9.6	8.9	9.3	6.4	7.2
Belgium	3.1	2.7	3.2	3.5	3.0	2.9	2.3	1.8
Bolivia	..	0.6	..	..	..	1.0	3.9	3.3
Brazil	..	..	..	0.0	0.0	0.0	0.0	0.0
Canada	8.2	8.5	9.7	17.7	17.6	15.6	16.1	11.3
Chile	0.3	0.5	0.5	0.6	0.8	1.1	0.9	0.9
Colombia	..	0.6	..	..	..	1.0	3.9	3.3
Costa Rica	0.1	0.2	0.3	0.3	0.3	0.3	0.3	0.3
Cuba	..	..	..	..	..	..	..	..
Czech Republic	1.7	1.9	1.8	1.6	2.0	2.4	2.5	2.1
Denmark	0.3	0.8	84.9	0.8	0.8	2.9	3.3	3.5
Dominican Republic	..	..	..	..	..	..	..	..
Ecuador	..	..	..	..	2.0	1.7	..	..
Egypt	..	..	..	..	..	..	..	..
El Salvador	..	..	..	..	..	..	..	5.1
Estonia	0.1	..	..	..	..	..	..	0.0
Finland	1.9	1.9	1.5	1.4	1.3	1.5	1.6	0.0
France	8.7	10.7	10.1	10.5	8.9	15.7	12.7	12.7
Germany	..	23.2	22.4	22.4	24.6	24.5	24.6	24.7
Greece	1.7	2.0	2.3	1.2	1.1	1.0	0.9	0.9
Guatemala	..	2.9	2.7	2.7	3.1	2.9	2.9	3.4
Honduras	..	..	0.0	0.0	0.0	..	..	..
Hong Kong, China	4.8	4.9	4.7	4.8	4.5	4.8	4.7	4.6
Hungary	0.7	1.0	1.3	0.9	1.0	1.0	1.5	1.1
India	1.7	..	..	..	0.7	..	5.8	..
Indonesia	..	4.2	4.9	2.5	2.1	2.0	1.8	1.8
Iceland	1.9	2.3	2.3	2.5	2.4	1.7	1.4	1.7
Ireland	1.6	2.0	1.8	1.9	1.9	2.2	1.2	3.0
Israel[1]	0.0	..	..	..	..	0.0	..	..
Italy	2.5	2.5	2.4	1.8	1.8	2.1	2.1	2.3
Japan	4.4	9.9	7.4	5.5	4.1	6.5	6.0	5.5
Korea	5.4	4.9	5.2	5.0	5.1	5.2	5.6	6.2
Latvia	1.5	1.4	0.0	0.0	0.0	0.0	0.0	0.0
Lithuania	0.1	0.1	0.1	0.0	0.0	0.0	0.0	0.0
Luxembourg	1.9	1.3	0.9	1.2	0.8	0.3	0.2	0.2
Malaysia	6.5	7.1	7.4	7.5	7.7	7.7	7.2	6.7
Mexico	2.0	1.8	1.7	1.8	1.7	1.6	1.7	1.7
Morocco	..	..	..	..	..	..	..	..
Netherlands	0.7	1.4	1.5	1.5	1.7	0.5	1.8	1.8
New Zealand	..	1.3	0.6	0.6	3.8	1.8	5.3	..
Nicaragua	..	..	0.0	..	..	..	..	..
Norway	..	..	..	..	..	..	..	..
Panama	..	6.7	6.2	..	..	..	..	..
Paraguay	..	2.0	1.5	..	1.1	1.0	0.7	..
Peru	1.5	1.4	1.0	0.7	0.6	0.6	0.7	0.6
Poland	0.9	1.0	1.2	1.0	2.7	3.5	3.2	3.7
Portugal	3.7	4.1	3.5	3.3	3.9	5.1	5.3	5.3
Puerto Rico	..	..	0.5	0.9	0.8	0.6	..	..
Russia	4.0	..	..	3.5	2.8	3.0	2.7	2.9
Singapore	25.1	20.6	19.6	19.2	19.7	21.7	17.6	..
Slovak Republic	0.9	1.0	0.9	1.4	2.0	..	0.2	..
Slovenia	12.0	12.3	11.3	11.3	12.5	12.1	12.1	11.7
South Africa	..	..	2.3	2.3	2.2	2.9	..	..
Spain	6.0	2.6	7.7	7.8	8.2	8.2	8.1	7.8
Sri Lanka	..	..	..	2.2	1.5	..	2.4	2.2
Sweden	6.0	7.9	6.3	4.1	3.1	3.0	3.1	3.1
Switzerland	12.3	13.5	14.5	13.8	12.7	13.3	14.2	15.0
Thailand	1.7	..	..	..	..	..	..	..
Tunisia	..	..	..	..	..	1.2	5.3	..
Turkey	3.2	2.9	2.7	5.0	3.1	5.9	6.0	8.5
United Kingdom	7.9	8.1	9.7	9.9	11.1	35.8	14.3	20.4
United States	20.5	20.7	21.5	21.8	22.8	22.3	23.0	11.9
Uruguay	..	0.0	0.0	0.0	0.0	..	0.0	..
OECD Total	13.0	15.0	15.5	15.4	16.7	18.5	17.2	11.8

.. Not available

Note: Detailed metadata at: *http://metalinks.oecd.org/ins/20200312/1e50.*

1. Information on data for Israel: *http://oe.cd/israel-disclaimer.*

Source: Insurance activity indicators, OECD Insurance Statistics (database)

Table 25. Ratio of reinsurance accepted (Life)

Per cent

	2011	2012	2013	2014	2015	2016	2017	2018
Argentina	..	1.1	0.6	3.0	2.3	3.0	2.9	2.8
Australia	6.4	7.6	8.1	7.5	8.4	9.7	12.2	14.3
Austria	..	..	0.2	0.2	0.2	0.2	0.2	0.2
Belgium	0.5	0.2	0.4	0.4	0.3	0.4	0.3	0.3
Bolivia	..	0.4	..	..	..	0.0	3.3	4.8
Brazil	..	..	..	0.0	0.0	0.0	0.0	0.0
Canada	8.3	8.8	9.7	16.6	17.5	15.0	14.4	11.8
Chile	0.1	0.0	0.0	0.1	0.4	1.0	0.8	0.8
Colombia	..	0.4	..	..	..	0.0	3.3	4.8
Costa Rica	0.0	0.1	0.0	0.0	0.0	0.0	0.0	0.0
Cuba	..	..	..	..	..	..	..	..
Czech Republic	0.0	0.0	0.0	0.0	0.0	0.6	0.6	0.7
Denmark	0.0	0.6	89.0	0.5	0.5	0.6	0.4	0.4
Dominican Republic	..	..	..	..	..	..	..	..
Ecuador	..	..	..	..	0.6	0.0	..	..
Egypt	..	..	..	..	..	..	..	..
El Salvador	..	..	..	..	..	..	..	5.0
Estonia	0.0	..	..	..	..	..	..	0.0
Finland	0.1	0.1	0.1	0.2	0.0	0.0	0.0	0.0
France	5.6	9.1	8.0	8.9	6.3	15.5	8.8	8.6
Germany	..	0.7	0.7	0.6	0.6	0.6	0.8	0.5
Greece	1.1	0.2	0.2	0.2	0.2	0.1	0.0	0.0
Guatemala	..	2.1	1.0	1.6	1.7	1.9	1.4	1.5
Honduras	..	..	0.0	0.0	0.0	..	..	..
Hong Kong, China	1.0	1.0	1.1	1.6	1.7	2.8	2.5	2.0
Hungary	0.0	0.0	0.0	0.0	0.0	0.0	0.0	0.0
India	0.0	..	..	..	0.0	..	0.2	..
Indonesia	..	0.0	0.0	..	..	..	..	..
Iceland	0.0	0.0	0.0	0.0	0.1	..	0.0	..
Ireland	0.9	1.2	1.1	1.1	1.2	0.7	0.2	0.1
Israel[1]	0.0	..	..	..	..	0.0	..	..
Italy	2.4	2.6	1.9	1.3	1.3	1.5	1.5	1.4
Japan	2.0	9.9	7.4	5.5	4.1	3.4	2.6	2.0
Korea	1.4	1.1	1.1	1.1	1.1	1.3	1.4	1.7
Latvia	0.0	0.0	0.0	0.0	0.0	0.0	0.0	0.0
Lithuania	0.0	0.0	0.0	0.0	0.0	0.0	0.0	0.0
Luxembourg	1.9	1.3	1.0	1.3	0.8	0.4	0.2	0.2
Malaysia	1.1	1.2	1.3	1.4	1.4	1.4	1.6	1.7
Mexico	0.6	0.5	0.6	0.7	0.4	0.5	0.6	0.4
Morocco	..	..	..	..	..	..	..	..
Netherlands	0.1	0.1	0.0	0.0	0.0	0.0	0.1	0.0
New Zealand	..	..	..	..	..	..	..	..
Nicaragua	..	..	0.0	..	..	..	..	..
Norway	..	..	..	..	..	..	..	..
Panama	..	5.1	5.5	..	..	..	..	..
Paraguay	..	..	0.8	..	0.7	0.0	0.2	..
Peru	1.8	1.6	1.2	0.6	0.5	0.3	0.1	0.0
Poland	0.1	0.1	0.1	0.1	0.1	0.1	0.1	0.0
Portugal	0.0	0.0	0.0	0.0	0.0	0.0	0.0	0.0
Puerto Rico	..	..	0.0	0.0	0.0	0.5	..	..
Russia	0.0	..	..	0.0	0.0	0.0	0.0	0.0
Singapore	10.2	11.8	10.9	10.8	10.4	14.7	11.0	..
Slovak Republic	0.0	0.0	0.0	0.0	0.0	..	0.0	..
Slovenia	0.0	..	..	..	..	..	..	..
South Africa	..	..	0.0	0.0	0.0	0.0	..	..
Spain	1.1	0.2	1.3	1.6	1.5	1.5	1.4	1.5
Sri Lanka	..	..	..	..	0.0	..	0.6	..
Sweden	0.2	2.3	0.2	0.0	0.0	0.0	0.0	0.0
Switzerland	0.5	1.1	1.5	1.4	1.5	1.7	1.3	1.2
Thailand	0.1	..	..	..	..	..	..	..
Tunisia	..	..	..	..	..	1.5	1.5	..
Turkey	2.0	1.6	2.1	1.5	1.6	4.3	3.6	3.9
United Kingdom	6.8	7.1	9.3	9.0	10.0	40.7	10.4	18.7
United States	9.2	9.8	11.3	10.4	15.1	13.8	14.9	20.2
Uruguay	..	0.0	0.0	0.0	0.0	..	0.0	..
OECD Total	5.5	7.4	7.5	6.8	8.8	12.5	9.0	12.4

.. Not available

Note: Detailed metadata at: *http://metalinks.oecd.org/ins/20200312/1e50*.

1. Information on data for Israel: *http://oe.cd/israel-disclaimer*.

Source: Insurance activity indicators, OECD Insurance Statistics (database)

Table 26. Ratio of reinsurance accepted (Non-life)

Per cent

	2011	2012	2013	2014	2015	2016	2017	2018
Argentina	..	0.4	0.3	8.0	7.8	7.5	7.2	6.0
Australia	14.8	15.2	14.2	14.3	14.7	16.0	13.9	14.3
Austria	..	..	18.2	14.7	13.6	13.7	9.2	10.2
Belgium	7.5	7.3	7.1	7.6	6.4	5.8	4.7	3.7
Bolivia	..	0.6	..	..	..	1.4	4.2	2.1
Brazil	..	..	..	0.1	0.0	0.0	0.0	0.0
Canada	8.2	8.3	9.7	18.1	17.7	15.8	16.7	11.1
Chile	0.7	1.2	1.4	1.5	1.6	1.3	1.1	1.1
Colombia	..	0.6	..	..	..	1.4	4.2	2.1
Costa Rica	0.1	0.2	0.4	0.3	0.4	0.3	0.3	0.4
Cuba	..	..	..	..	..	..	..	..
Czech Republic	3.2	3.5	3.3	2.9	3.4	3.7	3.7	2.9
Denmark	0.8	1.1	1.1	1.3	1.4	8.0	9.8	10.7
Dominican Republic	..	..	..	..	..	..	..	..
Ecuador	..	..	..	..	2.4	2.2	..	..
Egypt	..	..	..	..	..	..	..	..
El Salvador	..	..	..	..	..	..	..	5.2
Estonia	0.1	..	..	..	..	..	..	0.0
Finland	3.7	3.7	3.3	3.0	3.0	3.0	3.3	..
France	14.0	13.3	13.4	13.3	13.5	16.1	17.4	17.8
Germany	..	35.6	34.6	34.7	37.0	36.4	35.9	36.0
Greece	2.1	3.3	3.7	2.2	1.9	1.8	1.8	1.7
Guatemala	..	3.1	3.2	3.0	3.4	3.2	3.3	3.9
Honduras	..	..	0.0	0.0	0.0	..	..	..
Hong Kong, China	26.2	26.2	26.0	26.1	24.2	23.3	25.1	28.3
Hungary	1.5	2.2	2.9	1.9	2.1	2.0	2.9	2.0
India	11.6	..	..	..	3.0	..	19.4	..
Indonesia	..	14.4	15.2	7.3	6.8	7.5	7.2	6.6
Iceland	2.0	2.5	2.5	2.7	2.6	1.9	1.5	1.9
Ireland	4.1	5.3	5.0	5.3	4.6	5.5	5.3	6.5
Israel[1]	0.0	..	..	..	..	0.0	..	..
Italy	2.6	2.4	3.4	3.4	3.8	3.9	3.7	5.1
Japan	14.3	..	..	..	..	16.0	16.3	16.1
Korea	10.7	10.2	11.1	10.1	10.3	10.2	10.5	11.2
Latvia	1.8	1.7	0.0	0.0	0.0	0.0	0.0	0.0
Lithuania	0.2	0.2	0.2	0.0	0.0	0.0	0.0	0.0
Luxembourg	2.0	1.3	0.3	0.2	0.2	0.2	0.2	0.4
Malaysia	14.8	16.4	16.5	16.7	17.3	17.8	16.8	15.8
Mexico	3.1	2.9	2.7	2.7	2.7	2.6	2.6	2.7
Morocco	..	..	..	..	..	..	..	..
Netherlands	1.5	2.5	2.9	2.8	2.9	0.6	0.7	0.5
New Zealand	..	1.3	0.6	0.6	3.8	1.8	5.3	..
Nicaragua	..	..	0.0	..	..	..	..	..
Norway	..	..	..	..	..	..	..	..
Panama	..	7.7	6.6	..	..	..	..	..
Paraguay	..	2.2	1.5	..	1.2	1.0	0.8	..
Peru	1.4	1.3	1.0	0.8	0.7	0.8	1.3	1.1
Poland	1.9	2.3	2.5	2.1	5.3	6.1	5.2	5.7
Portugal	10.3	11.0	11.7	12.3	12.1	12.6	12.9	13.8
Puerto Rico	..	..	0.5	1.0	0.9	0.6	..	..
Russia	4.5	..	..	5.0	3.3	3.7	3.7	4.2
Singapore	55.3	37.6	38.1	37.3	40.7	39.2	37.0	..
Slovak Republic	1.9	2.1	2.1	3.1	4.0	..	0.8	..
Slovenia	15.4	15.8	14.6	14.6	16.3	15.7	15.5	14.9
South Africa	..	..	10.8	11.6	11.1	14.2	..	..
Spain	10.3	4.8	12.9	12.6	13.5	14.1	13.4	12.7
Sri Lanka	..	..	..	3.5	2.6	..	3.7	3.7
Sweden	11.8	14.6	12.9	13.5	11.4	11.8	13.0	12.6
Switzerland	23.3	24.9	26.6	25.4	23.4	23.6	24.8	26.0
Thailand	5.2	..	..	..	..	..	..	..
Tunisia	..	..	..	..	..	1.1	6.2	..
Turkey	3.5	3.1	2.8	5.4	3.3	6.1	6.5	9.3
United Kingdom	11.0	11.2	10.9	12.6	14.1	25.0	22.7	24.8
United States	28.1	28.2	27.8	28.2	27.4	27.0	27.4	5.6
Uruguay	..	0.0	0.0	0.0	0.0	..	0.0	..
OECD Total	21.6	23.6	23.5	24.2	24.3	23.7	24.0	11.1

.. Not available

Note: Detailed metadata at: *http://metalinks.oecd.org/ins/20200312/1e50.*

1. Information on data for Israel: *http://oe.cd/israel-disclaimer.*

Source: Insurance activity indicators, OECD Insurance Statistics (database)

Table 27. Market share of foreign companies in the domestic market (Life)

Per cent

	2011	2012	2013	2014	2015	2016	2017	2018
Argentina	..	18.3	31.8	31.4	30.8	30.4	30.0	27.9
Australia	10.3	15.8	16.8	15.5	17.7	20.8	25.5	29.8
Austria	..	..	37.5	39.2	37.7	39.3	39.7	39.7
Belgium	..	..	..	..	..	..	..	..
Bolivia	..	..	..	..	..	29.9	20.8	27.8
Brazil	..	..	..	18.6	18.3	17.2	21.3	28.3
Canada	7.9	6.3	5.6	26.0	21.0	18.7	18.1	15.2
Chile	37.6	43.7	46.7	45.0	41.8	41.6	44.5	43.0
Colombia	..	..	..	..	..	29.9	20.8	27.8
Costa Rica	3.4	5.5	12.4	17.0	23.0	25.0	33.9	37.4
Cuba	..	..	..	..	..	..	..	..
Czech Republic	97.2	97.1	96.8	96.7	96.3	96.8	96.4	95.9
Denmark	20.4	19.3	2.5	19.5	18.6	18.8	19.9	19.8
Dominican Republic	..	..	..	..	..	..	..	46.5
Ecuador	..	..	..	..	..	11.7	..	..
Egypt	..	..	..	..	..	..	..	..
El Salvador	9.3	9.7	17.4	9.6	9.4	9.6	..	10.3
Estonia	100.0	100.0	100.0	100.0	100.0	100.0	100.0	100.0
Finland	..	38.3	42.0	43.0	38.5	..	..	..
France	..	..	..	..	..	..	..	..
Germany	27.4	30.1	27.4	26.0	26.7	25.3	24.6	24.9
Greece	63.4	63.3	53.8	48.0	55.7	76.9	74.0	73.2
Guatemala	..	..	..	..	..	..	..	..
Honduras	..	..	13.8	59.6	62.2	..	..	62.7
Hong Kong, China	..	..	..	..	..	..	..	..
Hungary	92.8	93.5	95.6	96.2	95.8	96.9	96.6	96.3
India	0.0	..	..	..	0.0	..	0.1	..
Indonesia	..	..	..	..	..	..	..	..
Iceland	3.6	3.9	4.3	5.0	5.8	..	..	..
Ireland	4.7	3.9	4.9	4.5	4.7	..	5.3	2.5
Israel[1]	30.4	0.3	0.4	0.4	0.4	0.4	0.4	0.4
Italy	30.1	27.4	28.9	31.3	30.5	33.1	32.1	37.1
Japan	19.2	22.4	20.7	20.1	20.6	21.8	22.7	22.5
Korea	18.9	16.3	16.1	13.2	12.4	14.7	16.1	14.3
Latvia	90.1	90.0	91.8	91.0	89.8	90.8	91.3	91.6
Lithuania	96.9	96.8	97.0	97.4	97.4	97.5	97.1	97.3
Luxembourg	95.6	94.6	96.2	96.4	92.5	77.2	90.6	92.2
Malaysia	67.9	68.1	68.6	68.8	69.6	69.7	71.8	70.4
Mexico	69.9	71.1	6.3	74.0	72.3	70.6	68.0	68.8
Morocco	..	..	..	..	..	..	..	..
Netherlands	21.1	21.1	19.2	4.6	18.5	19.2	23.3	19.9
New Zealand	..	..	..	..	..	..	..	..
Nicaragua	..	32.6	29.1	26.6	26.4	18.0	..	25.8
Norway	9.3	10.7	12.3	13.3	15.1	0.7	0.7	0.5
Panama	..	54.1	59.9	..	..	..	..	..
Paraguay	..	..	6.2	..	0.0	0.0	5.5	..
Peru	22.3	20.7	23.5	30.7	56.8	28.1	27.6	23.4
Poland	50.9	51.1	48.8	50.0	50.7	54.3	45.2	44.0
Portugal	9.3	7.9	6.8	54.0	64.2	77.5	93.8	90.8
Puerto Rico	..	..	10.4	7.8	0.0	38.0	..	..
Russia	..	..	..	8.5	18.1	15.5	10.2	10.4
Singapore	61.0	66.3	67.2	71.3	70.6	70.0	53.3	..
Slovak Republic	90.4	90.2	90.4	90.0	89.0	..	5.6	..
Slovenia	17.1	16.8	17.6	17.2	17.0	17.1	15.7	15.4
South Africa	20.8	33.0	31.9	35.2	33.3	34.6	..	..
Spain	8.8	19.1	12.4	12.8	12.3	..	..	..
Sri Lanka	..	..	..	2.4	1.7	..	..	..
Sweden	17.3	18.4	19.5	7.9	8.8	11.2	12.2	13.2
Switzerland	29.9	30.6	31.2	27.9	26.9	25.6	25.3	26.1
Thailand	28.8	..	..	..	..	..	..	..
Tunisia	..	..	..	..	..	..	..	..
Turkey	27.7	27.1	47.1	47.9	59.7	54.2	56.4	59.2
United Kingdom	21.0	26.4	23.3	16.0	16.9	..	0.0	..
United States	19.8	19.6	20.0	21.0	17.4	22.5	21.7	23.0
Uruguay	..	33.5	32.8	33.4	30.1	..	21.3	..

.. Not available

Note: Detailed metadata at: *http://metalinks.oecd.org/ins/20200312/1e50.*

1. Information on data for Israel: *http://oe.cd/israel-disclaimer.*

Source: Insurance activity indicators, OECD Insurance Statistics (database)

Table 28. Market share of foreign undertakings in total domestic business (Life)

Branches or agencies

Per cent

	2011	2012	2013	2014	2015	2016	2017	2018
Argentina	..	1.5	1.8	3.9	3.2	3.4	3.5	3.7
Australia	..	..	..	..	..	..	..	..
Austria	..	..	0.0	0.0	0.0	0.0	0.0	0.0
Belgium	..	..	..	..	..	..	..	..
Bolivia	..	..	..	..	..	..	..	..
Brazil	..	..	..	..	0.0	0.0	0.0	0.0
Canada	2.4	2.6	2.2	15.5	15.8	13.2	12.7	9.0
Chile	..	..	..	..	..	..	..	..
Colombia	..	..	..	..	..	..	..	..
Costa Rica	0.0	0.0	0.2	0.6	1.1	1.0	1.3	1.6
Cuba	..	..	..	..	..	..	..	..
Czech Republic	8.3	8.1	7.5	7.2	10.8	10.9	11.4	11.5
Denmark	..	..	..	..	..	..	..	..
Dominican Republic	..	..	..	..	..	..	..	..
Ecuador	..	..	..	..	..	..	..	..
Egypt	..	..	..	..	..	..	..	..
El Salvador	9.3	9.7	17.4	9.6	9.4	9.6	..	10.3
Estonia	0.0	2.9	2.5	2.7	2.8	2.2	3.1	5.2
Finland	..	..	..	..	..	..	..	..
France	..	..	..	..	..	..	..	..
Germany	3.1	4.0	4.0	3.9	4.0	3.9	4.0	3.8
Greece	6.2	0.4	0.0	0.0	0.0	0.0	0.0	0.0
Guatemala	..	..	..	..	..	..	..	..
Honduras	..	..	13.8	25.6	23.1	..	..	62.7
Hong Kong, China	..	..	..	..	..	..	..	..
Hungary	..	..	..	..	..	..	..	..
India	0.0	..	..	..	0.0	..	0.1	..
Indonesia	..	..	..	..	..	..	..	..
Iceland	0.0	..	..	..	..	..	..	..
Ireland	4.7	3.9	4.9	4.5	4.7	..	5.3	2.5
Israel[1]	..	..	..	..	..	..	..	..
Italy	0.0	0.0	0.0	0.0	0.0	0.0	0.0	..
Japan	9.2	5.5	4.9	4.2	4.1	4.3	4.5	0.1
Korea	2.7	2.2	2.2	2.4	0.2	2.0	2.1	2.3
Latvia	51.5	55.7	56.3	58.5	59.3	61.4	63.1	65.5
Lithuania	46.7	41.5	41.6	43.1	41.8	40.8	41.4	43.3
Luxembourg	0.4	0.3	0.5	0.1	0.1	0.1	0.1	0.1
Malaysia	0.4	0.4	0.5	0.5	0.5	0.5	0.6	0.7
Mexico	..	..	..	..	..	..	..	..
Morocco	..	..	..	..	..	..	..	..
Netherlands	2.7	2.7	2.0	0.0	0.0	..	..	..
New Zealand	..	..	..	..	..	..	..	..
Nicaragua	..	..	..	..	..	..	..	..
Norway	1.0	0.8	1.3	1.4	0.7	0.7	0.7	0.5
Panama	..	10.3	10.0	..	..	..	..	..
Paraguay	..	..	..	..	0.0	0.0	..	..
Peru	..	..	..	..	..	..	..	..
Poland	..	..	..	..	..	..	..	..
Portugal	0.8	0.0	0.0	0.0	0.0	0.0	0.0	0.0
Puerto Rico	..	..	..	..	..	..	..	..
Russia	..	..	..	..	..	..	0.0	0.0
Singapore	29.8	15.1	15.0	32.6	30.7	32.3	8.7	..
Slovak Republic	4.5	4.3	5.4	4.4	4.8	..	5.6	..
Slovenia	..	..	..	..	..	..	..	..
South Africa	..	..	0.0	..	..	..	..	..
Spain	0.3	0.2	0.0	0.0	0.0	..	..	..
Sri Lanka	..	..	..	..	0.0	..	..	..
Sweden	..	..	..	0.7	..	..	..	..
Switzerland	1.6	2.1	1.5	0.0	0.0	0.0	0.0	0.0
Thailand	28.8	..	..	..	..	..	..	..
Tunisia	..	..	..	..	..	..	..	..
Turkey	..	..	..	..	..	0.0	0.0	0.0
United Kingdom	0.1	0.0	0.0	0.0	0.0	..	0.0	..
United States	0.0	..	..	..	..	0.0	0.0	0.0
Uruguay	..	..	0.0	0.0	0.0	..	0.0	..

.. Not available

Note: Detailed metadata at: *http://metalinks.oecd.org/ins/20200312/1e50.*

1. Information on data for Israel: *http://oe.cd/israel-disclaimer.*

Source: Insurance activity indicators, OECD Insurance Statistics (database)

Table 29. Market share of foreign companies in the domestic market (Non-life)

Per cent

	2011	2012	2013	2014	2015	2016	2017	2018
Argentina	..	17.6	20.1	21.1	22.0	23.4	30.5	30.0
Australia	27.3	27.1	27.7	28.7	28.2	28.7	29.5	34.8
Austria	..	..	35.2	37.5	36.9	36.6	33.2	32.9
Belgium	..	..	..	..	..	..	..	..
Bolivia	..	..	..	..	..	27.9	29.1	25.5
Brazil	..	..	..	51.3	32.4	35.7	39.4	53.9
Canada	29.8	29.0	27.9	44.8	41.6	40.9	41.3	37.5
Chile	66.5	65.7	63.7	63.5	62.7	79.0	75.6	73.8
Colombia	..	..	..	..	..	27.9	29.1	25.5
Costa Rica	5.8	7.6	10.0	14.2	17.5	20.5	22.8	25.6
Cuba	..	..	..	..	..	..	..	..
Czech Republic	88.6	88.6	88.2	89.4	90.0	89.1	88.6	87.8
Denmark	16.0	16.6	16.4	27.5	27.9	28.3	25.3	23.1
Dominican Republic	..	..	..	..	..	..	..	28.4
Ecuador	..	..	..	..	..	0.4	..	..
Egypt	..	..	..	..	..	..	..	..
El Salvador	2.3	2.4	0.0	0.0	0.0	0.0	..	4.5
Estonia	90.4	92.7	94.3	95.1	95.2	94.8	100.0	95.4
Finland	..	25.0	23.8	23.7	100.0	..	..	..
France	0.1	0.1	0.1	0.1	0.1	..	..	..
Germany	18.2	13.2	14.0	14.5	14.3	13.3	13.6	14.4
Greece	36.6	41.2	34.5	41.2	43.0	57.3	57.3	56.4
Guatemala	..	..	..	..	..	..	..	..
Honduras	..	..	10.5	40.3	42.8	..	..	49.3
Hong Kong, China	..	..	..	..	..	..	..	..
Hungary	96.8	95.7	94.9	94.7	92.8	91.7	91.4	91.4
India	0.0	..	..	..	..	..	2.9	..
Indonesia	..	..	..	..	..	..	..	..
Iceland	9.7	9.9	10.4	10.9	11.3	..	..	..
Ireland	8.2	17.6	14.3	24.3	22.2	..	17.1	16.6
Israel[1]	11.2	3.3	3.3	3.4	4.0	3.8	3.8	3.8
Italy	27.6	27.5	27.8	28.9	32.2	31.8	31.1	30.0
Japan	12.8	..	..	..	..	9.4	7.5	9.4
Korea	3.9	3.8	4.0	3.7	3.7	3.7	3.8	4.1
Latvia	44.3	48.1	49.4	48.7	57.1	79.0	77.2	79.5
Lithuania	98.0	98.5	98.8	99.0	99.0	99.3	99.5	99.5
Luxembourg	62.7	58.9	52.1	53.3	52.8	51.7	51.1	50.2
Malaysia	42.7	43.9	45.8	46.6	47.8	48.5	51.9	52.9
Mexico	51.1	52.4	9.7	48.7	52.2	48.5	50.3	48.1
Morocco	..	..	..	..	..	..	..	..
Netherlands	29.4	29.4	22.7	11.6	16.3	2.6	2.3	1.7
New Zealand	..	..	..	..	..	..	..	..
Nicaragua	..	24.6	25.7	24.7	25.7	26.0	..	29.4
Norway	42.3	43.9	43.4	41.1	40.2	40.3	37.8	37.3
Panama	..	39.2	47.0	..	..	..	..	..
Paraguay	..	0.0	26.4	..	0.0	22.8	24.7	..
Peru	18.8	19.1	19.9	20.6	45.9	24.8	25.7	25.0
Poland	61.1	62.8	61.3	61.3	61.8	59.1	58.4	59.1
Portugal	26.7	26.5	26.6	84.2	84.3	91.0	91.6	91.0
Puerto Rico	..	..	52.6	51.8	41.0	55.6	..	..
Russia	..	..	..	2.2	13.7	13.7	14.0	13.9
Singapore	85.6	86.8	86.2	89.0	89.2	90.2	80.0	..
Slovak Republic	94.4	94.0	93.8	93.6	93.2	..	8.3	..
Slovenia	5.1	4.9	5.1	5.2	5.3	5.7	5.9	5.8
South Africa	27.3	63.5	45.2	39.5	34.6	37.4	..	..
Spain	17.0	32.2	29.1	28.8	23.6	..	..	..
Sri Lanka	..	..	..	4.7	4.8	..	16.0	10.6
Sweden	51.9	63.8	57.6	55.4	44.8	46.7	48.0	52.6
Switzerland	19.8	20.4	20.6	19.6	20.3	20.1	18.7	17.4
Thailand	7.1	..	..	..	..	..	..	..
Tunisia	..	..	..	..	..	..	..	..
Turkey	57.9	53.8	62.2	59.3	66.7	63.7	57.1	54.2
United Kingdom	55.2	55.2	58.0	57.8	57.5	0.3	0.4	0.4
United States	13.9	10.1	10.4	9.4	9.5	10.2	10.0	0.8
Uruguay	..	31.3	31.4	32.2	33.6	..	34.7	..

.. Not available

Note: Detailed metadata at: *http://metalinks.oecd.org/ins/20200312/1e50.*

1. Information on data for Israel: *http://oe.cd/israel-disclaimer.*

Source: Insurance activity indicators, OECD Insurance Statistics (database)

Table 30. Market share of foreign undertakings in total domestic business (Non-life)

Branches or agencies

Per cent

	2011	2012	2013	2014	2015	2016	2017	2018
Argentina	..	0.1	0.1	3.2	2.5	2.4	2.6	2.1
Australia	9.7	9.7	9.7	10.1	9.1	9.9	9.6	11.9
Austria	..	..	0.1	0.1	0.0	0.0	0.1	0.1
Belgium	..	..	..	..	..	..	..	..
Bolivia	..	..	..	..	..	..	..	..
Brazil	..	..	..	..	0.0	0.0	0.0	0.0
Canada	14.3	13.4	13.1	23.2	21.0	19.4	19.0	15.1
Chile	..	..	..	..	..	..	..	..
Colombia	..	..	..	..	..	..	..	..
Costa Rica	0.0	0.1	0.3	0.4	0.8	1.3	1.5	1.7
Cuba	..	..	..	..	..	..	..	..
Czech Republic	3.1	2.7	3.7	4.7	4.9	5.3	5.4	4.4
Denmark	..	..	..	..	..	..	..	..
Dominican Republic	..	..	..	..	..	..	..	..
Ecuador	..	..	..	..	..	..	..	..
Egypt	..	..	..	..	..	..	..	..
El Salvador	2.3	2.4	0.0	0.0	0.0	0.0	..	4.5
Estonia	0.0	14.5	13.6	14.8	13.5	15.0	15.1	15.3
Finland	..	..	..	..	..	..	..	..
France	0.1	0.1	0.1	0.1	0.1	..	..	..
Germany	3.0	3.1	2.7	3.2	3.5	3.1	3.8	4.0
Greece	4.6	7.9	0.0	0.0	0.0	0.0	0.0	0.0
Guatemala	..	..	..	..	..	..	..	..
Honduras	..	..	10.5	4.4	3.6	..	..	49.3
Hong Kong, China	..	..	..	..	..	..	..	..
Hungary	..	..	..	..	..	..	..	..
India	0.0	..	..	..	..	..	2.9	..
Indonesia	..	..	..	..	..	..	..	..
Iceland	0.0	..	..	..	..	..	..	..
Ireland	8.2	17.6	14.3	24.3	22.2	..	17.1	16.6
Israel[1]	..	..	..	..	..	..	..	..
Italy	1.1	1.1	1.1	1.1	1.4	1.6	1.5	1.6
Japan	7.8	..	..	..	..	2.3	2.5	2.8
Korea	2.6	2.0	3.1	2.3	2.3	2.3	2.4	2.8
Latvia	10.9	13.3	18.5	20.4	20.2	22.6	27.0	28.1
Lithuania	40.4	39.7	52.9	53.1	53.9	46.8	48.4	51.4
Luxembourg	7.2	7.5	6.5	3.6	3.6	3.5	3.3	3.6
Malaysia	4.4	5.8	6.7	7.3	8.4	9.6	8.9	8.8
Mexico	..	..	..	..	..	..	..	..
Morocco	..	..	..	..	..	..	..	..
Netherlands	1.9	1.9	0.3	0.3	0.0	..	..	..
New Zealand	..	..	..	..	..	..	..	..
Nicaragua	..	..	..	..	..	..	..	..
Norway	41.5	43.2	43.4	41.1	40.2	40.3	37.8	37.3
Panama	..	7.9	7.7	..	..	..	..	..
Paraguay	..	..	..	..	0.0	0.0	..	..
Peru	..	..	..	..	..	..	..	..
Poland	..	..	..	..	..	..	..	..
Portugal	0.3	0.0	0.0	0.0	0.0	0.0	0.0	0.0
Puerto Rico	..	..	..	..	..	..	..	..
Russia	..	..	..	..	..	0.1	0.0	0.0
Singapore	44.0	42.7	46.8	39.6	38.2	37.4	36.5	..
Slovak Republic	6.2	7.1	8.0	8.7	8.5	..	8.3	..
Slovenia	..	..	..	..	..	..	..	..
South Africa	..	..	0.0	..	..	..	..	..
Spain	0.2	0.2	0.0	0.0	0.0	..	..	..
Sri Lanka	..	..	..	..	0.0	..	..	..
Sweden	..	..	..	8.2	..	..	..	..
Switzerland	4.8	4.9	5.0	5.5	6.0	7.1	7.5	5.8
Thailand	7.1	..	..	..	..	..	..	..
Tunisia	..	..	..	..	..	..	..	..
Turkey	0.2	0.3	0.3	0.3	0.4	0.4	0.5	0.7
United Kingdom	5.4	4.7	3.7	4.1	4.6	0.3	0.4	0.4
United States	0.1	0.1	0.0	0.0	0.1	0.1	0.1	0.1
Uruguay	..	..	0.0	0.0	0.0	..	0.0	..

.. Not available

Note: Detailed metadata at: *http://metalinks.oecd.org/ins/20200312/1e50.*

1. Information on data for Israel: *http://oe.cd/israel-disclaimer.*

Source: Insurance activity indicators, OECD Insurance Statistics (database)

Country tables

AUSTRALIA

Table 1. Selected aggregates

Million AUD

	2011	2012	2013	2014	2015	2016	2017	2018
1.1 Insurance business written in the reporting country								
1.1.1 Insurance business, by ownership								
Gross premiums								
Domestic undertakings	78 509	79 230	86 754	103 414	100 992	95 348	90 032	88 064
Foreign controlled undertakings	11 038	13 757	15 722	17 983	19 150	19 836	21 498	24 659
Foreign companies (branches)	3 450	3 713	3 977	4 206	3 893	4 393	4 353	5 613
All undertakings	81 959	82 943	90 731	107 620	104 885	99 741	94 385	93 677
Premiums ceded								
Domestic undertakings	11 246	11 507	12 121	13 268	15 209	17 826	19 711	18 794
Foreign controlled undertakings	3 170	4 111	4 666	5 483	5 986	6 268	8 647	8 223
Foreign companies (branches)	1 442	1 659	1 947	1 842	1 739	1 759	1 873	1 875
All undertakings	12 688	13 166	14 068	15 110	16 948	19 585	21 584	20 669
Net written premiums								
Domestic undertakings	67 263	67 724	74 633	90 147	85 783	77 522	70 321	69 270
Foreign controlled undertakings	7 868	9 646	11 055	12 500	13 164	13 568	12 851	16 436
Foreign companies (branches)	2 008	2 054	2 030	2 365	2 154	2 634	2 480	3 738
All undertakings	69 271	69 778	76 663	92 511	87 937	80 156	72 801	73 008
1.1.2 Insurance business on foreign risks, gross premiums								
Life	475	491	574	686	701	711	706	880
Non-life	..	..	..	..	..	..	..	..
Composite total	..	..	..	..	..	..	..	..
Total	475	491	574	686	701	711	706	880
1.1.3 Life insurance payments, by class, gross premiums								
Annuities	..	..	..	..	..	..	..	..
Unit linked	..	..	..	..	..	..	..	..
Other life insurance	..	..	..	..	..	..	..	..
Total life insurance	..	41 091	45 794	60 881	56 868	49 890	43 141	39 741
***of which:** Pension contracts*	..	..	..	..	..	..	..	..
1.1.4 Non-life insurance payments, by class, gross premiums								
Motor vehicle insurance	11 474	12 114	12 924	13 467	13 749	14 512	15 447	15 789
Marine, aviation and other transport insurance	1 457	1 484	1 523	1 598	1 673	1 648	1 739	1 871
Freight insurance	..	..	..	..	..	..	..	..
Fire and other property damage insurance	9 537	10 918	12 038	11 836	12 031	12 297	12 713	13 428
Pecuniary loss insurance	1 161	1 207	1 258	1 454	1 493	1 443	1 352	1 230
General liability insurance	4 821	5 008	5 283	5 418	5 435	5 348	5 491	5 893
Accident and health	1 038	1 049	1 134	1 124	1 130	1 064	1 021	1 006
***of which:** Health*	..	..	..	..	..	..	..	..
Other non-life insurance	751	835	900	951	1 029	1 071	1 205	1 325
Treaty reinsurance	5 235	5 836	5 823	5 970	6 271	7 115	6 269	6 742
Total non-life insurance	35 475	38 450	40 884	41 818	42 811	44 498	45 237	47 283
1.2 Gross claims payments								
Life								
Domestic undertakings	44 988	45 777	47 647	64 828	56 547	59 350	47 307	46 989
Foreign controlled undertakings	4 301	4 181	5 212	5 876	6 681	7 133	9 207	8 564
Foreign companies (branches)	..	..	..	..	..	..	..	..
All undertakings	44 988	45 777	47 647	64 828	56 547	59 350	47 307	46 989
Non-life								
Domestic undertakings	31 597	22 048	24 141	26 293	29 311	28 026	29 946	30 252
Foreign controlled undertakings	6 668	4 538	4 542	5 446	6 183	5 534	6 453	8 199
Foreign companies (branches)	7 061	1 749	1 984	3 318	2 585	3 217	3 124	3 853
All undertakings	38 658	23 797	26 126	29 611	31 896	31 243	33 070	34 105
Composite, all undertakings	..	..	..	..	..	..	..	..
Total								
Domestic undertakings	76 585	67 825	71 788	91 121	85 858	87 376	77 253	77 241
Foreign controlled undertakings	10 969	8 719	9 754	11 322	12 864	12 667	15 660	16 763
Foreign companies (branches)	7 061	1 749	1 984	3 318	2 585	3 217	3 124	3 853
All undertakings	83 646	69 574	73 773	94 439	88 443	90 593	80 377	81 094
1.3 Commissions								
Life								
Domestic undertakings	2 852	3 007	3 015	3 118	3 087	3 129	2 514	2 402
Foreign controlled undertakings	455	252	447	451	460	464	494	483
Foreign companies (branches)	..	..	..	..	..	..	..	..
All undertakings	2 852	3 007	3 015	3 118	3 087	3 129	2 514	2 402
Non-life								
Domestic undertakings	..	..	506	566	816	1 038	1 070	1 310
Foreign controlled undertakings	..	..	239	270	276	308	341	418
Foreign companies (branches)	..	..	264	287	301	327	324	250
All undertakings	..	..	770	853	1 117	1 364	1 394	1 560
Composite, all undertakings	..	..	..	..	..	..	..	..
Total								
Domestic undertakings	2 852	3 007	3 521	3 684	3 903	4 167	3 584	3 712
Foreign controlled undertakings	455	252	686	721	736	772	835	901
Foreign companies (branches)	..	..	264	287	301	327	324	250
All undertakings	2 852	3 007	3 785	3 971	4 204	4 493	3 908	3 962

Table 1. Selected aggregates *(cont.)*

Million AUD

	2011	2012	2013	2014	2015	2016	2017	2018
1.4 Gross operating expenses								
Life								
Domestic undertakings	6 777	7 274	7 830	8 128	8 041	8 666	8 457	9 370
Foreign controlled undertakings	1 709	1 430	2 392	2 393	2 487	3 038	3 239	4 439
Foreign companies (branches)	..	..	..	..	..	..	..	..
All undertakings	6 777	7 274	7 830	8 128	8 041	8 666	8 457	9 370
Non-life								
Domestic undertakings	6 658	7 197	7 361	7 502	7 497	7 368	7 475	7 517
Foreign controlled undertakings	1 370	1 490	1 618	1 704	1 850	1 829	1 975	2 378
Foreign companies (branches)	571	559	597	629	660	618	563	790
All undertakings	7 229	7 756	7 959	8 131	8 157	7 987	8 038	8 307
Composite, all undertakings	..	..	..	..	..	..	..	..
Total								
Domestic undertakings	13 435	14 471	15 191	15 630	15 538	16 034	15 932	16 887
Foreign controlled undertakings	3 079	2 920	4 010	4 097	4 337	4 867	5 214	6 817
Foreign companies (branches)	571	559	597	629	660	618	563	790
All undertakings	14 006	15 030	15 789	16 259	16 198	16 653	16 495	17 677
1.5 Insurance business written abroad by branches, gross premiums								
Life								
Branches and agencies	..	..	..	..	..	..	..	..
Subsidaries	..	..	..	..	..	..	..	..
Total	..	..	..	..	..	..	..	..
Non-life								
Branches and agencies	..	..	..	..	..	..	..	..
Subsidaries	..	..	..	..	..	..	..	..
Total	..	..	..	..	..	..	..	..
Composite total	..	..	..	..	..	..	..	..
Total								
Branches and agencies	..	..	..	..	..	..	..	..
Subsidaries	..	..	..	..	..	..	..	..
Total	..	..	..	..	..	..	..	..

.. Not available

Note: Detailed metadata at: *http://metalinks.oecd.org/ins/20200312/0732.*

Source: OECD Insurance Statistics (database)

AUSTRALIA

Table 2. Number of companies and employees

	2011	2012	2013	2014	2015	2016	2017	2018
2.1 Number of companies								
Life								
Domestic undertakings	31	28	28	28	28	29	29	29
Foreign controlled undertakings	14	14	14	14	13	13	13	14
Foreign companies (branches)	..	..	..	..	..	..	..	..
All undertakings	31	28	28	28	28	29	29	29
Non-life								
Domestic undertakings	81	79	75	74	70	68	58	58
Foreign controlled undertakings	19	17	18	19	19	17	15	17
Foreign companies (branches)	31	30	29	29	29	31	28	28
All undertakings	112	109	104	103	99	99	86	86
Composite, all undertakings	..	..	..	..	0	..	..	..
Reinsurance								
Domestic undertakings	3	3	3	3	2	2	2	2
Foreign controlled undertakings	1	1	1	1	1	1	1	1
Foreign companies (branches)	9	9	9	9	9	8	8	8
All undertakings	12	12	12	12	11	10	10	10
Total								
Domestic undertakings	115	110	106	105	100	99	89	89
Foreign controlled undertakings	34	32	33	34	33	31	29	32
Foreign companies (branches)	40	39	38	38	38	39	36	36
All undertakings	155	149	144	143	138	138	125	125
2.2 Number of employees								
Insurance undertakings	..	..	..	..	..	..	..	..
Intermediaries	..	..	..	..	..	..	..	..
Total	..	..	..	..	..	..	..	..

.. Not available

Note: Detailed metadata at: *http://metalinks.oecd.org/ins/20200312/0732.*

Source: OECD Insurance Statistics (database)

AUSTRIA

Table 1. Selected aggregates

Million EUR

	2011	2012	2013	2014	2015	2016	2017	2018
1.1 Insurance business written in the reporting country								
1.1.1 Insurance business, by ownership								
Gross premiums								
Domestic undertakings	..	..	18 879	18 889	19 003	18 647	18 126	18 520
Foreign controlled undertakings	..	..	6 781	7 196	7 060	6 979	6 390	6 467
Foreign companies (branches)	..	..	8	6	6	6	7	8
All undertakings	..	..	18 887	18 895	19 009	18 653	18 134	18 527
Premiums ceded								
Domestic undertakings	..	..	3 539	3 102	2 996	3 521	3 130	2 376
Foreign controlled undertakings	..	..	1 127	1 171	1 113	1 636	1 280	475
Foreign companies (branches)	..	..	0	0	0	0	0	0
All undertakings	..	..	3 539	3 102	2 996	3 522	3 131	2 376
Net written premiums								
Domestic undertakings	..	..	15 340	15 787	16 007	15 126	14 996	16 144
Foreign controlled undertakings	..	..	5 654	6 024	5 948	5 343	5 110	5 991
Foreign companies (branches)	..	..	8	6	6	6	7	7
All undertakings	..	..	15 348	15 793	16 013	15 131	15 003	16 151
1.1.2 Insurance business on foreign risks, gross premiums								
Life	174	72	157	22	20	14	3	4
Non-life	722	662	717	726	702	753	777	931
Composite	523	626	595	489	391	371	363	358
of which:								
Life	252	188	202	158	111	95	89	82
Non-life	270	438	393	331	280	276	274	276
Total	1 419	1 360	1 469	1 237	1 114	1 138	1 143	1 293
1.1.3 Life insurance payments, by class, gross premiums								
Annuities	..	..	1 441	1 822	1 946	1 531	1 434	1 367
Unit linked	2 255	1 846	1 248	1 011	933	864	812	972
Other life insurance	4 644	4 588	3 738	3 852	3 812	3 646	3 488	3 188
Total life insurance	6 899	6 434	6 427	6 685	6 692	6 041	5 735	5 527
***of which:** Pension contracts*	..	..	997	1 116	1 031	940	964	923
1.1.4 Non-life insurance payments, by class, gross premiums								
Motor vehicle insurance	1 316	1 386	1 487	1 447	3 920	4 043	3 980	4 207
Marine, aviation and other transport insurance	140	165	174	138	11	9	10	9
Freight insurance	..	..	..	..	155	148	137	165
Fire and other property damage insurance	978	1 008	1 081	1 058	3 153	3 178	3 013	3 030
Pecuniary loss insurance	237	167	174	183	178	176	166	169
General liability insurance	922	834	860	886	889	905	868	903
Accident and health	2 873	3 024	3 150	3 143	3 257	3 391	3 473	3 627
***of which:** Health*	1 704	1 762	1 841	1 905	2 007	2 096	2 167	2 264
Other non-life insurance	5 517	5 672	5 517	5 340	742	749	739	877
Treaty reinsurance	..	..	..	..	..	..	..	..
Total non-life insurance	11 983	12 255	12 444	12 195	12 303	12 599	12 386	12 987
1.2 Gross claims payments								
Life								
Domestic undertakings	314	360	358	1 110	1 254	947	977	933
Foreign controlled undertakings	0	145	140	714	837	920	959	914
Foreign companies (branches)	0	..	0	0	0	0	0	0
All undertakings	314	360	358	1 110	1 254	947	977	933
Non-life								
Domestic undertakings	2 290	2 675	1 107	1 632	2 072	2 203	1 939	1 936
Foreign controlled undertakings	875	1 490	905	873	1 288	2 620	1 893	1 862
Foreign companies (branches)	5	5	4	3	2	3	3	3
All undertakings	2 296	2 681	1 111	1 636	2 075	2 206	1 942	1 939
Composite								
Domestic undertakings	10 854	11 652	11 676	11 289	12 780	12 440	12 173	11 700
Foreign controlled undertakings	3 751	3 829	3 846	3 026	3 760	10 479	9 813	9 865
Foreign companies (branches)	0	..	0	0	0	0	0	0
All undertakings	10 854	11 652	11 676	11 289	12 780	12 440	12 173	11 700
of which:								
Life	6 338	6 047	6 011	5 955	7 193	6 817	6 194	5 688
Domestic undertakings	6 338	6 047	6 011	5 955	7 193	6 817	6 194	5 688
Foreign controlled undertakings	2 297	2 281	2 274	1 630	2 235	3 500	3 281	3 307
Foreign companies (branches)	0	..	0	0	0	0	0	0
All undertakings	6 338	6 047	6 011	5 955	7 193	6 817	6 194	5 688
Non-life	4 516	5 605	5 665	5 335	5 588	5 623	5 980	6 012
Domestic undertakings	4 516	5 605	5 665	5 335	5 588	5 623	5 980	6 012
Foreign controlled undertakings	1 454	1 549	1 572	1 396	1 525	6 979	6 532	6 558
Foreign companies (branches)	0	..	0	0	0	0	0	0
All undertakings	4 516	5 605	5 665	5 335	5 588	5 623	5 980	6 012
Total								
Domestic undertakings	13 458	14 687	13 141	14 032	16 107	15 590	15 089	14 568
Foreign controlled undertakings	4 626	5 464	4 891	4 613	5 885	14 018	12 665	12 641
Foreign companies (branches)	5	5	4	3	2	3	3	3
All undertakings	13 463	14 692	13 145	14 036	16 109	15 593	15 092	14 572

Table 1. Selected aggregates *(cont.)*

Million EUR

	2011	2012	2013	2014	2015	2016	2017	2018
1.3 Commissions								
Life								
Domestic undertakings	138	75	99	98	98	80	73	73
Foreign controlled undertakings	0	17	5	70	70	79	72	72
Foreign companies (branches)	0	..	0	0	0	0	0	0
All undertakings	138	75	99	98	98	80	73	73
Non-life								
Domestic undertakings	548	338	354	398	386	399	408	411
Foreign controlled undertakings	302	309	319	329	341	348	352	350
Foreign companies (branches)	2	2	2	1	1	1	2	2
All undertakings	549	340	356	399	387	400	410	413
Composite								
Domestic undertakings	1 962	2 309	2 285	2 279	2 354	2 392	2 365	2 335
Foreign controlled undertakings	717	750	752	666	739	734	725	706
Foreign companies (branches)	0	..	0	0	0	0	0	0
All undertakings	1 962	2 309	2 285	2 279	2 354	2 392	2 365	2 335
of which:								
Life	669	692	644	624	623	579	538	454
Domestic undertakings	669	692	644	624	623	579	538	454
Foreign controlled undertakings	255	253	238	163	188	163	149	106
Foreign companies (branches)	0	..	0	0	0	0	0	0
All undertakings	669	692	644	624	623	579	538	454
Non-life	1 292	1 616	1 641	1 655	1 731	1 812	1 827	1 881
Domestic undertakings	1 292	1 616	1 641	1 655	1 731	1 812	1 827	1 881
Foreign controlled undertakings	462	497	514	503	551	571	576	600
Foreign companies (branches)	0	..	0	0	0	0	0	0
All undertakings	1 292	1 616	1 641	1 655	1 731	1 812	1 827	1 881
Total								
Domestic undertakings	2 647	2 722	2 738	2 775	2 839	2 871	2 846	2 819
Foreign controlled undertakings	1 019	1 077	1 076	1 065	1 150	1 161	1 149	1 128
Foreign companies (branches)	2	2	2	1	1	1	2	2
All undertakings	2 649	2 724	2 740	2 776	2 840	2 872	2 848	2 821
1.4 Gross operating expenses								
Life								
Domestic undertakings	157	95	120	43	40	37	42	37
Foreign controlled undertakings	0	0	14	30	30	36	41	37
Foreign companies (branches)	0	..	0	0	0	0	0	0
All undertakings	157	95	120	43	40	37	42	37
Non-life								
Domestic undertakings	672	860	697	153	143	192	191	210
Foreign controlled undertakings	263	447	414	116	92	111	105	103
Foreign companies (branches)	3	3	3	1	1	1	1	1
All undertakings	675	863	700	154	144	193	192	210
Composite								
Domestic undertakings	2 054	1 918	2 306	623	678	702	696	741
Foreign controlled undertakings	667	695	699	167	185	177	181	178
Foreign companies (branches)	0	..	0	0	0	0	0	0
All undertakings	2 054	1 918	2 306	623	678	702	696	741
of which:								
Life	879	513	848	194	202	223	224	236
Domestic undertakings	879	513	848	194	202	223	224	236
Foreign controlled undertakings	344	339	323	61	68	63	58	60
Foreign companies (branches)	0	..	0	0	0	0	0	0
All undertakings	879	513	848	194	202	223	224	236
Non-life	1 175	1 405	1 458	428	476	479	472	505
Domestic undertakings	1 175	1 405	1 458	428	476	479	472	505
Foreign controlled undertakings	323	356	376	106	117	114	123	118
Foreign companies (branches)	0	..	0	0	0	0	0	0
All undertakings	1 175	1 405	1 458	428	476	479	472	505
Total								
Domestic undertakings	2 883	2 873	3 124	819	861	930	929	988
Foreign controlled undertakings	930	1 143	1 128	313	308	324	328	318
Foreign companies (branches)	3	3	3	1	1	1	1	1
All undertakings	2 885	2 876	3 127	820	862	931	930	989

AUSTRIA

Table 1. Selected aggregates *(cont.)*

Million EUR

	2011	2012	2013	2014	2015	2016	2017	2018
1.5 Insurance business written abroad by branches, gross premiums								
Life								
Branches and agencies	174	72	157	22	19	13	11	10
Subsidaries	..	..	..	..	..	..	..	..
Total	174	72	157	22	19	13	11	10
Non-life								
Branches and agencies	219	149	159	198	204	217	215	220
Subsidaries	..	..	..	..	..	..	..	..
Total	219	149	159	198	204	217	215	220
Composite								
Branches and agencies	480	557	480	368	284	251	275	279
Subsidaries	..	..	..	..	..	..	..	..
Total	480	557	480	368	284	251	275	279
of which:								
Life	233	168	140	103	78	83	78	73
Branches and agencies	233	168	140	103	78	83	78	73
Subsidaries	..	..	..	..	..	..	..	..
Total	233	168	140	103	78	83	78	73
Non-life	246	389	340	266	206	168	198	206
Branches and agencies	246	389	340	266	206	168	198	206
Subsidaries	..	..	..	..	..	..	..	..
Total	246	389	340	266	206	168	198	206
Total								
Branches and agencies	873	778	796	587	507	481	501	510
Subsidaries	..	..	..	..	..	..	..	..
Total	873	778	796	587	507	481	501	510

.. Not available

Note: Detailed metadata at: *http://metalinks.oecd.org/ins/20200312/f820.*

Source: OECD Insurance Statistics (database)

AUSTRIA

Table 2. Number of companies and employees

	2011	2012	2013	2014	2015	2016	2017	2018
2.1 Number of companies								
Life								
Domestic undertakings	3	3	3	7	7	6	6	6
Foreign controlled undertakings	0	1	1	3	3	4	4	4
Foreign companies (branches)	0	0	0	0	0	0	0	0
All undertakings	3	3	3	7	7	6	6	6
Non-life								
Domestic undertakings	17	14	14	12	12	12	12	12
Foreign controlled undertakings	8	7	7	8	8	8	8	7
Foreign companies (branches)	1	1	1	1	1	1	1	1
All undertakings	18	15	15	13	13	13	13	13
Composite								
Domestic undertakings	28	27	26	21	20	17	17	16
Foreign controlled undertakings	10	10	9	6	5	4	4	4
Foreign companies (branches)	0	0	0	0	0	0	0	0
All undertakings	28	27	26	21	20	17	17	16
Reinsurance								
Domestic undertakings	3	3	3	3	2	3	2	1
Foreign controlled undertakings	2	2	1	2	1	1	0	0
Foreign companies (branches)	0	0	0	0	0	0	0	0
All undertakings	3	3	3	3	2	3	2	1
Total								
Domestic undertakings	51	47	46	43	41	38	37	35
Foreign controlled undertakings	20	20	18	19	17	17	16	15
Foreign companies (branches)	1	1	1	1	1	1	1	1
All undertakings	52	48	47	44	42	39	38	36
2.2 Number of employees								
Insurance undertakings	27 671	27 430	27 738	27 791	27 911	28 336	28 367	27 804
Intermediaries	9 839	9 255	..	..	..	..	..	..
Total	27 671	27 430	27 738	27 791	27 911	28 336	28 367	27 804

.. Not available

Note: Detailed metadata at: *http://metalinks.oecd.org/ins/20200312/f820.*

Source: OECD Insurance Statistics (database)

BELGIUM

Table 1. Selected aggregates

Million EUR

	2011	2012	2013	2014	2015	2016	2017	2018
1.1 Insurance business written in the reporting country								
1.1.1 Insurance business, by ownership								
Gross premiums								
Domestic undertakings	29 363	32 640	28 251	28 863	27 712	27 493	27 299	28 539
Foreign controlled undertakings	..	..	..	..	..	..	..	..
Foreign companies (branches)	..	..	..	..	..	..	..	..
All undertakings	29 363	32 640	28 251	28 863	27 712	27 493	27 299	28 539
Premiums ceded								
Domestic undertakings	1 441	2 417	2 474	3 251	3 183	3 520	3 412	3 656
Foreign controlled undertakings	..	..	..	..	..	..	..	..
Foreign companies (branches)	..	..	..	..	..	..	..	..
All undertakings	1 441	2 417	2 474	3 251	3 183	3 520	3 412	3 656
Net written premiums								
Domestic undertakings	27 922	30 223	25 777	25 612	24 529	23 973	23 887	24 882
Foreign controlled undertakings	..	..	..	..	..	..	..	..
Foreign companies (branches)	..	..	..	..	..	..	..	..
All undertakings	27 922	30 223	25 777	25 612	24 529	23 973	23 887	24 882
1.1.2 Insurance business on foreign risks, gross premiums								
Life	..	31	25	15	24	20	17	6
Non-life	..	242	268	563	436	515	553	611
Composite	..	230	218	223	321	331	331	378
of which:								
Life	..	77	53	39	38	23	17	14
Non-life	..	153	165	184	282	308	313	364
Total	..	502	511	801	781	866	901	995
1.1.3 Life insurance payments, by class, gross premiums								
Annuities	..	..	..	..	..	..	..	..
Unit linked	2 142	4 844	2 743	2 524	3 008	2 221	3 182	3 520
Other life insurance	16 324	16 235	13 501	13 723	12 302	12 674	11 424	12 051
Total life insurance	18 467	21 078	16 244	16 247	15 310	14 895	14 606	15 571
***of which:** Pension contracts*	..	..	..	..	..	..	..	..
1.1.4 Non-life insurance payments, by class, gross premiums								
Motor vehicle insurance	..	3 459	3 487	3 542	3 585	..	..	..
Marine, aviation and other transport insurance	..	78	71	69	81	..	..	..
Freight insurance	..	116	104	100	73	..	..	..
Fire and other property damage insurance	..	2 573	2 696	2 755	2 708	..	..	..
Pecuniary loss insurance	..	407	404	725	598	..	..	..
General liability insurance	..	780	770	785	762	..	..	..
Accident and health	..	3 361	3 592	3 695	3 653	..	..	..
***of which:** Health*	..	1 517	1 618	1 708	1 849	..	..	..
Other non-life insurance	..	737	825	885	888	..	..	..
Treaty reinsurance	..	7	..	..	..	..	..	..
Total non-life insurance	..	11 516	11 949	12 556	12 349	12 532	12 652	12 926
1.2 Gross claims payments								
Life								
Domestic undertakings	547	592	528	626	469	642	521	731
Foreign controlled undertakings	..	..	..	..	..	..	..	..
Foreign companies (branches)	..	..	..	..	..	..	..	..
All undertakings	..	592	528	626	469	642	521	731
Non-life								
Domestic undertakings	1 512	1 898	1 960	2 272	2 363	2 539	2 316	1 489
Foreign controlled undertakings	..	..	..	..	..	..	..	..
Foreign companies (branches)	..	..	..	..	..	..	..	..
All undertakings	..	1 898	1 960	2 272	2 363	2 539	2 316	1 489
Composite								
Domestic undertakings	20 798	23 438	23 890	24 323	25 926	25 229	24 184	22 308
Foreign controlled undertakings	..	..	..	..	..	..	..	..
Foreign companies (branches)	..	..	..	..	..	..	..	..
All undertakings	..	23 438	23 890	24 323	25 926	25 229	24 184	22 308
of which:								
Life	..	17 427	17 746	17 418	19 244	18 328	17 466	16 063
Domestic undertakings	15 232	17 427	17 746	17 418	19 244	18 328	17 466	16 063
Foreign controlled undertakings	..	..	..	..	..	..	..	..
Foreign companies (branches)	..	..	..	..	..	..	..	..
All undertakings	..	17 427	17 746	17 418	19 244	18 328	17 466	16 063
Non-life	..	6 010	6 144	6 905	6 682	6 901	6 717	6 244
Domestic undertakings	5 566	6 010	6 144	6 905	6 682	6 901	6 717	6 244
Foreign controlled undertakings	..	..	..	..	..	..	..	..
Foreign companies (branches)	..	..	..	..	..	..	..	..
All undertakings	..	6 010	6 144	6 905	6 682	6 901	6 717	6 244
Total								
Domestic undertakings	22 857	25 928	26 378	27 222	28 758	28 410	27 020	24 527
Foreign controlled undertakings	..	..	..	..	..	..	..	..
Foreign companies (branches)	..	..	..	..	..	..	..	..
All undertakings	..	25 928	26 378	27 222	28 758	28 410	27 020	24 527

Table 1. Selected aggregates *(cont.)*

Million EUR

	2011	2012	2013	2014	2015	2016	2017	2018
1.3 Commissions								
Life								
Domestic undertakings	54	59	55	45	47	55	56	64
Foreign controlled undertakings	..	..	..	..	..	..	..	..
Foreign companies (branches)	..	..	..	..	..	..	..	..
All undertakings	..	59	55	45	47	55	56	64
Non-life								
Domestic undertakings	318	394	391	450	550	616	607	303
Foreign controlled undertakings	..	..	..	..	..	..	..	..
Foreign companies (branches)	..	..	..	..	..	..	..	..
All undertakings	..	394	391	450	550	616	607	303
Composite								
Domestic undertakings	2 209	2 397	2 446	2 478	2 493	2 484	2 536	2 161
Foreign controlled undertakings	..	..	..	..	..	..	..	..
Foreign companies (branches)	..	..	..	..	..	..	..	..
All undertakings	..	2 397	2 446	2 478	2 493	2 484	2 536	2 161
of which:								
Life	..	905	875	852	833	765	756	730
Domestic undertakings	826	905	875	852	833	765	756	730
Foreign controlled undertakings	..	..	..	..	..	..	..	..
Foreign companies (branches)	..	..	..	..	..	..	..	..
All undertakings	..	905	875	852	833	765	756	730
Non-life	..	1 493	1 572	1 626	1 660	1 719	1 779	1 431
Domestic undertakings	1 382	1 493	1 572	1 626	1 660	1 719	1 779	1 431
Foreign controlled undertakings	..	..	..	..	..	..	..	..
Foreign companies (branches)	..	..	..	..	..	..	..	..
All undertakings	..	1 493	1 572	1 626	1 660	1 719	1 779	1 431
Total								
Domestic undertakings	2 581	2 851	2 892	2 973	3 090	3 155	3 198	2 529
Foreign controlled undertakings	..	..	..	..	..	..	..	..
Foreign companies (branches)	..	..	..	..	..	..	..	..
All undertakings	..	2 851	2 892	2 973	3 090	3 155	3 198	2 529
1.4 Gross operating expenses								
Life								
Domestic undertakings	115	118	58	41	45	47	51	61
Foreign controlled undertakings	..	..	..	..	..	..	..	..
Foreign companies (branches)	..	..	..	..	..	..	..	..
All undertakings	..	118	58	41	45	47	51	61
Non-life								
Domestic undertakings	621	806	386	643	618	641	678	382
Foreign controlled undertakings	..	..	..	..	..	..	..	..
Foreign companies (branches)	..	..	..	..	..	..	..	..
All undertakings	..	806	386	643	618	641	678	382
Composite								
Domestic undertakings	4 176	4 401	2 084	2 197	2 205	2 320	2 402	2 306
Foreign controlled undertakings	..	..	..	..	..	..	..	..
Foreign companies (branches)	..	..	..	..	..	..	..	..
All undertakings	..	4 401	2 084	2 197	2 205	2 320	2 402	2 306
of which:								
Life	..	1 702	830	833	824	859	869	883
Domestic undertakings	1 597	1 702	830	833	824	859	869	883
Foreign controlled undertakings	..	..	..	..	..	..	..	..
Foreign companies (branches)	..	..	..	..	..	..	..	..
All undertakings	..	1 702	830	833	824	859	869	883
Non-life	..	2 699	1 254	1 364	1 382	1 461	1 533	1 423
Domestic undertakings	2 579	2 699	1 254	1 364	1 382	1 461	1 533	1 423
Foreign controlled undertakings	..	..	..	..	..	..	..	..
Foreign companies (branches)	..	..	..	..	..	..	..	..
All undertakings	..	2 699	1 254	1 364	1 382	1 461	1 533	1 423
Total								
Domestic undertakings	4 912	5 325	2 528	2 881	2 868	3 008	3 130	2 749
Foreign controlled undertakings	..	..	..	..	..	..	..	..
Foreign companies (branches)	..	..	..	..	..	..	..	..
All undertakings	..	5 325	2 528	2 881	2 868	3 008	3 130	2 749

Table 1. Selected aggregates *(cont.)*

Million EUR

	2011	2012	2013	2014	2015	2016	2017	2018
1.5 Insurance business written abroad by branches, gross premiums								
Life								
Branches and agencies	..	2	2	2	0	0	0	0
Subsidaries	..	..	..	..	..	..	..	..
Total	..	2	2	2	..	0	0	0
Non-life								
Branches and agencies	..	698	727	1 572	1 931	1 854	1 843	1 912
Subsidaries	..	..	..	..	..	..	..	..
Total	..	698	727	1 572	1 931	1 854	1 843	1 912
Composite								
Branches and agencies	..	442	448	1 121	1 156	1 197	1 337	1 246
Subsidaries	..	..	..	..	..	..	..	..
Total	..	442	448	1 121	1 156	1 197	1 337	1 246
of which:								
Life	..	32	28	16	16	14	61	57
Branches and agencies	..	32	28	16	16	14	61	57
Subsidaries	..	..	..	..	..	..	..	..
Total	..	32	28	16	16	14	61	57
Non-life	..	409	421	1 105	1 141	1 183	1 276	1 189
Branches and agencies	..	409	421	1 105	1 141	1 183	1 276	1 189
Subsidaries	..	..	..	..	..	..	..	..
Total	..	409	421	1 105	1 141	1 183	1 276	1 189
Total								
Branches and agencies	..	1 142	1 178	2 696	3 087	3 051	3 181	3 158
Subsidaries	..	..	..	..	..	..	..	..
Total	..	1 142	1 178	2 696	3 087	3 051	3 181	3 158

.. Not available

Note: Detailed metadata at: *http://metalinks.oecd.org/ins/20200312/03ef.*

Source: OECD Insurance Statistics (database)

Table 2. Number of companies and employees

	2011	2012	2013	2014	2015	2016	2017	2018
2.1 Number of companies								
Life								
Domestic undertakings	18	17	16	15	15	12	10	9
Foreign controlled undertakings	..	..	..	..	..	..	..	..
Foreign companies (branches)	8	7	7	8	8	10	10	7
All undertakings	26	24	23	23	23	22	20	16
Non-life								
Domestic undertakings	53	49	44	42	41	38	34	36
Foreign controlled undertakings	..	..	..	..	..	..	..	..
Foreign companies (branches)	44	36	36	36	32	32	33	36
All undertakings	97	85	80	78	73	70	67	72
Composite								
Domestic undertakings	24	23	23	23	23	22	23	22
Foreign controlled undertakings	..	..	..	..	..	..	..	..
Foreign companies (branches)	2	2	2	2	2	2	2	2
All undertakings	26	25	25	25	25	24	25	24
Reinsurance								
Domestic undertakings	2	1	1	1	1	1	1	2
Foreign controlled undertakings	..	..	..	..	..	..	..	..
Foreign companies (branches)	0	1	1	1	1	1	1	1
All undertakings	2	2	2	2	2	2	2	3
Total								
Domestic undertakings	97	90	84	81	80	73	68	69
Foreign controlled undertakings	..	..	..	..	..	..	..	..
Foreign companies (branches)	54	46	46	47	43	45	46	46
All undertakings	151	136	130	128	123	118	114	115
2.2 Number of employees								
Insurance undertakings	25 083	..	..	..	..	..	..	..
Intermediaries	..	..	..	..	..	..	..	..
Total	..	..	..	..	..	..	..	..

.. Not available

Note: Detailed metadata at: *http://metalinks.oecd.org/ins/20200312/03ef.*

Source: OECD Insurance Statistics (database)

CANADA

Table 1. Selected aggregates

Million CAD

	2011	2012	2013	2014	2015	2016	2017	2018
1.1 Insurance business written in the reporting country								
1.1.1 Insurance business, by ownership								
Gross premiums								
Domestic undertakings	83 513	87 337	91 830	81 347	86 082	89 439	93 962	97 815
Foreign controlled undertakings	11 273	11 465	11 237	18 957	17 321	18 250	19 658	19 804
Foreign companies (branches)	9 502	9 621	9 651	21 604	20 840	19 141	19 488	14 937
All undertakings	93 014	96 958	101 481	102 951	106 922	108 580	113 450	112 752
Premiums ceded								
Domestic undertakings	21 174	23 483	25 176	22 771	25 855	23 885	26 759	19 135
Foreign controlled undertakings	2 550	2 413	2 504	5 070	4 912	5 107	7 154	6 751
Foreign companies (branches)	1 923	2 405	2 094	4 469	4 735	4 370	4 568	4 467
All undertakings	23 097	25 888	27 270	27 240	30 590	28 255	31 327	23 602
Net written premiums								
Domestic undertakings	62 338	63 854	66 655	58 576	60 227	65 554	67 204	78 680
Foreign controlled undertakings	8 723	9 052	8 733	13 888	12 410	13 142	12 504	13 053
Foreign companies (branches)	7 579	7 216	7 557	17 135	16 104	14 771	14 920	10 470
All undertakings	69 917	71 070	74 212	75 710	76 331	80 325	82 123	89 150
1.1.2 Insurance business on foreign risks, gross premiums								
Life	..	..	..	..	..	..	..	..
Non-life	..	..	..	..	..	..	..	..
Composite	..	..	..	..	..	..	..	..
of which:								
Life	..	..	..	..	..	..	..	..
Non-life	..	..	..	..	..	..	..	..
Total	..	..	..	..	..	..	..	..
1.1.3 Life insurance payments, by class, gross premiums								
Annuities	6 457	5 276	6 263	5 562	5 539	5 966	6 558	7 390
Unit linked	..	..	..	..	..	..	..	..
Other life insurance	..	..	..	..	..	..	..	..
Total life insurance	..	..	..	..	..	..	..	..
of which: *Pension contracts*	..	..	..	..	..	..	..	..
1.1.4 Non-life insurance payments, by class, gross premiums								
Motor vehicle insurance	20 277	21 805	22 857	21 007	21 426	21 938	23 234	24 519
Marine, aviation and other transport insurance	656	672	630	773	716	769	700	1 143
Freight insurance	..	..	..	..	..	..	..	..
Fire and other property damage insurance	15 268	16 577	16 687	18 994	19 992	20 599	21 593	28 429
Pecuniary loss insurance	1 716	1 785	1 748	2 271	2 613	2 659	2 708	2 559
General liability insurance	5 054	5 197	5 267	5 830	6 289	6 339	6 398	10 463
Accident and health	25 743	19 672	20 262	25 708	26 370	25 944	26 471	24 315
of which: *Health*	..	..	..	..	..	..	..	..
Other non-life insurance	8	14	32	138	275	368	440	170
Treaty reinsurance	..	..	..	..	..	..	..	..
Total non-life insurance	68 723	65 723	67 482	74 721	77 682	78 616	81 545	91 598
1.2 Gross claims payments								
Life								
Domestic undertakings	0	0	0	0	0	3	..	3
Foreign controlled undertakings	0	0	0	0	0	0	..	0
Foreign companies (branches)	27	28	36	41	13	3	3	3
All undertakings	27	28	36	41	13	6	3	6
Non-life								
Domestic undertakings	23 354	24 435	28 506	25 194	25 500	30 110	29 433	30 596
Foreign controlled undertakings	5 150	4 939	5 566	8 332	8 552	11 171	11 043	11 435
Foreign companies (branches)	5 840	4 875	5 242	5 901	4 694	6 748	4 566	6 479
All undertakings	29 193	29 310	33 748	31 095	30 193	36 858	33 999	37 075
Composite								
Domestic undertakings	10 525	10 851	11 227	9 477	10 030	11 984	12 753	18 600
Foreign controlled undertakings	666	731	736	881	303	336	396	435
Foreign companies (branches)	160	163	159	7 182	7 161	5 671	5 797	1 025
All undertakings	10 685	11 014	11 386	16 659	17 190	17 654	18 549	19 626
of which:								
Life	4 599	4 749	4 969	5 480	5 747	5 919	6 342	6 699
Domestic undertakings	4 523	4 650	4 869	3 858	4 186	4 581	4 981	6 073
Foreign controlled undertakings	190	189	190	344	188	210	256	301
Foreign companies (branches)	76	99	99	1 622	1 561	1 339	1 361	626
All undertakings	4 599	4 749	4 969	5 480	5 747	5 919	6 342	6 699
Non-life	6 085	6 264	6 417	11 179	11 444	11 735	12 207	12 927
Domestic undertakings	6 002	6 201	6 357	5 620	5 844	7 403	7 772	12 528
Foreign controlled undertakings	475	542	546	537	115	127	139	134
Foreign companies (branches)	83	63	60	5 560	5 600	4 332	4 435	399
All undertakings	6 085	6 264	6 417	11 179	11 444	11 735	12 207	12 927
Total								
Domestic undertakings	33 879	35 286	39 733	34 671	35 529	42 097	42 186	49 199
Foreign controlled undertakings	5 816	5 670	6 301	9 213	8 854	11 508	11 439	11 870
Foreign companies (branches)	6 026	5 066	5 437	13 124	11 867	12 422	10 366	7 507
All undertakings	39 905	40 351	45 170	47 795	47 396	54 518	52 552	56 706

CANADA

Table 1. Selected aggregates *(cont.)*

Million CAD

	2011	2012	2013	2014	2015	2016	2017	2018
1.3 Commissions								
Life								
Domestic undertakings	0	0	0	..	0	0	0	..
Foreign controlled undertakings	0	0	0	..	..	..	..	..
Foreign companies (branches)	10	12	10	..	0	0	0	..
All undertakings	10	12	10	..	0	0	0	..
Non-life								
Domestic undertakings	4 305	4 719	4 781	..	5 441	5 666	5 434	6 103
Foreign controlled undertakings	91	1 115	1 092	..	1 882	1 938	2 087	2 182
Foreign companies (branches)	1 102	1 077	1 095	..	1 104	1 177	1 299	1 492
All undertakings	5 407	5 796	5 876	..	6 545	6 843	6 733	7 595
Composite								
Domestic undertakings	5 539	5 505	5 558	..	4 787	5 363	5 218	5 127
Foreign controlled undertakings	377	258	239	..	97	94	97	150
Foreign companies (branches)	158	147	145	..	193	156	197	174
All undertakings	5 697	5 652	5 703	..	4 980	5 519	5 416	5 301
of which:								
Life	4 212	4 239	4 291	..	3 572	4 059	3 893	3 812
Domestic undertakings	4 115	4 150	4 213	..	3 457	3 982	3 801	3 734
Foreign controlled undertakings	285	172	173	..	65	72	75	93
Foreign companies (branches)	97	89	78	..	115	77	93	78
All undertakings	4 212	4 239	4 291	..	3 572	4 059	3 893	3 812
Non-life	1 485	1 413	1 412	..	1 408	1 460	1 522	1 489
Domestic undertakings	1 424	1 355	1 345	..	1 330	1 381	1 418	1 393
Foreign controlled undertakings	91	86	66	..	32	22	22	57
Foreign companies (branches)	61	58	67	..	78	79	105	97
All undertakings	1 485	1 413	1 412	..	1 408	1 460	1 522	1 489
Total								
Domestic undertakings	9 844	10 224	10 339	..	10 228	11 029	10 653	11 230
Foreign controlled undertakings	467	1 373	1 331	..	1 979	2 032	2 184	2 332
Foreign companies (branches)	1 270	1 235	1 249	..	1 298	1 333	1 496	1 666
All undertakings	11 114	11 460	11 588	..	11 526	12 362	12 149	12 896
1.4 Gross operating expenses								
Life								
Domestic undertakings	20	22	23	24	22	30	29	25
Foreign controlled undertakings	0	0	..	0	0	0	0	0
Foreign companies (branches)	29	32	27	28	15	10	9	10
All undertakings	49	53	50	52	37	40	38	36
Non-life								
Domestic undertakings	5 235	5 774	6 023	4 032	4 493	4 725	4 694	4 658
Foreign controlled undertakings	1 385	1 465	1 409	1 385	1 488	1 756	1 635	1 548
Foreign companies (branches)	931	1 001	1 017	855	689	673	672	704
All undertakings	6 166	6 775	7 040	4 887	5 182	5 398	5 366	5 362
Composite								
Domestic undertakings	10 675	12 274	13 728	12 612	14 400	17 159	17 966	19 399
Foreign controlled undertakings	558	557	571	736	187	194	248	251
Foreign companies (branches)	119	110	117	206	272	518	713	259
All undertakings	10 794	12 384	13 845	12 818	14 672	17 677	18 679	19 658
of which:								
Life	..	..	..	..	..	..	..	..
Domestic undertakings	..	..	..	..	..	..	..	..
Foreign controlled undertakings	..	..	..	..	..	..	..	..
Foreign companies (branches)	..	..	..	..	..	..	..	..
All undertakings	..	..	..	..	..	..	..	..
Non-life	..	..	..	..	..	..	..	..
Domestic undertakings	..	..	..	..	..	..	..	..
Foreign controlled undertakings	..	..	..	..	..	..	..	..
Foreign companies (branches)	..	..	..	..	..	..	..	..
All undertakings	..	..	..	..	..	..	..	..
Total								
Domestic undertakings	15 930	18 069	19 774	16 668	18 915	21 914	22 689	24 082
Foreign controlled undertakings	1 943	2 021	1 981	2 121	1 675	1 950	1 883	1 799
Foreign companies (branches)	1 079	1 143	1 161	1 089	976	1 201	1 394	973
All undertakings	17 009	19 212	20 934	17 757	19 891	23 115	24 083	25 055

CANADA

Table 1. Selected aggregates *(cont.)*

Million CAD

	2011	2012	2013	2014	2015	2016	2017	2018
1.5 Insurance business written abroad by branches, gross premiums								
Life								
Branches and agencies	..	..	..	..	..	..	..	..
Subsidaries	..	..	..	..	..	..	..	..
Total	..	..	..	0	0	0	0	0
Non-life								
Branches and agencies	..	..	..	..	..	..	..	..
Subsidaries	..	..	..	..	..	..	..	..
Total	545	548	1 018	1 320	1 500	1 502	1 522	2 658
Composite								
Branches and agencies	..	..	..	..	..	..	..	..
Subsidaries	..	..	..	..	..	..	..	..
Total	34 423	37 741	7 942	31 162	40 235	50 713	54 040	57 636
of which:								
Life	..	..	..	27 224	..	..	..	..
Branches and agencies	..	..	..	..	..	..	..	..
Subsidaries	..	..	..	..	..	..	..	..
Total	..	..	..	27 224	..	..	..	..
Non-life	..	..	..	3 939	..	..	..	..
Branches and agencies	..	..	..	..	..	..	..	..
Subsidaries	..	..	..	..	..	..	..	..
Total	..	..	..	3 939	..	..	..	..
Total								
Branches and agencies	..	..	..	..	..	..	..	..
Subsidaries	..	..	..	..	..	..	..	..
Total	34 968	38 289	8 959	32 482	41 736	52 215	55 562	60 294

.. Not available

Note: Detailed metadata at: *http://metalinks.oecd.org/ins/20200312/bbd1.*

Source: *OECD Insurance Statistics (database)*

Table 2. Number of companies and employees

	2011	2012	2013	2014	2015	2016	2017	2018
2.1 Number of companies								
Life								
Domestic undertakings	1	1	1	1	1	3	3	3
Foreign controlled undertakings	0	0	0	0	0	0	0	0
Foreign companies (branches)	5	5	5	5	5	2	2	2
All undertakings	6	6	6	6	6	5	5	5
Non-life								
Domestic undertakings	86	84	60	66	66	63	61	57
Foreign controlled undertakings	23	23	22	28	28	27	27	25
Foreign companies (branches)	61	60	60	60	58	54	54	54
All undertakings	147	144	120	126	124	117	115	111
Composite								
Domestic undertakings	43	43	34	34	33	31	31	29
Foreign controlled undertakings	10	10	10	9	7	7	8	7
Foreign companies (branches)	26	21	26	23	22	20	20	20
All undertakings	69	64	60	57	55	51	51	49
Reinsurance								
Domestic undertakings	6	6	6	5	5	5	5	5
Foreign controlled undertakings	6	6	6	5	5	5	5	5
Foreign companies (branches)	28	27	28	25	26	28	28	28
All undertakings	34	33	34	30	31	33	33	33
Total								
Domestic undertakings	136	134	101	106	105	102	100	94
Foreign controlled undertakings	39	39	38	42	40	39	40	37
Foreign companies (branches)	120	113	119	113	111	104	104	104
All undertakings	256	247	220	219	216	206	204	198
2.2 Number of employees								
Insurance undertakings	..	..	..	..	..	..	..	..
Intermediaries	..	..	..	..	..	..	..	..
Total	..	..	..	..	..	..	..	..

.. Not available

Note: Detailed metadata at: *http://metalinks.oecd.org/ins/20200312/bbd1*.

Source: OECD Insurance Statistics (database)

Table 1. Selected aggregates

Million CLP

	2011	2012	2013	2014	2015	2016	2017	2018
1.1 Insurance business written in the reporting country								
1.1.1 Insurance business, by ownership								
Gross premiums								
Domestic undertakings	4 691 200	5 496 223	5 832 221	6 260 019	7 465 743	8 394 971	8 344 320	8 981 504
Foreign controlled undertakings	2 270 671	2 821 041	3 056 166	3 211 682	3 614 011	4 422 880	4 504 671	4 722 316
Foreign companies (branches)	..	..	..	..	..	..	..	..
All undertakings	4 691 200	5 496 223	5 832 221	6 260 019	7 465 743	8 394 971	8 344 320	8 981 504
Premiums ceded								
Domestic undertakings	911 543	930 906	906 942	998 507	1 135 872	1 310 392	1 382 346	1 428 339
Foreign controlled undertakings	648 512	671 333	647 814	676 439	749 522	953 240	901 373	921 260
Foreign companies (branches)	..	..	..	..	..	..	..	..
All undertakings	911 543	930 906	906 942	998 507	1 135 872	1 310 392	1 382 346	1 428 339
Net written premiums								
Domestic undertakings	3 779 657	4 565 317	4 925 279	5 261 513	6 329 871	7 084 578	6 961 974	7 553 165
Foreign controlled undertakings	1 622 159	2 149 709	2 408 352	2 535 243	2 864 489	3 469 640	3 603 299	3 801 056
Foreign companies (branches)	..	..	..	..	..	..	..	..
All undertakings	3 779 657	4 565 317	4 925 279	5 261 513	6 329 871	7 084 578	6 961 974	7 553 165
1.1.2 Insurance business on foreign risks, gross premiums								
Life	0	..	..	..	..	..	..	..
Non-life	0	..	..	..	..	..	..	..
Composite total	..	..	..	..	..	..	..	..
Total	0	..	..	..	..	..	..	..
1.1.3 Life insurance payments, by class, gross premiums								
Annuities	1 105 236	1 623 894	1 729 819	1 692 693	2 343 736	2 759 473	2 456 649	2 767 820
Unit linked	201 183	213 028	318 975	475 508	613 110	712 539	728 441	582 074
Other life insurance	1 625 966	1 761 476	1 827 419	1 948 628	2 123 123	2 373 130	2 560 094	2 775 274
Total life insurance	2 932 385	3 598 399	3 876 213	4 116 829	5 079 969	5 845 142	5 745 185	6 125 167
***of which:** Pension contracts*	1 340 726	..	..	..	..	..	..	..
1.1.4 Non-life insurance payments, by class, gross premiums								
Motor vehicle insurance	420 964	480 767	467 370	509 632	554 020	607 928	658 852	741 818
Marine, aviation and other transport insurance	92 530	93 208	117 884	129 698	148 074	132 318	134 870	152 066
Freight insurance	0	0	0	0	0	0	0	0
Fire and other property damage insurance	663 739	726 707	711 066	788 536	901 636	926 988	899 548	999 817
Pecuniary loss insurance	58 737	62 661	55 877	62 708	73 291	81 763	83 750	89 411
General liability insurance	69 048	80 035	52 154	56 828	41 342	34 468	30 188	41 483
Accident and health	115 563	117 127	25 789	30 296	46 180	53 105	66 796	74 322
***of which:** Health*	943	1 362	1 349	6 186	2 268	8 145	7 442	15 661
Other non-life insurance	336 427	335 850	524 059	561 863	602 569	651 596	675 973	705 464
Treaty reinsurance	0	0	0	0	0	0	0	0
Total non-life insurance	1 757 008	1 896 354	1 954 198	2 139 562	2 367 113	2 488 165	2 549 976	2 804 382
1.2 Gross claims payments								
Life								
Domestic undertakings	2 914 714	3 393 850	3 714 398	4 027 828	2 853 170	3 342 724	3 838 076	4 106 073
Foreign controlled undertakings	989 305	1 353 122	1 551 286	1 580 430	1 020 903	1 219 666	1 524 203	1 999 198
Foreign companies (branches)	0	..	..	..	..	..	..	..
All undertakings	2 914 714	3 393 850	3 714 398	4 027 828	2 853 170	3 342 724	3 838 076	4 106 073
Non-life								
Domestic undertakings	658 815	874 913	896 672	260 092	1 421 296	1 491 740	1 515 015	1 432 942
Foreign controlled undertakings	420 283	524 939	541 982	157 970	889 183	1 193 951	1 168 469	1 032 572
Foreign companies (branches)	0	..	..	..	..	..	..	..
All undertakings	658 815	874 913	896 672	260 092	1 421 296	1 491 740	1 515 015	1 432 942
Composite, all undertakings	..	..	..	..	..	..	..	..
Total								
Domestic undertakings	3 573 529	4 268 763	4 611 070	4 287 920	4 274 466	4 834 464	5 353 090	5 539 015
Foreign controlled undertakings	1 409 588	1 878 061	2 093 268	1 738 400	1 910 087	2 413 617	2 692 672	3 031 770
Foreign companies (branches)	0	..	..	..	..	..	..	..
All undertakings	3 573 529	4 268 763	4 611 070	4 287 920	4 274 466	4 834 464	5 353 090	5 539 015
1.3 Commissions								
Life								
Domestic undertakings	182 335	228 573	248 645	263 060	301 418	318 445	330 472	360 325
Foreign controlled undertakings	86 321	118 560	131 550	139 650	164 172	159 299	171 055	186 888
Foreign companies (branches)	0	..	..	..	..	..	..	..
All undertakings	182 335	228 573	248 645	263 060	301 418	318 445	330 472	360 325
Non-life								
Domestic undertakings	205 222	224 665	230 945	260 092	287 918	312 001	322 793	360 936
Foreign controlled undertakings	134 674	142 291	140 238	157 970	171 469	242 835	238 778	261 147
Foreign companies (branches)	0	..	..	..	..	..	..	..
All undertakings	205 222	224 665	230 945	260 092	287 918	312 001	322 793	360 936
Composite, all undertakings	..	..	..	..	..	..	..	..
Total								
Domestic undertakings	387 557	453 238	479 590	523 153	589 336	630 445	653 265	721 261
Foreign controlled undertakings	220 996	260 851	271 787	297 621	335 641	402 134	409 832	448 035
Foreign companies (branches)	0	..	..	..	..	..	..	..
All undertakings	387 557	453 238	479 590	523 153	589 336	630 445	653 265	721 261

Table 1. Selected aggregates *(cont.)*

Million CLP

	2011	2012	2013	2014	2015	2016	2017	2018
1.4 Gross operating expenses								
Life								
Domestic undertakings	502 620	519 184	549 344	583 313	612 178	664 997	732 176	776 679
Foreign controlled undertakings	242 660	250 271	268 515	284 692	308 320	316 103	364 993	390 610
Foreign companies (branches)	0	..	..	..	..	..	..	..
All undertakings	502 620	519 184	549 344	583 313	612 178	664 997	732 176	776 679
Non-life								
Domestic undertakings	331 560	339 044	359 066	382 886	412 676	457 861	501 804	533 252
Foreign controlled undertakings	241 486	239 100	251 791	266 721	288 658	367 114	406 682	414 288
Foreign companies (branches)	0	..	..	..	..	..	..	..
All undertakings	331 560	339 044	359 066	382 886	412 676	457 861	501 804	533 252
Composite, all undertakings	..	..	..	..	..	..	..	..
Total								
Domestic undertakings	834 180	858 228	908 410	966 199	1 024 854	1 122 857	1 233 980	1 309 931
Foreign controlled undertakings	484 145	489 370	520 306	551 413	596 978	683 216	771 674	804 898
Foreign companies (branches)	0	..	..	..	..	..	..	..
All undertakings	834 180	858 228	908 410	966 199	1 024 854	1 122 857	1 233 980	1 309 931
1.5 Insurance business written abroad by branches, gross premiums								
Life								
Branches and agencies	0	..	..	..	..	..	..	..
Subsidaries	0	..	..	..	..	..	..	..
Total	0	..	..	..	..	..	..	..
Non-life								
Branches and agencies	0	..	..	..	..	..	..	..
Subsidaries	0	..	..	..	..	..	..	..
Total	0	..	..	..	..	..	..	..
Composite total	..	..	..	..	..	..	..	..
Total								
Branches and agencies	0	..	..	..	..	..	..	..
Subsidaries	0	..	..	..	..	..	..	..
Total	0	..	..	..	..	..	..	..

.. Not available

Note: Detailed metadata at: *http://metalinks.oecd.org/ins/20200312/0015*.

Source: *OECD Insurance Statistics (database)*

Table 2. Number of companies and employees

	2011	2012	2013	2014	2015	2016	2017	2018
2.1 Number of companies								
Life								
Domestic undertakings	30	32	33	34	36	36	36	37
Foreign controlled undertakings	12	11	12	12	13	13	15	16
Foreign companies (branches)	0	..	..	..	..	0	..	..
All undertakings	30	32	33	34	36	36	36	37
Non-life								
Domestic undertakings	27	28	29	29	30	30	32	32
Foreign controlled undertakings	16	16	18	17	18	11	19	17
Foreign companies (branches)	0	..	..	..	..	0	..	..
All undertakings	27	28	29	29	30	30	32	32
Composite, all undertakings	**0**	**0**	**0**	**0**	**0**	**0**	**..**	**..**
Reinsurance								
Domestic undertakings	1	1	1	1	1	1	1	1
Foreign controlled undertakings	1	1	1	1	..	1	1	1
Foreign companies (branches)	0	..	..	..	..	0	..	..
All undertakings	1	1	1	1	1	1	1	1
Total								
Domestic undertakings	58	61	63	64	67	67	69	70
Foreign controlled undertakings	29	28	31	30	31	25	35	33
Foreign companies (branches)	0	..	..	..	..	0	..	..
All undertakings	58	61	63	64	67	67	69	70
2.2 Number of employees								
Insurance undertakings	14 366	16 304	16 686	17 039	15 368	16 414	16 859	16 908
Intermediaries	7 211	6 828	7 046	6 959	7 499	7 599	7 663	7 945
Total	21 577	23 132	23 732	23 998	22 867	24 013	24 522	24 853

.. Not available

Note: Detailed metadata at: *http://metalinks.oecd.org/ins/20200312/0015.*

Source: OECD Insurance Statistics (database)

CZECH REPUBLIC

Table 1. Selected aggregates

Million CZK

	2011	2012	2013	2014	2015	2016	2017	2018
1.1 Insurance business written in the reporting country								
1.1.1 Insurance business, by ownership								
Gross premiums								
Domestic undertakings	146 494	145 572	147 955	148 755	140 688	135 581	138 186	142 473
Foreign controlled undertakings	134 999	134 114	135 671	137 200	129 432	124 165	125 585	128 377
Foreign companies (branches)	8 598	8 026	8 567	9 164	11 159	11 102	11 459	10 768
All undertakings	155 092	153 597	156 522	157 919	151 846	146 683	149 645	153 241
Premiums ceded								
Domestic undertakings	27 642	27 730	29 333	29 915	29 857	28 913	30 449	31 057
Foreign controlled undertakings	24 903	24 826	26 054	26 601	26 578	25 450	26 230	26 704
Foreign companies (branches)	1 120	984	1 016	1 250	1 561	1 993	1 484	1 048
All undertakings	28 762	28 714	30 349	31 165	31 418	30 905	31 933	32 105
Net written premiums								
Domestic undertakings	118 852	117 842	118 623	118 839	110 831	106 669	107 737	111 416
Foreign controlled undertakings	110 096	109 288	109 617	110 598	102 854	98 714	99 356	101 673
Foreign companies (branches)	7 478	7 041	7 550	7 914	9 598	9 109	9 976	9 720
All undertakings	126 330	124 884	126 173	126 754	120 429	115 778	117 713	121 136
1.1.2 Insurance business on foreign risks, gross premiums								
Life	2	3	0	0	0	0	0	0
Non-life	814	931	741	993	524	274	738	874
Composite	1 553	1 681	1 780	2 121	1 867	1 843	2 777	3 561
of which:								
Life	1	0	37	360	4	0	1 805	1 897
Non-life	1 553	1 681	1 742	1 761	1 863	1 843	972	1 664
Total	2 370	2 614	2 521	3 113	2 390	2 117	3 515	4 435
1.1.3 Life insurance payments, by class, gross premiums								
Annuities	1 881	1 810	1 775	1 505	1 413	..	..	..
Unit linked	36 584	37 799	34 764	37 632	35 125	26 131	25 608	25 199
Other life insurance	33 543	32 437	35 030	32 042	25 876	33 110	31 425	30 653
Total life insurance	72 008	72 046	71 569	71 179	62 414	59 240	57 033	55 852
***of which:** Pension contracts*	..	..	..	..	..	..	0	0
1.1.4 Non-life insurance payments, by class, gross premiums								
Motor vehicle insurance	35 827	34 350	35 804	37 855	39 633	38 212	40 533	44 078
Marine, aviation and other transport insurance	274	243	214	294	331	912	1 073	1 072
Freight insurance	385	336	393	461	466	0	..	..
Fire and other property damage insurance	20 586	20 832	21 442	21 687	22 655	23 042	24 244	24 997
Pecuniary loss insurance	5 413	5 190	5 920	4 933	3 770	3 959	4 030	3 309
General liability insurance	12 416	12 420	12 869	13 164	13 810	13 609	14 559	15 207
Accident and health	5 708	5 523	5 482	5 342	5 393	5 136	5 460	5 802
***of which:** Health*	0	0	0	0	0	0	2 474	2 575
Other non-life insurance	2 477	2 656	2 825	3 002	3 374	2 223	2 364	2 489
Treaty reinsurance	0	0	0	0	0	0	..	..
Total non-life insurance	83 084	81 550	84 950	86 738	89 431	87 092	92 263	96 954
1.2 Gross claims payments								
Life								
Domestic undertakings	934	968	765	1 307	702	.. c	.. c	.. c
Foreign controlled undertakings	934	968	765	1 307	702	.. c	.. c	.. c
Foreign companies (branches)	4 193	4 402	7 219	6 044	6 376	6 094	6 249	5 572
All undertakings	5 127	5 370	7 984	7 352	7 077	6 456	6 567	5 875
Non-life								
Domestic undertakings	2 981	3 594	5 208	6 045	2 285	2 103	2 172	2 681
Foreign controlled undertakings	1 463	1 648	2 171	1 734	1 288	1 072	1 070	1 349
Foreign companies (branches)	922	746	1 184	1 353	1 216	1 674	1 764	1 344
All undertakings	3 903	4 340	6 392	7 398	3 501	3 777	3 936	4 025
Composite								
Domestic undertakings	76 178	78 484	86 244	90 284	84 909	81 024	80 221	80 773
Foreign controlled undertakings	72 105	74 012	81 355	84 712	79 681	75 835	75 301	75 653
Foreign companies (branches)	0	0	0	0	0	0	0	0
All undertakings	76 178	78 484	86 244	90 284	84 909	81 024	80 221	80 773
of which:								
Life	36 944	41 040	43 395	50 972	44 105	37 676	36 087	37 421
Domestic undertakings	36 944	41 040	43 395	50 972	44 105	37 676	36 087	37 421
Foreign controlled undertakings	35 822	39 685	42 174	49 092	42 631	36 570	35 018	36 422
Foreign companies (branches)	0	0	0	0	0	0	0	0
All undertakings	36 944	41 040	43 395	50 972	44 105	37 676	36 087	37 421
Non-life	39 235	37 444	42 849	39 312	40 805	43 348	44 134	43 352
Domestic undertakings	39 235	37 444	42 849	39 312	40 805	43 348	44 134	43 352
Foreign controlled undertakings	36 283	34 327	39 180	35 620	37 050	39 265	40 283	39 231
Foreign companies (branches)	0	0	0	0	0	0	0	0
All undertakings	39 235	37 444	42 849	39 312	40 805	43 348	44 134	43 352
Total								
Domestic undertakings	80 094	83 046	92 217	97 636	87 896	83 490	82 712	83 757
Foreign controlled undertakings	74 502	76 628	84 291	87 754	81 671	77 269	76 690	77 305
Foreign companies (branches)	5 116	5 148	8 403	7 397	7 592	7 767	8 012	6 916
All undertakings	85 209	88 194	100 620	105 033	95 488	91 257	90 724	90 673

Table 1. Selected aggregates *(cont.)*

Million CZK

	2011	2012	2013	2014	2015	2016	2017	2018
1.3 Commissions								
Life								
Domestic undertakings	628	..	..	..	..	..	..	..
Foreign controlled undertakings	628	..	..	..	..	..	..	..
Foreign companies (branches)	486	..	..	..	..	..	..	..
All undertakings	1 114	..	..	..	..	..	..	..
Non-life								
Domestic undertakings	466	..	..	..	..	..	..	..
Foreign controlled undertakings	273	..	..	..	..	..	..	..
Foreign companies (branches)	418	..	..	..	..	..	..	..
All undertakings	884	..	..	..	..	..	..	..
Composite								
Domestic undertakings	12 386	..	..	..	..	..	..	..
Foreign controlled undertakings	11 419	..	..	..	..	..	..	..
Foreign companies (branches)	0	..	..	..	..	..	..	..
All undertakings	12 386	..	..	..	..	..	..	..
of which:								
Life	7 407	..	..	..	..	..	..	..
Domestic undertakings	7 407	..	..	..	..	..	..	..
Foreign controlled undertakings	7 243	..	..	..	..	..	..	..
Foreign companies (branches)	0	..	..	..	..	..	..	..
All undertakings	7 407	..	..	..	..	..	..	..
Non-life	4 980	..	..	..	..	..	..	..
Domestic undertakings	4 980	..	..	..	..	..	..	..
Foreign controlled undertakings	4 176	..	..	..	..	..	..	..
Foreign companies (branches)	0	..	..	..	..	..	..	..
All undertakings	4 980	..	..	..	..	..	..	..
Total								
Domestic undertakings	13 481	..	..	..	..	..	..	..
Foreign controlled undertakings	12 320	..	..	..	..	..	..	..
Foreign companies (branches)	904	..	..	..	..	..	..	..
All undertakings	14 384	..	..	..	..	..	..	..
1.4 Gross operating expenses								
Life								
Domestic undertakings	1 085	1 132	748	759	739	.. c	.. c	.. c
Foreign controlled undertakings	1 085	1 132	748	759	739	.. c	.. c	.. c
Foreign companies (branches)	1 617	1 659	1 587	1 459	2 036	2 015	1 894	1 905
All undertakings	2 702	2 791	2 335	2 219	2 775	2 520	2 251	2 232
Non-life								
Domestic undertakings	2 559	1 970	1 795	1 805	1 571	1 203	2 170	2 988
Foreign controlled undertakings	1 509	1 152	987	937	883	622	979	1 044
Foreign companies (branches)	933	277	715	841	1 203	1 224	1 412	1 401
All undertakings	3 491	2 247	2 510	2 646	2 773	2 427	3 582	4 389
Composite								
Domestic undertakings	33 219	21 405	21 863	22 207	20 341	21 319	36 095	41 260
Foreign controlled undertakings	31 001	20 417	20 499	21 233	19 120	19 893	32 685	36 930
Foreign companies (branches)	0	0	0	0	0	0	0	0
All undertakings	33 219	21 405	21 863	22 207	20 341	21 319	36 095	41 260
of which:								
Life	13 363	12 009	11 670	11 475	9 613	9 217	11 707	12 405
Domestic undertakings	13 363	12 009	11 670	11 475	9 613	9 217	11 707	12 405
Foreign controlled undertakings	12 861	11 604	11 231	11 050	9 059	8 637	10 795	11 445
Foreign companies (branches)	0	0	0	0	0	0	0	0
All undertakings	13 363	12 009	11 670	11 475	9 613	9 217	11 707	12 405
Non-life	19 856	9 396	10 193	10 733	10 728	12 102	24 388	28 855
Domestic undertakings	19 856	9 396	10 193	10 733	10 728	12 102	24 388	28 855
Foreign controlled undertakings	18 140	8 814	9 268	10 184	10 061	11 256	21 890	25 485
Foreign companies (branches)	0	0	0	0	0	0	0	0
All undertakings	19 856	9 396	10 193	10 733	10 728	12 102	24 388	28 855
Total								
Domestic undertakings	36 863	24 507	24 407	24 772	22 650	23 027	38 621	44 574
Foreign controlled undertakings	33 595	22 701	22 234	22 929	20 742	21 020	34 020	38 301
Foreign companies (branches)	2 550	1 936	2 302	2 301	3 239	3 239	3 307	3 307
All undertakings	39 413	26 443	26 708	27 072	25 889	26 266	41 928	47 881

Table 1. Selected aggregates *(cont.)*

Million CZK

	2011	2012	2013	2014	2015	2016	2017	2018
1.5 Insurance business written abroad by branches, gross premiums								
Life								
Branches and agencies	0	0	0	0	0	0	0	0
Subsidaries	..	..	..	..	..	..	..	..
Total	0	0	0	0	0	..	0	0
Non-life								
Branches and agencies	318	307	323	313	351	377	596	804
Subsidaries	..	..	..	..	..	..	..	..
Total	318	307	323	313	351	377	596	804
Composite								
Branches and agencies	1 294	1 359	3 714	4 528	5 164	1 697	1 805	1 897
Subsidaries	..	..	..	..	..	..	..	..
Total	1 294	1 359	3 714	4 528	5 164	1 697	1 805	1 897
of which:								
Life	1 244	1 317	1 737	1 434	1 460	1 697	1 805	1 897
Branches and agencies	1 244	1 317	1 737	1 434	1 460	1 697	1 805	1 897
Subsidaries	..	..	..	..	..	..	..	..
Total	1 244	1 317	1 737	1 434	1 460	1 697	1 805	1 897
Non-life	49	42	1 977	3 095	3 704	..	0	0
Branches and agencies	49	42	1 977	3 095	3 704	0	0	0
Subsidaries	..	..	..	..	..	..	..	..
Total	49	42	1 977	3 095	3 704	..	0	0
Total								
Branches and agencies	1 612	1 666	4 037	4 841	5 516	2 074	2 401	2 700
Subsidaries	..	..	..	..	..	..	..	..
Total	1 612	1 666	4 037	4 841	5 516	2 074	2 401	2 700

.. Not available; c Confidential data

Note: Detailed metadata at: *http://metalinks.oecd.org/ins/20200312/a906*.

Source: *OECD Insurance Statistics (database)*

CZECH REPUBLIC

Table 2. Number of companies and employees

	2011	2012	2013	2014	2015	2016	2017	2018
2.1 Number of companies								
Life								
Domestic undertakings	3	3	2	2	2	1	1	1
Foreign controlled undertakings	3	3	2	2	2	1	1	1
Foreign companies (branches)	4	3	3	4	5	5	5	6
All undertakings	7	6	5	6	7	6	6	7
Non-life								
Domestic undertakings	17	16	16	15	15	13	11	11
Foreign controlled undertakings	9	8	8	7	5	4	3	3
Foreign companies (branches)	14	15	15	16	18	19	17	14
All undertakings	31	31	31	31	33	32	28	25
Composite								
Domestic undertakings	15	15	15	15	14	14	14	14
Foreign controlled undertakings	12	12	12	12	11	11	11	11
Foreign companies (branches)	0	0	0	0	0	0	0	0
All undertakings	15	15	15	15	14	14	14	14
Reinsurance								
Domestic undertakings	1	1	1	1	1	1	1	1
Foreign controlled undertakings	1	1	1	1	1	1	1	1
Foreign companies (branches)	..	..	..	..	..	..	0	0
All undertakings	1	1	1	1	1	1	1	1
Total								
Domestic undertakings	36	35	34	33	32	29	27	27
Foreign controlled undertakings	25	24	23	22	19	17	16	16
Foreign companies (branches)	18	18	18	20	23	24	22	20
All undertakings	54	53	52	53	55	53	49	47
2.2 Number of employees								
Insurance undertakings	..	..	..	..	..	..	..	..
Intermediaries	..	..	..	..	..	..	..	..
Total	..	..	..	..	..	..	..	..

.. Not available

Note: Detailed metadata at: *http://metalinks.oecd.org/ins/20200312/a906.*

Source: OECD Insurance Statistics (database)

DENMARK

Table 1. Selected aggregates

Million DKK

	2011	2012	2013	2014	2015	2016	2017	2018
1.1 Insurance business written in the reporting country								
1.1.1 Insurance business, by ownership								
Gross premiums								
Domestic undertakings	181 700	189 673	1 268 025	208 213	215 276	225 500	247 934	258 749
Foreign controlled undertakings	34 560	34 996	39 736	46 022	46 192	49 042	53 373	53 706
Foreign companies (branches)	..	..	..	..	..	..	..	..
All undertakings	181 700	189 673	1 268 025	208 213	215 276	225 500	247 934	258 749
Premiums ceded								
Domestic undertakings	7 676	7 009	7 417	5 875	6 309	6 943	8 079	7 160
Foreign controlled undertakings	3 427	3 293	3 199	2 080	2 462	2 355	2 024	1 666
Foreign companies (branches)	..	..	..	..	..	..	..	..
All undertakings	7 676	7 009	7 417	5 875	6 309	6 943	8 079	7 160
Net written premiums								
Domestic undertakings	174 024	182 664	1 260 608	202 338	208 966	218 557	239 855	251 589
Foreign controlled undertakings	31 132	31 703	36 537	43 942	43 730	46 687	51 349	52 040
Foreign companies (branches)	..	..	..	..	..	..	..	..
All undertakings	174 024	182 664	1 260 608	202 338	208 966	218 557	239 855	251 589
1.1.2 Insurance business on foreign risks, gross premiums								
Life	3 099	3 530	1 125	631	631	..	..	..
Non-life	13 950	14 359	14 611	23 099	22 611	..	..	..
Composite total	..	..	..	..	..	..	..	..
Total	17 050	17 889	15 737	23 730	23 242	..	..	..
1.1.3 Life insurance payments, by class, gross premiums								
Annuities	..	..	..	..	..	..	..	..
Unit linked	..	..	..	..	..	..	..	..
Other life insurance	..	..	..	..	..	..	..	..
Total life insurance	..	129 477	133 294	140 314	147 662	153 907	170 623	180 289
***of which:** Pension contracts*	..	..	..	..	..	..	..	..
1.1.4 Non-life insurance payments, by class, gross premiums								
Motor vehicle insurance	16 520	16 511	16 304	19 310	19 146	21 247	23 487	25 929
Marine, aviation and other transport insurance	1 328	1 397	1 263	1 174	1 105	1 857	1 844	1 769
Freight insurance	..	..	..	..	0	..	..	..
Fire and other property damage insurance	15 003	20 461	20 737	22 855	22 642	25 107	26 732	26 184
Pecuniary loss insurance	336	359	372	402	417	1 113	2 045	1 921
General liability insurance	1 857	2 023	2 061	2 377	2 314	3 203	3 411	3 494
Accident and health	13 403	13 553	12 611	15 063	15 282	15 965	16 727	16 051
***of which:** Health*	900	1 013	1 051	1 265	1 337	4 498	4 657	4 129
Other non-life insurance	3 983	4 465	4 659	5 156	5 052	1 635	1 759	1 710
Treaty reinsurance	451	638	653	867	937	538	616	687
Total non-life insurance	52 882	59 407	58 661	67 204	66 895	70 665	76 621	77 745
1.2 Gross claims payments								
Life								
Domestic undertakings	86 498	92 230	111 119	124 323	98 376	115 270	112 996	128 844
Foreign controlled undertakings	20 780	22 286	24 154	24 385	20 765	23 573	22 740	25 299
Foreign companies (branches)	..	..	..	..	..	..	..	..
All undertakings	86 498	92 230	111 119	124 323	98 376	115 270	112 996	128 844
Non-life								
Domestic undertakings	45 935	40 906	43 547	46 601	47 833	44 773	45 620	46 939
Foreign controlled undertakings	7 484	6 308	6 731	13 007	13 316	11 816	11 605	11 136
Foreign companies (branches)	..	..	..	..	..	..	..	..
All undertakings	45 935	40 906	43 547	46 601	47 833	44 773	45 620	46 939
Composite, all undertakings	..	..	..	..	..	..	..	..
Total								
Domestic undertakings	132 433	133 136	154 666	170 924	146 209	160 043	158 616	175 783
Foreign controlled undertakings	28 264	28 594	30 885	37 392	34 081	35 389	34 345	36 435
Foreign companies (branches)	..	..	..	..	..	..	..	..
All undertakings	132 433	133 136	154 666	170 924	146 209	160 043	158 616	175 783
1.3 Commissions								
Life								
Domestic undertakings	235	194	182	195	199	175	207	246
Foreign controlled undertakings	77	59	43	60	36	34	26	30
Foreign companies (branches)	..	..	..	..	..	..	..	..
All undertakings	235	194	182	195	199	175	207	246
Non-life								
Domestic undertakings	1 257	1 434	1 380	1 613	1 879	1 361	1 320	1 262
Foreign controlled undertakings	257	367	361	579	891	494	463	446
Foreign companies (branches)	..	..	..	..	..	..	..	..
All undertakings	1 257	1 434	1 380	1 613	1 879	1 361	1 320	1 262
Composite, all undertakings	..	..	..	..	..	..	..	..
Total								
Domestic undertakings	1 492	1 629	1 562	1 808	2 079	1 536	1 527	1 508
Foreign controlled undertakings	334	426	405	639	927	528	489	476
Foreign companies (branches)	..	..	..	..	..	..	..	..
All undertakings	1 492	1 629	1 562	1 808	2 079	1 536	1 527	1 508

Table 1. Selected aggregates *(cont.)*

Million DKK

	2011	2012	2013	2014	2015	2016	2017	2018
1.4 Gross operating expenses								
Life								
Domestic undertakings	5 136	5 088	4 954	4 887	4 570	4 788	4 971	5 138
Foreign controlled undertakings	1 325	1 316	1 326	1 377	1 284	1 268	1 386	1 349
Foreign companies (branches)	..	..	..	..	..	..	..	..
All undertakings	5 136	5 088	4 954	4 887	4 570	4 788	4 971	5 138
Non-life								
Domestic undertakings	10 241	10 292	10 391	11 564	11 856	12 050	12 003	11 298
Foreign controlled undertakings	1 940	2 124	2 200	3 867	4 065	3 780	3 542	2 778
Foreign companies (branches)	..	..	..	..	..	..	..	..
All undertakings	10 241	10 292	10 391	11 564	11 856	12 050	12 003	11 322
Composite, all undertakings	..	..	..	..	..	..	..	..
Total								
Domestic undertakings	15 377	15 380	15 345	16 451	16 426	16 838	16 974	16 436
Foreign controlled undertakings	3 265	3 440	3 526	5 244	5 349	5 048	4 928	4 127
Foreign companies (branches)	..	..	..	..	..	..	..	..
All undertakings	15 377	15 380	15 345	16 451	16 426	16 838	16 974	16 460
1.5 Insurance business written abroad by branches, gross premiums								
Life								
Branches and agencies	353	..	..	..	..	..	..	..
Subsidaries	..	..	..	..	..	..	..	..
Total	353	..	..	..	..	..	..	..
Non-life								
Branches and agencies	9 995	10 646	10 031	9 286	8 607	19 043	19 072	18 499
Subsidaries	..	..	..	..	..	..	..	..
Total	9 995	10 646	10 031	9 286	8 607	19 043	19 072	18 499
Composite total	..	..	..	..	..	..	..	..
Total								
Branches and agencies	10 348	10 646	10 031	9 286	8 607	19 043	19 072	18 499
Subsidaries	..	..	..	..	..	..	..	..
Total	10 348	10 646	10 031	9 286	8 607	19 043	19 072	18 499

.. Not available

Note: Detailed metadata at: *http://metalinks.oecd.org/ins/20200312/99d2.*

Source: OECD Insurance Statistics (database)

Table 2. Number of companies and employees

	2011	2012	2013	2014	2015	2016	2017	2018
2.1 Number of companies								
Life								
Domestic undertakings	55	47	39	37	33	33	33	31
Foreign controlled undertakings	8	7	5	4	4	4	4	4
Foreign companies (branches)	6	6	1	1	1	1	2	2
All undertakings	61	53	40	38	34	34	35	33
Non-life								
Domestic undertakings	85	76	77	63	63	63	59	55
Foreign controlled undertakings	8	6	6	6	6	6	6	5
Foreign companies (branches)	41	38	48	49	49	53	56	67
All undertakings	126	114	125	112	112	116	115	122
Composite, all undertakings	**0**	**0**	**0**	**0**	**0**	**0**	..	..
Reinsurance								
Domestic undertakings	9	9	7	7	7	5	6	5
Foreign controlled undertakings	0	..	..	..	..	0	..	..
Foreign companies (branches)	..	..	..	..	..	..	..	..
All undertakings	9	9	7	7	7	5	6	5
Total								
Domestic undertakings	149	132	123	107	103	101	98	91
Foreign controlled undertakings	16	13	11	10	10	10	10	9
Foreign companies (branches)	47	44	49	50	50	54	58	69
All undertakings	196	176	172	157	153	155	156	160
2.2 Number of employees								
Insurance undertakings	16 130	15 835	15 377	17 057	16 472	16 112	13 640	11 568
Intermediaries	..	..	..	..	..	..	..	..
Total	16 130	15 835	15 377	17 057	16 472	16 112	13 640	11 568

.. Not available

Note: Detailed metadata at: *http://metalinks.oecd.org/ins/20200312/99d2.*

Source: OECD Insurance Statistics (database)

ESTONIA

Table 1. Selected aggregates

Million EUR

	2011	2012	2013	2014	2015	2016	2017	2018
1.1 Insurance business written in the reporting country								
1.1.1 Insurance business, by ownership								
Gross premiums								
Domestic undertakings	403	430	523	561	619	654	721	807
Foreign controlled undertakings	380	407	499	539	596	627	721	775
Foreign companies (branches)	0	51	60	70	70	82	97	118
All undertakings	403	480	583	631	689	736	818	925
Premiums ceded								
Domestic undertakings	20	..	27	28	29	31	31	45
Foreign controlled undertakings	11	..	18	2	20	22	22	34
Foreign companies (branches)	0	..	..	..	..	..	..	..
All undertakings	20	..	..	..	..	..	..	..
Net written premiums								
Domestic undertakings	383	..	496	534	590	624	690	762
Foreign controlled undertakings	368	..	481	217	576	605	670	741
Foreign companies (branches)	0	..	..	..	..	..	..	..
All undertakings	383	..	..	..	..	..	..	..
1.1.2 Insurance business on foreign risks, gross premiums								
Life	90	..	..	..	..	..	..	..
Non-life	68	..	..	..	..	..	..	..
Composite	..	..	..	..	..	..	..	..
of which:								
Life	..	..	..	..	..	..	..	..
Non-life	..	..	..	..	..	..	..	..
Total	158	..	..	..	..	..	..	..
1.1.3 Life insurance payments, by class, gross premiums								
Annuities	9	10	17	19	24	27	27	..
Unit linked	84	27	87	109	118	116	116	120
Other life insurance	67	30	66	63	72	80	80	113
Total life insurance	160	68	171	191	215	221	223	233
***of which:** Pension contracts*	26	30	33	37	36	40	39	39
1.1.4 Non-life insurance payments, by class, gross premiums								
Motor vehicle insurance	142	143	229	244	259	292	345	404
Marine, aviation and other transport insurance	1	3	2	2	2	6	6	6
Freight insurance	2	..	3	4	4	..	..	..
Fire and other property damage insurance	63	59	99	107	115	127	140	159
Pecuniary loss insurance	5	5	8	9	9	12	17	21
General liability insurance	9	6	15	16	19	21	22	26
Accident and health	30	15	40	42	42	54	43	70
***of which:** Health*	..	..	9	..	..	..	..	20
Other non-life insurance	1	1	9	16	23	4	7	6
Treaty reinsurance	0	..	8	..	..	..	..	..
Total non-life insurance	253	231	412	440	474	515	580	692
1.2 Gross claims payments								
Life								
Domestic undertakings	115	112	101	..	97	87	.. c	.. c
Foreign controlled undertakings	115	112	101	..	97	87	.. c	.. c
Foreign companies (branches)	0	..	..	..	..	0	2	12
All undertakings	115	112	101	..	97	87	93	80
Non-life								
Domestic undertakings	154	147	197	..	230	243	270	315
Foreign controlled undertakings	141	134	184	..	217	228	253	297
Foreign companies (branches)	0	..	33	..	40	43	49	55
All undertakings	154	147	230	246	271	287	319	370
Composite								
Domestic undertakings	..	..	..	..	..	38	36	48
Foreign controlled undertakings	..	..	..	..	..	38	36	48
Foreign companies (branches)	..	..	..	..	..	3	4	4
All undertakings	..	..	..	..	..	42	40	52
of which:								
Life	..	..	..	..	..	34	40	39
Domestic undertakings	..	..	..	..	..	31	36	35
Foreign controlled undertakings	..	..	..	..	..	31	36	35
Foreign companies (branches)	..	..	..	..	..	3	4	4
All undertakings	..	..	..	..	..	34	40	39
Non-life	..	..	..	..	..	8	0	13
Domestic undertakings	..	..	..	..	..	8	0	13
Foreign controlled undertakings	..	..	..	..	..	8	0	13
Foreign companies (branches)	..	..	..	..	..	0	0	0
All undertakings	..	..	..	..	..	8	0	13
Total								
Domestic undertakings	270	259	298	..	328	369	397	431
Foreign controlled undertakings	256	246	285	..	314	354	380	413
Foreign companies (branches)	0	..	33	..	40	47	55	71
All undertakings	270	259	331	246	368	416	452	502

ESTONIA

Table 1. Selected aggregates *(cont.)*

Million EUR

	2011	2012	2013	2014	2015	2016	2017	2018
1.3 Commissions								
Life								
Domestic undertakings	8	9	19	21	23	..	..	..
Foreign controlled undertakings	8	9	19	21	23	..	..	..
Foreign companies (branches)	0	..	..	..	..	..	..	..
All undertakings	8	9	19	..	23	..	..	..
Non-life								
Domestic undertakings	17	4	72	73	78	..	..	..
Foreign controlled undertakings	15	2	67	69	73	..	..	..
Foreign companies (branches)	0	..	..	..	..	..	..	..
All undertakings	17	4	72	..	78	..	..	..
Composite								
Domestic undertakings	..	..	..	..	..	..	..	..
Foreign controlled undertakings	..	..	..	..	..	..	..	..
Foreign companies (branches)	..	..	..	..	..	..	..	..
All undertakings	..	..	..	..	..	..	..	..
of which:								
Life	..	..	..	..	..	..	..	..
Domestic undertakings	..	..	..	..	..	..	..	..
Foreign controlled undertakings	..	..	..	..	..	..	..	..
Foreign companies (branches)	..	..	..	..	..	..	..	..
All undertakings	..	..	..	..	..	..	..	..
Non-life	..	..	..	..	..	..	..	..
Domestic undertakings	..	..	..	..	..	..	..	..
Foreign controlled undertakings	..	..	..	..	..	..	..	..
Foreign companies (branches)	..	..	..	..	..	..	..	..
All undertakings	..	..	..	..	..	..	..	..
Total								
Domestic undertakings	25	13	90	94	101	..	..	..
Foreign controlled undertakings	23	11	86	89	95	..	..	..
Foreign companies (branches)	0	..	..	..	..	..	..	..
All undertakings	25	13	90	..	101	..	..	..
1.4 Gross operating expenses								
Life								
Domestic undertakings	24	23	9	9	11	..	..	.. c
Foreign controlled undertakings	24	23	9	9	11	..	..	.. c
Foreign companies (branches)	0	..	..	..	..	..	..	..
All undertakings	24	23	9	..	11	..	..	..
Non-life								
Domestic undertakings	74	73	27	30	27	115	137	153
Foreign controlled undertakings	67	67	25	29	26	..	..	142
Foreign companies (branches)	0	..	..	..	..	..	..	..
All undertakings	74	73	27	..	27	..	..	..
Composite								
Domestic undertakings	..	..	..	..	..	..	..	25
Foreign controlled undertakings	..	..	..	..	..	..	..	25
Foreign companies (branches)	..	..	..	..	..	..	..	..
All undertakings	..	..	..	..	..	..	..	..
of which:								
Life	..	..	..	..	..	..	..	..
Domestic undertakings	..	..	..	..	..	..	..	21
Foreign controlled undertakings	..	..	..	..	..	..	..	21
Foreign companies (branches)	..	..	..	..	..	..	..	..
All undertakings	..	..	..	..	..	..	..	..
Non-life	..	..	..	..	..	..	..	..
Domestic undertakings	..	..	..	..	..	..	..	4
Foreign controlled undertakings	..	..	..	..	..	..	..	4
Foreign companies (branches)	..	..	..	..	..	..	..	..
All undertakings	..	..	..	..	..	..	..	..
Total								
Domestic undertakings	98	96	37	40	38	115	137	188
Foreign controlled undertakings	91	90	35	38	36	..	..	177
Foreign companies (branches)	0	..	..	..	..	..	..	..
All undertakings	98	96	37	..	38	..	..	..

Table 1. Selected aggregates *(cont.)*

Million EUR

	2011	2012	2013	2014	2015	2016	2017	2018
1.5 Insurance business written abroad by branches, gross premiums								
Life								
Branches and agencies	90	85	94	114	130	96	..	84
Subsidaries	0	..	..	..	..	..	..	..
Total	90	85	94	114	130	96	..	..
Non-life								
Branches and agencies	68	96	170	174	190	201	243	289
Subsidaries	0	..	..	..	..	..	..	..
Total	68	96	170	174	190	201	243	289
Composite								
Branches and agencies	..	..	..	..	..	52	..	73
Subsidaries	..	..	..	..	..	..	..	..
Total	..	..	..	..	..	52	..	..
of which:								
Life	..	..	..	..	..	42	..	..
Branches and agencies	..	..	..	..	..	42	..	56
Subsidaries	..	..	..	..	..	..	..	..
Total	..	..	..	..	..	42	..	..
Non-life	..	..	..	..	..	10	..	..
Branches and agencies	..	..	..	..	..	10	..	17
Subsidaries	..	..	..	..	..	..	..	..
Total	..	..	..	..	..	10	..	..
Total								
Branches and agencies	158	181	264	288	320	349	243	446
Subsidaries	0	..	..	..	..	..	..	..
Total	158	181	264	288	320	349	243	289

.. Not available; c Confidential data
Note: Detailed metadata at: *http://metalinks.oecd.org/ins/20200312/3571*.
Source: OECD Insurance Statistics (database)

Table 2. Number of companies and employees

	2011	2012	2013	2014	2015	2016	2017	2018
2.1 Number of companies								
Life								
Domestic undertakings	4	4	4	4	4	2	1	1
Foreign controlled undertakings	4	4	4	4	4	2	1	1
Foreign companies (branches)	0	1	1	1	1	0	1	1
All undertakings	4	5	5	5	5	2	2	2
Non-life								
Domestic undertakings	8	8	8	8	8	8	7	7
Foreign controlled undertakings	5	5	5	5	5	5	4	4
Foreign companies (branches)	0	4	4	4	3	4	4	6
All undertakings	8	12	12	12	11	12	11	13
Composite								
Domestic undertakings	0	0	0	0	0	2	2	2
Foreign controlled undertakings	0	0	0	0	0	2	2	2
Foreign companies (branches)	0	0	0	0	0	1	1	1
All undertakings	0	0	0	0	0	3	3	3
Reinsurance								
Domestic undertakings	0	..	0	0	0	0	0	0
Foreign controlled undertakings	0	..	0	0	0	0	..	0
Foreign companies (branches)	0	..	..	..	0	0	..	0
All undertakings	0	..	..	..	0	0	..	0
Total								
Domestic undertakings	12	12	12	12	12	12	10	10
Foreign controlled undertakings	9	9	9	9	9	9	7	7
Foreign companies (branches)	0	5	5	5	4	5	6	8
All undertakings	12	17	17	17	16	17	16	18
2.2 Number of employees								
Insurance undertakings	1 867	1 903	2 596	2 561	2 581	..	..	..
Intermediaries	814	849	1 271	1 217	1 232	..	..	..
Total	2 681	2 752	3 867	3 778	3 813	..	..	..

.. Not available

Note: Detailed metadata at: *http://metalinks.oecd.org/ins/20200312/3571.*

Source: OECD Insurance Statistics (database)

FINLAND

Table 1. Selected aggregates

Million EUR

	2011	2012	2013	2014	2015	2016	2017	2018
1.1 Insurance business written in the reporting country								
1.1.1 Insurance business, by ownership								
Gross premiums								
Domestic undertakings	7 279	7 279	9 834	10 632	10 741	9 045	8 926	7 922
Foreign controlled undertakings	..	2 317	3 357	3 698	6 892	..	..	..
Foreign companies (branches)	..	..	..	..	..	..	..	..
All undertakings	7 279	7 279	9 834	10 632	10 741	9 045	8 926	4 366
Premiums ceded								
Domestic undertakings	240	240	257	259	246	241	230	-251
Foreign controlled undertakings	..	20	19	15	217	..	..	..
Foreign companies (branches)	..	..	..	..	..	..	..	..
All undertakings	240	240	257	259	246	241	230	-24
Net written premiums								
Domestic undertakings	7 039	7 039	9 577	10 373	10 495	8 804	8 696	7 671
Foreign controlled undertakings	..	2 297	3 338	3 683	6 675	..	..	..
Foreign companies (branches)	..	..	..	..	..	..	..	..
All undertakings	7 039	7 039	9 577	10 373	10 495	8 804	8 696	4 342
1.1.2 Insurance business on foreign risks, gross premiums								
Life	..	..	..	..	..	..	..	..
Non-life	..	..	..	..	..	..	..	..
Composite total	..	..	..	..	..	..	..	..
Total	..	..	..	..	..	..	..	..
1.1.3 Life insurance payments, by class, gross premiums								
Annuities	1 988	1 988	2 458	2 544	2 287	694	621	608
Unit linked	1 255	1 255	2 509	2 929	3 224	2 446	2 265	1 757
Other life insurance	505	505	614	619	745	1 433	1 641	2 000
Total life insurance	3 749	3 749	5 581	6 092	6 256	4 573	4 527	4 365
***of which:** Pension contracts*	828	828	819	756	597	675	2 265	593
1.1.4 Non-life insurance payments, by class, gross premiums								
Motor vehicle insurance	1 389	1 474	1 520	1 591	1 639	1 639	1 586	1 213
Marine, aviation and other transport insurance	64	68	70	70	68	73	69	69
Freight insurance	50	53	55	56	52	57	55	43
Fire and other property damage insurance	828	864	929	985	1 030	1 028	972	790
Pecuniary loss insurance	38	33	33	30	28	22	20	19
General liability insurance	191	191	239	392	385	234	218	193
Accident and health	938	1 024	1 048	1 060	1 058	1 119	1 183	957
***of which:** Health*	218	245	264	299	290	368	395	343
Other non-life insurance	129	131	144	152	88	163	151	124
Treaty reinsurance	132	149	149	135	135	136	144	148
Total non-life insurance	3 759	3 986	4 187	4 471	4 483	4 471	4 398	3 556
1.2 Gross claims payments								
Life								
Domestic undertakings	3 592	3 917	3 927	3 871	3 957	4 324	4 233	4 632
Foreign controlled undertakings	1 013	1 479	1 399	1 160	1 124	.. c	.. c	.. c
Foreign companies (branches)	..	..	..	..	..	..	..	..
All undertakings	3 592	3 917	3 927	3 871	3 957	4 324	4 233	4 632
Non-life								
Domestic undertakings	2 706	2 873	2 858	2 939	2 872	3 103	3 179	2 538
Foreign controlled undertakings	676	696	741	724	2 872	.. c	.. c	.. c
Foreign companies (branches)	..	..	..	..	..	..	..	.. c
All undertakings	2 706	2 873	2 858	2 939	2 872	3 103	3 179	.. c
Composite, all undertakings	..	..	..	..	..	..	..	..
Total								
Domestic undertakings	6 298	6 790	6 785	6 810	6 829	7 427	7 412	7 170
Foreign controlled undertakings	1 689	2 175	2 140	1 884	3 996	..	..	..
Foreign companies (branches)	..	..	..	..	..	..	..	..
All undertakings	6 298	6 790	6 785	6 810	6 829	7 427	7 412	4 632
1.3 Commissions								
Life								
Domestic undertakings	81	68	90	-83	101	126	121	116
Foreign controlled undertakings	7	6	9	-10	15	.. c	.. c	.. c
Foreign companies (branches)	..	..	..	..	..	..	..	..
All undertakings	81	68	90	-83	101	126	121	..
Non-life								
Domestic undertakings	90	102	58	-142	113	166	160	131
Foreign controlled undertakings	13	16	21	-18	23	.. c	.. c	.. c
Foreign companies (branches)	..	..	..	..	..	..	..	..
All undertakings	90	102	58	-142	113	166	160	..
Composite, all undertakings	..	..	..	..	..	..	..	..
Total								
Domestic undertakings	171	170	148	-225	214	292	281	247
Foreign controlled undertakings	21	22	30	-28	38	..	..	..
Foreign companies (branches)	..	..	..	..	..	..	..	..
All undertakings	171	170	148	-225	214	292	281	..

Table 1. Selected aggregates *(cont.)*

Million EUR

	2011	2012	2013	2014	2015	2016	2017	2018
1.4 Gross operating expenses								
Life								
Domestic undertakings	275	283	302	317	316	341	355	359
Foreign controlled undertakings	39	36	34	36	34	.. c	.. c	.. c
Foreign companies (branches)	..	..	..	..	..	..	..	..
All undertakings	275	283	302	317	316	341	355	359
Non-life								
Domestic undertakings	738	778	827	844	847	876	884	746
Foreign controlled undertakings	138	143	161	158	847	.. c	.. c	.. c
Foreign companies (branches)	..	..	..	..	..	..	..	..
All undertakings	738	778	827	844	847	876	884	..
Composite, all undertakings	..	..	..	..	..	..	..	..
Total								
Domestic undertakings	1 013	1 061	1 129	1 161	1 163	1 217	1 239	1 105
Foreign controlled undertakings	177	179	195	194	881	..	..	..
Foreign companies (branches)	..	..	..	..	..	..	..	..
All undertakings	1 013	1 061	1 129	1 161	1 163	1 217	1 239	359
1.5 Insurance business written abroad by branches, gross premiums								
Life								
Branches and agencies	614	203	162	107	17	..	..	..
Subsidaries	..	..	..	..	..	..	..	..
Total	614	203	162	107	17	..	..	..
Non-life								
Branches and agencies	..	..	..	..	..	..	..	..
Subsidaries	..	..	..	..	..	..	..	..
Total	..	..	..	..	..	..	..	..
Composite total	..	..	..	..	..	..	..	..
Total								
Branches and agencies	614	203	162	107	17	..	..	..
Subsidaries	..	..	..	..	..	..	..	..
Total	614	203	162	107	17	..	..	..

.. Not available; c Confidential data

Note: Detailed metadata at: *http://metalinks.oecd.org/ins/20200312/d93d.*

Source: OECD Insurance Statistics (database)

Table 2. Number of companies and employees

	2011	2012	2013	2014	2015	2016	2017	2018
2.1 Number of companies								
Life								
Domestic undertakings	11	13	13	13	13	11	10	10
Foreign controlled undertakings	1	1	1	1	1	1	1	1
Foreign companies (branches)	..	..	..	..	..	..	..	10
All undertakings	11	13	13	13	13	11	10	20
Non-life								
Domestic undertakings	78	42	42	38	38	37	37	40
Foreign controlled undertakings	1	1	1	1	1	2	2	1
Foreign companies (branches)	..	..	..	..	..	..	..	8
All undertakings	78	42	42	38	38	37	37	48
Composite, all undertakings	..	..	..	..	..	..	..	0
Reinsurance								
Domestic undertakings	2	..	..	..	..	..	..	0
Foreign controlled undertakings	..	..	..	..	..	..	..	0
Foreign companies (branches)	..	..	..	..	..	..	..	0
All undertakings	2	..	..	..	..	..	..	0
Total								
Domestic undertakings	91	55	55	51	51	48	47	50
Foreign controlled undertakings	2	2	2	2	2	3	3	2
Foreign companies (branches)	..	..	..	..	..	..	..	18
All undertakings	91	55	55	51	51	48	47	68
2.2 Number of employees								
Insurance undertakings	9 321	9 321	9 231	8 980	8 750	8 815	7 751	7 866
Intermediaries	338	342	203	216	221	244	265	265
Total	9 659	9 663	9 434	9 196	8 971	9 059	8 016	8 131

.. Not available

Note: Detailed metadata at: *http://metalinks.oecd.org/ins/20200312/d93d.*

Source: OECD Insurance Statistics (database)

FRANCE

Table 1. Selected aggregates

Million EUR

	2011	2012	2013	2014	2015	2016	2017	2018
1.1 Insurance business written in the reporting country								
1.1.1 Insurance business, by ownership								
Gross premiums								
Domestic undertakings	207 586	201 207	207 521	221 223	226 000	..	..	286 809
Foreign controlled undertakings	..	..	..	..	..	..	..	..
Foreign companies (branches)	95	104	103	103	111	..	..	..
All undertakings	207 680	201 310	207 624	221 327	226 111	283 901	278 237	286 809
Premiums ceded								
Domestic undertakings	20 994	21 638	22 115	19 932	25 840	..	..	35 307
Foreign controlled undertakings	..	..	..	..	..	..	..	..
Foreign companies (branches)	19	18	19	22	21	..	..	..
All undertakings	21 013	21 657	22 135	19 954	25 861	43 153	33 277	35 307
Net written premiums								
Domestic undertakings	186 592	179 568	185 406	201 291	200 160	..	..	251 502
Foreign controlled undertakings	..	..	..	..	..	..	..	..
Foreign companies (branches)	76	85	84	82	90	..	..	..
All undertakings	186 668	179 654	185 490	201 373	200 250	240 747	244 960	251 502
1.1.2 Insurance business on foreign risks, gross premiums								
Life	107	83	259	73	60	..	..	..
Non-life	1 592	1 589	1 735	1 876	2 188	..	..	..
Composite	227	206	636	468	485	..	..	..
of which:								
Life	226	206	167	456	482	..	..	..
Non-life	1	1	469	12	3	..	..	..
Total	1 926	1 879	2 631	2 416	2 734	..	..	..
1.1.3 Life insurance payments, by class, gross premiums								
Annuities	..	..	..	..	..	..	..	..
Unit linked	..	..	..	..	..	28 208	38 135	38 569
Other life insurance	..	..	..	..	..	111 059	102 007	106 170
Total life insurance	..	..	..	..	..	139 267	140 142	144 740
***of which:** Pension contracts*	..	..	..	..	..	..	..	..
1.1.4 Non-life insurance payments, by class, gross premiums								
Motor vehicle insurance	..	..	..	..	..	..	..	..
Marine, aviation and other transport insurance	..	..	..	..	..	..	..	..
Freight insurance	..	..	..	..	..	..	..	..
Fire and other property damage insurance	..	..	..	..	..	..	..	..
Pecuniary loss insurance	..	..	..	..	..	..	..	..
General liability insurance	..	..	..	..	..	..	..	..
Accident and health	..	..	..	..	..	..	..	..
***of which:** Health*	..	..	..	..	..	..	..	..
Other non-life insurance	..	..	..	..	..	..	..	..
Treaty reinsurance	..	..	..	..	..	..	..	..
Total non-life insurance	71 324	76 295	..	..	..	119 104	124 560	128 064
1.2 Gross claims payments								
Life								
Domestic undertakings	30 961	31 131	25 663	26 144	26 794	..	..	21 986
Foreign controlled undertakings	..	..	..	..	..	..	..	..
Foreign companies (branches)	..	..	..	..	..	..	..	..
All undertakings	30 961	31 131	25 663	26 144	26 794	133 135	145 577	21 986
Non-life								
Domestic undertakings	48 584	50 472	45 317	61 895	63 029	..	..	56 407
Foreign controlled undertakings	..	..	..	..	..	..	..	..
Foreign companies (branches)	51	59	59	52	51	..	..	..
All undertakings	48 635	50 531	45 376	61 947	63 080	95 217	101 007	56 407
Composite								
Domestic undertakings	93 502	98 016	97 287	86 518	91 862	..	..	158 076
Foreign controlled undertakings	..	..	..	..	..	..	..	..
Foreign companies (branches)	..	..	..	..	..	..	..	..
All undertakings	93 502	98 016	97 287	86 518	91 862	..	..	158 076
of which:								
Life	..	..	88 620	..	..	..	..	111 830
Domestic undertakings	..	..	88 620	..	..	..	..	111 830
Foreign controlled undertakings	..	..	..	..	..	..	..	..
Foreign companies (branches)	..	..	..	..	..	..	..	..
All undertakings	..	..	88 620	..	..	..	..	111 830
Non-life	..	..	8 667	..	..	..	..	46 246
Domestic undertakings	..	..	8 667	..	..	..	..	46 246
Foreign controlled undertakings	..	..	..	..	..	..	..	..
Foreign companies (branches)	..	..	..	..	..	..	..	..
All undertakings	..	..	8 667	..	..	..	..	46 246
Total								
Domestic undertakings	173 047	179 619	168 267	174 557	181 685	..	..	236 469
Foreign controlled undertakings	..	..	..	..	..	..	..	..
Foreign companies (branches)	51	59	59	52	51	..	..	..
All undertakings	173 098	179 678	168 326	174 608	181 736	228 352	246 584	236 469

Table 1. Selected aggregates *(cont.)*

Million EUR

	2011	2012	2013	2014	2015	2016	2017	2018
1.3 Commissions								
Life								
Domestic undertakings	1 682	1 705	..	..	..	..	..	..
Foreign controlled undertakings	..	..	..	..	..	..	..	..
Foreign companies (branches)	..	..	..	..	..	..	..	..
All undertakings	1 682	1 705	..	..	..	..	..	..
Non-life								
Domestic undertakings	10 449	10 610	..	..	..	..	..	..
Foreign controlled undertakings	..	..	..	..	..	..	..	..
Foreign companies (branches)	19	22	..	..	..	..	..	..
All undertakings	10 468	10 633	..	..	..	..	..	..
Composite								
Domestic undertakings	5 915	5 717	..	..	..	..	..	..
Foreign controlled undertakings	..	..	..	..	..	..	..	..
Foreign companies (branches)	..	..	..	..	..	..	..	..
All undertakings	5 915	5 717	..	..	..	..	..	..
of which:								
Life	4 985	4 677	..	..	..	..	..	..
Domestic undertakings	4 985	4 677	..	..	..	..	..	..
Foreign controlled undertakings	..	..	..	..	..	..	..	..
Foreign companies (branches)	..	..	..	..	..	..	..	..
All undertakings	4 985	4 677	..	..	..	..	..	..
Non-life	930	1 041	..	..	..	..	..	..
Domestic undertakings	930	1 041	..	..	..	..	..	..
Foreign controlled undertakings	..	..	..	..	..	..	..	..
Foreign companies (branches)	..	..	..	..	..	..	..	..
All undertakings	930	1 041	..	..	..	..	..	..
Total								
Domestic undertakings	18 046	18 033	..	..	..	..	..	..
Foreign controlled undertakings	..	..	..	..	..	..	..	..
Foreign companies (branches)	19	22	..	..	..	..	..	..
All undertakings	18 065	18 055	..	..	..	..	..	..
1.4 Gross operating expenses								
Life								
Domestic undertakings	842	2 982	2 828	2 893	2 914	..	..	2 545
Foreign controlled undertakings	..	..	..	..	..	..	..	..
Foreign companies (branches)	..	..	..	..	..	..	..	..
All undertakings	842	2 982	2 828	2 893	2 914	15 848	16 123	2 545
Non-life								
Domestic undertakings	5 487	15 726	15 969	16 156	15 936	..	..	18 654
Foreign controlled undertakings	..	..	..	..	..	..	..	..
Foreign companies (branches)	10	9	..	8	..	..	..	..
All undertakings	5 497	15 726	15 969	16 164	15 936	27 415	27 948	18 654
Composite								
Domestic undertakings	4 937	12 392	12 957	13 439	14 727	..	..	24 734
Foreign controlled undertakings	..	..	..	..	..	..	..	..
Foreign companies (branches)	..	..	..	..	..	..	..	..
All undertakings	4 937	12 392	12 957	13 439	14 727	..	..	24 734
of which:								
Life	..	..	10 533	10 808	11 414	..	..	13 366
Domestic undertakings	..	..	10 533	..	..	..	..	13 366
Foreign controlled undertakings	..	..	..	..	..	..	..	..
Foreign companies (branches)	..	..	..	..	..	..	..	..
All undertakings	..	..	10 533	10 808	11 414	..	..	13 366
Non-life	..	..	2 424	2 631	3 313	..	..	11 368
Domestic undertakings	..	..	2 424	..	..	..	..	11 368
Foreign controlled undertakings	..	..	..	..	..	..	..	..
Foreign companies (branches)	..	..	..	..	..	..	..	..
All undertakings	..	..	2 424	2 631	3 313	..	..	11 368
Total								
Domestic undertakings	11 266	31 100	31 754	32 488	33 578	..	..	45 933
Foreign controlled undertakings	..	..	..	..	..	..	..	..
Foreign companies (branches)	10	9	..	8	..	..	..	..
All undertakings	11 276	31 100	31 754	32 497	33 578	43 263	44 071	45 933

FRANCE

Table 1. Selected aggregates *(cont.)*

Million EUR

	2011	2012	2013	2014	2015	2016	2017	2018
1.5 Insurance business written abroad by branches, gross premiums								
Life								
Branches and agencies	1 929	1 895	2 691	2 860	3 373	4 393	5 050	..
Subsidaries	..	..	..	..	..	..	..	..
Total	1 929	1 895	2 691	2 860	3 373	4 393	5 050	..
Non-life								
Branches and agencies	5 592	4 107	4 176	4 960	5 460	8 837	9 719	..
Subsidaries	..	..	..	..	..	..	..	..
Total	5 592	4 107	4 176	4 960	5 460	8 837	9 719	..
Composite								
Branches and agencies	..	..	..	..	..	..	..	..
Subsidaries	..	..	..	..	..	..	..	..
Total	..	..	..	..	..	..	..	..
of which:								
Life	..	..	..	..	..	..	..	..
Branches and agencies	..	..	..	..	..	..	..	..
Subsidaries	..	..	..	..	..	..	..	..
Total	..	..	..	..	..	..	..	..
Non-life	..	..	..	..	..	..	..	..
Branches and agencies	..	..	..	..	..	..	..	..
Subsidaries	..	..	..	..	..	..	..	..
Total	..	..	..	..	..	..	..	..
Total								
Branches and agencies	7 521	6 001	6 867	7 820	8 834	13 230	14 769	..
Subsidaries	..	..	..	..	..	..	..	..
Total	7 521	6 001	6 867	7 820	8 834	13 230	14 769	..

.. Not available

Note: Detailed metadata at: *http://metalinks.oecd.org/ins/20200312/9f15*.

Source: OECD Insurance Statistics (database)

FRANCE

Table 2. Number of companies and employees

	2011	2012	2013	2014	2015	2016	2017	2018
2.1 Number of companies								
Life								
Domestic undertakings	61	62	59	55	51	..	..	..
Foreign controlled undertakings	..	..	..	..	..	..	..	..
Foreign companies (branches)	..	..	..	..	..	..	..	..
All undertakings	61	62	59	55	51	..	..	..
Non-life								
Domestic undertakings	250	221	212	206	191	..	..	..
Foreign controlled undertakings	7	5	..	..	..	..	..	..
Foreign companies (branches)	..	..	4	4	4	..	..	..
All undertakings	250	221	216	210	195	394	381	364
Composite								
Domestic undertakings	40	40	38	38	39	..	..	..
Foreign controlled undertakings	..	..	..	..	..	..	..	..
Foreign companies (branches)	..	..	..	..	..	..	..	..
All undertakings	40	40	38	38	39	239	236	239
Reinsurance								
Domestic undertakings	20	16	16	15	16	..	..	..
Foreign controlled undertakings	..	..	..	..	..	..	..	..
Foreign companies (branches)	..	..	..	..	..	..	..	..
All undertakings	20	16	16	15	16	14	14	12
Total								
Domestic undertakings	371	339	325	314	297	..	..	..
Foreign controlled undertakings	7	5	..	..	..	..	..	..
Foreign companies (branches)	..	..	4	4	4	..	..	..
All undertakings	371	339	329	318	301	647	631	615
2.2 Number of employees								
Insurance undertakings	..	..	..	..	..	..	..	..
Intermediaries	..	..	..	..	..	..	..	..
Total	..	..	..	..	..	..	..	..

.. Not available

Note: Detailed metadata at: *http://metalinks.oecd.org/ins/20200312/9f15*.

Source: OECD Insurance Statistics (database)

Table 1. Selected aggregates

Million EUR

	2011	2012	2013	2014	2015	2016	2017	2018
1.1 Insurance business written in the reporting country								
1.1.1 Insurance business, by ownership								
Gross premiums								
Domestic undertakings	178 145	233 661	243 304	246 201	254 407	257 208	264 933	273 036
Foreign controlled undertakings	35 602	37 194	39 396	38 694	39 170	36 978	36 644	39 215
Foreign companies (branches)	5 560	8 062	7 963	8 796	9 751	8 994	10 550	11 199
All undertakings	183 705	235 634	251 267	254 997	264 158	266 203	275 483	284 235
Premiums ceded								
Domestic undertakings	15 996	23 045	25 709	27 853	32 499	31 990	34 336	39 483
Foreign controlled undertakings	3 905	3 947	4 645	4 615	4 593	4 041	4 046	4 482
Foreign companies (branches)	..	100	108	103	114	112	132	127
All undertakings	..	23 145	25 817	27 956	32 613	32 102	34 469	39 609
Net written premiums								
Domestic undertakings	162 149	210 616	217 596	218 348	221 907	225 218	230 596	233 553
Foreign controlled undertakings	31 696	33 247	34 751	34 078	34 577	32 937	32 598	34 732
Foreign companies (branches)	..	1 873	7 854	8 693	9 637	8 882	10 418	11 073
All undertakings	..	212 489	225 450	227 041	231 545	234 100	241 014	244 626
1.1.2 Insurance business on foreign risks, gross premiums								
Life	..	..	..	..	..	..	..	..
Non-life	..	..	..	..	..	..	..	..
Composite total	..	..	..	..	..	..	..	..
Total	..	..	..	..	..	..	..	..
1.1.3 Life insurance payments, by class, gross premiums								
Annuities	27 237	29 443	32 863	34 019	31 782	31 215	30 000	31 730
Unit linked	12 808	12 721	12 919	13 863	13 863	15 351	15 994	17 293
Other life insurance	40 660	40 822	41 934	40 891	41 214	38 845	41 612	40 959
Total life insurance	80 705	82 986	87 716	88 774	86 859	85 411	87 606	89 982
***of which:** Pension contracts*	..	..	..	..	..	..	..	..
1.1.4 Non-life insurance payments, by class, gross premiums								
Motor vehicle insurance	26 350	27 577	28 592	31 425	32 589	36 521	40 579	44 565
Marine, aviation and other transport insurance	4 156	4 537	4 476	4 379	5 116	4 749	4 933	5 050
Freight insurance	..	..	..	..	..	..	..	..
Fire and other property damage insurance	36 611	34 420	36 832	35 422	38 830	42 499	46 541	50 056
Pecuniary loss insurance	2 979	2 754	2 815	2 088	2 197	2 376	3 872	3 857
General liability insurance	12 321	12 623	13 265	14 213	15 425	16 126	17 517	18 440
Accident and health	47 235	48 823	49 395	48 811	49 176	49 721	52 572	52 301
***of which:** Health*	39 555	41 036	41 747	40 924	41 627	37 178	39 328	40 220
Other non-life insurance	4 316	4 794	4 841	4 865	31 030	25 991	21 153	19 528
Treaty reinsurance	..	..	..	..	..	..	..	..
Total non-life insurance	133 968	135 526	140 215	141 203	174 363	177 983	187 167	193 798
1.2 Gross claims payments								
Life								
Domestic undertakings	85 244	66 288	69 267	74 625	73 307	78 596	69 073	70 871
Foreign controlled undertakings	..	15 284	17 017	17 510	17 929	17 942	16 501	16 759
Foreign companies (branches)	..	..	..	..	..	..	..	..
All undertakings	85 244	66 288	69 267	74 625	73 307	78 596	69 073	70 871
Non-life								
Domestic undertakings	93 574	101 839	113 293	72 709	77 667	78 086	84 787	87 989
Foreign controlled undertakings	..	12 192	12 402	8 955	3 653	9 227	9 500	10 110
Foreign companies (branches)	..	..	..	..	..	..	..	..
All undertakings	93 574	101 839	113 293	72 709	77 667	78 086	84 787	87 989
Composite, all undertakings	..	..	..	..	..	..	..	..
Total								
Domestic undertakings	178 818	168 127	182 560	147 334	150 974	156 682	153 859	158 861
Foreign controlled undertakings	..	27 475	29 419	26 465	21 581	27 169	26 001	26 869
Foreign companies (branches)	..	..	..	..	..	..	..	..
All undertakings	178 818	168 127	182 560	147 334	150 974	156 682	153 859	158 861
1.3 Commissions								
Life								
Domestic undertakings	6 312	6 005	5 367	5 583	5 069	4 987	4 794	4 961
Foreign controlled undertakings	..	1 771	1 604	1 533	1 488	1 238	1 138	1 211
Foreign companies (branches)	..	..	..	..	..	..	..	..
All undertakings	6 312	6 005	5 367	5 583	5 069	4 987	4 794	4 961
Non-life								
Domestic undertakings	9 908	10 069	10 048	10 221	10 740	11 105	12 173	12 647
Foreign controlled undertakings	..	1 985	1 720	1 626	257	1 594	1 623	1 806
Foreign companies (branches)	..	..	..	..	..	..	..	..
All undertakings	9 908	10 069	10 048	10 221	10 740	11 105	12 173	12 647
Composite, all undertakings	..	..	..	..	..	..	..	..
Total								
Domestic undertakings	16 220	16 074	15 416	15 805	15 810	16 092	16 967	17 609
Foreign controlled undertakings	..	3 756	3 323	3 159	1 745	2 832	2 760	3 017
Foreign companies (branches)	..	..	..	..	..	..	..	..
All undertakings	16 220	16 074	15 416	15 805	15 810	16 092	16 967	17 609

GERMANY

Table 1. Selected aggregates *(cont.)*

Million EUR

	2011	2012	2013	2014	2015	2016	2017	2018
1.4 Gross operating expenses								
Life								
Domestic undertakings	14 545	4 051	3 954	3 963	4 008	3 902	3 907	3 901
Foreign controlled undertakings	..	925	921	894	1 036	938	952	1 001
Foreign companies (branches)	..	..	..	..	..	..	..	..
All undertakings	14 545	4 051	3 954	3 963	4 008	3 902	3 907	3 901
Non-life								
Domestic undertakings	28 382	11 593	11 599	10 296	10 627	10 807	11 161	11 390
Foreign controlled undertakings	..	1 528	1 400	1 187	324	1 183	1 210	1 297
Foreign companies (branches)	..	..	..	..	..	..	..	..
All undertakings	28 382	11 593	11 599	10 296	10 627	10 807	11 161	11 390
Composite, all undertakings	..	..	..	..	..	..	..	..
Total								
Domestic undertakings	42 927	15 644	15 553	14 259	14 635	14 709	15 068	15 291
Foreign controlled undertakings	..	2 453	2 321	2 081	1 361	2 121	2 163	2 297
Foreign companies (branches)	..	..	..	..	..	..	..	..
All undertakings	42 927	15 644	15 553	14 259	14 635	14 709	15 068	15 291
1.5 Insurance business written abroad by branches, gross premiums								
Life								
Branches and agencies	..	..	..	..	..	..	..	200
Subsidaries	..	..	..	..	..	..	..	..
Total	..	..	..	..	..	..	..	200
Non-life								
Branches and agencies	..	..	..	..	..	..	..	22 495
Subsidaries	..	..	..	..	..	..	..	..
Total	..	..	..	..	..	..	..	22 495
Composite total	..	..	..	..	..	..	..	..
Total								
Branches and agencies	..	..	..	..	..	..	..	22 695
Subsidaries	..	..	..	..	..	..	..	..
Total	..	..	..	..	..	..	..	22 695

.. Not available

Note: Detailed metadata at: *http://metalinks.oecd.org/ins/20200312/74fa*.

Source: OECD Insurance Statistics (database)

Table 2. Number of companies and employees

	2011	2012	2013	2014	2015	2016	2017	2018
2.1 Number of companies								
Life								
Domestic undertakings	95	90	91	91	85	85	86	86
Foreign controlled undertakings	20	19	17	17	14	14	15	16
Foreign companies (branches)	20	19	2	2	2	2	1	1
All undertakings	115	109	93	93	87	87	87	87
Non-life								
Domestic undertakings	265	256	259	255	257	252	251	250
Foreign controlled undertakings	25	25	23	21	22	18	17	21
Foreign companies (branches)	69	62	3	3	3	2	2	1
All undertakings	334	318	262	258	260	254	253	251
Composite, all undertakings	**0**	**0**	**0**	**0**	**0**	**0**	..	..
Reinsurance								
Domestic undertakings	33	30	29	27	27	27	27	28
Foreign controlled undertakings	5	6	4	3	3	3	3	3
Foreign companies (branches)	7	7	1	1	1	1	1	1
All undertakings	40	37	30	28	28	28	28	29
Total								
Domestic undertakings	393	376	379	373	369	364	364	364
Foreign controlled undertakings	50	50	44	41	39	35	35	40
Foreign companies (branches)	96	88	6	6	6	5	4	3
All undertakings	489	464	385	379	375	369	368	367
2.2 Number of employees								
Insurance undertakings	125 783	126 625	128 755	126 755	128 784	..	..	..
Intermediaries	27 952	27 407	27 331	26 982	25 917	..	..	..
Total	153 735	154 032	156 086	153 737	154 701	156 675	154 262	152 888

.. Not available

Note: Detailed metadata at: *http://metalinks.oecd.org/ins/20200312/74fa.*

Source: OECD Insurance Statistics (database)

GREECE

Table 1. Selected aggregates

Million EUR

	2011	2012	2013	2014	2015	2016	2017	2018
1.1 Insurance business written in the reporting country								
1.1.1 Insurance business, by ownership								
Gross premiums								
Domestic undertakings	4 691	4 289	4 071	3 806	3 573	3 531	3 729	3 798
Foreign controlled undertakings	2 130	2 071	1 730	1 696	1 766	2 350	2 450	2 458
Foreign companies (branches)	261	211	0	0	0	0	0	0
All undertakings	4 952	4 499	4 071	3 806	3 573	3 531	3 729	3 798
Premiums ceded								
Domestic undertakings	737	534	824	471	459	396	402	429
Foreign controlled undertakings	439	235	214	206	201	244	260	274
Foreign companies (branches)	90	0	0	0	0	0	0	0
All undertakings	827	534	824	471	459	396	402	429
Net written premiums								
Domestic undertakings	3 954	3 754	3 247	3 334	3 114	3 135	3 328	3 369
Foreign controlled undertakings	1 691	1 836	1 516	1 490	1 565	2 106	2 190	2 183
Foreign companies (branches)	171	211	0	0	0	0	0	0
All undertakings	4 125	3 965	3 247	3 335	3 114	3 135	3 328	3 369
1.1.2 Insurance business on foreign risks, gross premiums								
Life	..	..	..	..	..	..	..	..
Non-life	..	..	..	..	..	..	..	..
Composite	..	..	..	..	..	..	..	..
of which:								
Life	..	..	..	..	..	..	..	..
Non-life	..	..	..	..	..	..	..	..
Total	..	..	..	..	..	..	..	..
1.1.3 Life insurance payments, by class, gross premiums								
Annuities	..	165	142	129	125	0	0	0
Unit linked	..	368	240	396	326	250	347	380
Other life insurance	..	1 406	1 299	1 353	1 348	1 416	1 533	1 499
Total life insurance	..	1 939	1 681	1 879	1 799	1 666	1 881	1 879
***of which:** Pension contracts*	..	205	143	151	156	..	..	..
1.1.4 Non-life insurance payments, by class, gross premiums								
Motor vehicle insurance	1 840	1 569	1 417	1 154	1 006	911	938	948
Marine, aviation and other transport insurance	25	21	19	19	20	32	34	38
Freight insurance	27	24	24	21	21	..	0	0
Fire and other property damage insurance	529	538	529	448	440	410	398	409
Pecuniary loss insurance	69	78	69	30	30	40	28	31
General liability insurance	73	78	76	67	68	65	63	75
Accident and health	76	68	64	57	57	300	242	263
***of which:** Health*	19	20	0	0	..	..	0	0
Other non-life insurance	146	179	188	128	129	137	146	153
Treaty reinsurance	0	0	0	0	..	..	0	0
Total non-life insurance	2 786	2 556	2 386	1 924	1 770	1 896	1 848	1 918
1.2 Gross claims payments								
Life								
Domestic undertakings	822	1 300	1 072	900	744	..	..	..
Foreign controlled undertakings	591	1 017	707	1	502	..	..	..
Foreign companies (branches)	263	0	0	0	0	..	..	..
All undertakings	1 085	1 300	1 072	900	744	..	..	..
Non-life								
Domestic undertakings	501	431	373	355	314	..	..	..
Foreign controlled undertakings	146	142	121	224	109	..	..	..
Foreign companies (branches)	47	0	1	1	0	..	..	..
All undertakings	549	431	375	356	314	..	..	..
Composite								
Domestic undertakings	1 408	1 291	1 096	1 018	931	..	..	..
Foreign controlled undertakings	430	441	364	412	347	..	..	..
Foreign companies (branches)	0	0	0	0	0	..	..	..
All undertakings	1 408	1 291	1 096	1 018	931	..	..	..
of which:								
Life	866	791	669	613	573	..	..	..
Domestic undertakings	866	791	669	613	573	..	..	..
Foreign controlled undertakings	285	282	226	7	220	..	..	..
Foreign companies (branches)	0	0	0	0	0	..	..	..
All undertakings	866	791	669	613	573	..	..	..
Non-life	541	501	426	405	358	..	..	..
Domestic undertakings	541	501	426	405	358	..	..	..
Foreign controlled undertakings	145	159	138	405	126	..	..	..
Foreign companies (branches)	0	0	0	0	0	..	..	..
All undertakings	541	501	426	405	358	..	..	..
Total								
Domestic undertakings	2 731	3 022	2 541	2 273	1 989	..	..	..
Foreign controlled undertakings	1 167	1 600	1 192	637	957	..	..	..
Foreign companies (branches)	310	0	1	1	0	..	..	..
All undertakings	3 042	3 022	2 542	2 274	1 989	..	..	..

GREECE

Table 1. Selected aggregates *(cont.)*

Million EUR

	2011	2012	2013	2014	2015	2016	2017	2018
1.3 Commissions								
Life								
Domestic undertakings	..	..	..	95	91	..	..	..
Foreign controlled undertakings	..	..	..	70	70	..	..	..
Foreign companies (branches)	..	..	..	0	0	..	..	..
All undertakings	..	..	..	95	91	..	..	..
Non-life								
Domestic undertakings	..	..	..	161	158	..	..	..
Foreign controlled undertakings	..	..	..	63	66	..	..	..
Foreign companies (branches)	..	..	..	0	0	..	..	..
All undertakings	..	..	..	162	158	..	..	..
Composite								
Domestic undertakings	..	..	..	276	709	..	..	..
Foreign controlled undertakings	..	..	..	115	115	..	..	..
Foreign companies (branches)	..	..	..	0	0	..	..	..
All undertakings	..	..	..	276	709	..	..	..
of which:								
Life	..	..	..	102	544	..	..	..
Domestic undertakings	..	..	..	102	544	..	..	..
Foreign controlled undertakings	..	..	..	39	40	..	..	..
Foreign companies (branches)	..	..	..	0	0	..	..	..
All undertakings	..	..	..	102	544	..	..	..
Non-life	..	..	..	174	164	..	..	..
Domestic undertakings	..	..	..	174	164	..	..	..
Foreign controlled undertakings	..	..	..	76	75	..	..	..
Foreign companies (branches)	..	..	..	0	0	..	..	..
All undertakings	..	..	..	174	164	..	..	..
Total								
Domestic undertakings	..	..	..	532	957	..	..	..
Foreign controlled undertakings	..	..	..	248	251	..	..	..
Foreign companies (branches)	..	..	..	0	0	..	..	..
All undertakings	..	..	..	532	957	..	..	..
1.4 Gross operating expenses								
Life								
Domestic undertakings	182	82	79	176	163	35	38	39
Foreign controlled undertakings	139	75	66	141	132	32	35	35
Foreign companies (branches)	57	0	0	0	..	0	0	0
All undertakings	239	82	79	176	163	35	38	39
Non-life								
Domestic undertakings	373	104	124	264	247	248	301	242
Foreign controlled undertakings	137	59	61	115	116	145	168	104
Foreign companies (branches)	60	1	0	0	0	0	0	0
All undertakings	432	106	124	264	247	248	301	242
Composite								
Domestic undertakings	543	67	169	404	371	700	701	811
Foreign controlled undertakings	191	16	57	154	150	448	438	550
Foreign companies (branches)	0	0	0	0	..	0	0	0
All undertakings	543	67	169	404	371	700	701	811
of which:								
Life	176	36	53	144	145	315	322	312
Domestic undertakings	176	36	53	144	145	315	322	312
Foreign controlled undertakings	69	11	21	53	52	231	223	219
Foreign companies (branches)	0	0	0	0	..	0	0	0
All undertakings	176	36	53	144	145	315	322	312
Non-life	368	31	116	260	226	385	379	499
Domestic undertakings	368	31	116	260	226	385	379	499
Foreign controlled undertakings	122	4	36	101	98	217	215	331
Foreign companies (branches)	0	0	0	0	..	0	0	0
All undertakings	368	31	116	260	226	385	379	499
Total								
Domestic undertakings	1 098	253	372	844	781	983	1 041	1 092
Foreign controlled undertakings	467	150	184	410	398	625	641	689
Foreign companies (branches)	117	1	0	0	0	0	0	0
All undertakings	1 215	254	372	844	781	983	1 041	1 092

Table 1. Selected aggregates *(cont.)*

Million EUR

	2011	2012	2013	2014	2015	2016	2017	2018
1.5 Insurance business written abroad by branches, gross premiums								
Life								
Branches and agencies	0	..	..	..	..	..	0	0
Subsidaries	..	..	..	..	..	..	0	0
Total	0	..	..	..	..	..	0	0
Non-life								
Branches and agencies	0	..	..	..	..	..	1	3
Subsidaries	..	..	..	..	..	..	0	0
Total	0	..	..	..	..	..	1	3
Composite								
Branches and agencies	..	..	..	..	..	..	0	18
Subsidaries	..	..	..	..	..	..	0	0
Total	..	..	..	..	..	..	0	18
of which:								
Life	..	..	..	..	..	..	0	0
Branches and agencies	..	..	..	..	..	..	0	0
Subsidaries	..	..	..	..	..	..	0	0
Total	..	..	..	..	..	..	0	0
Non-life	..	..	..	..	..	..	0	17
Branches and agencies	..	..	..	..	..	..	0	17
Subsidaries	..	..	..	..	..	..	0	0
Total	..	..	..	..	..	..	0	17
Total								
Branches and agencies	0	..	..	..	..	..	1	21
Subsidaries	..	..	..	..	..	..	0	0
Total	0	..	..	..	..	..	1	21

.. Not available

Note: Detailed metadata at: *http://metalinks.oecd.org/ins/20200312/cf94.*

Source: *OECD Insurance Statistics (database)*

Table 2. Number of companies and employees

	2011	2012	2013	2014	2015	2016	2017	2018
2.1 Number of companies								
Life								
Domestic undertakings	10	11	11	11	11	4	3	2
Foreign controlled undertakings	6	7	7	7	7	2	2	1
Foreign companies (branches)	1	0	0	0	0	0	0	0
All undertakings	11	11	11	11	11	4	3	2
Non-life								
Domestic undertakings	31	31	28	24	24	24	22	20
Foreign controlled undertakings	7	7	7	6	5	7	6	5
Foreign companies (branches)	2	2	2	2	2	0	0	0
All undertakings	33	33	30	26	26	24	22	20
Composite								
Domestic undertakings	11	11	11	11	11	17	17	17
Foreign controlled undertakings	4	4	4	4	4	10	10	10
Foreign companies (branches)	0	0	0	0	0	0	0	0
All undertakings	11	11	11	11	11	17	17	17
Reinsurance								
Domestic undertakings	0	0	0	0	0	0	0	0
Foreign controlled undertakings	0	0	0	0	0	0	0	0
Foreign companies (branches)	0	0	0	0	0	0	0	0
All undertakings	0	0	0	0	0	0	0	0
Total								
Domestic undertakings	52	53	50	46	46	45	42	39
Foreign controlled undertakings	17	18	18	17	16	19	18	16
Foreign companies (branches)	3	2	2	2	2	0	0	0
All undertakings	55	55	52	48	48	45	42	39
2.2 Number of employees								
Insurance undertakings	..	..	..	..	..	..	..	..
Intermediaries	..	..	..	..	..	..	..	..
Total	..	..	..	..	..	..	..	..

.. Not available

Note: Detailed metadata at: *http://metalinks.oecd.org/ins/20200312/cf94.*

Source: OECD Insurance Statistics (database)

HUNGARY

Table 1. Selected aggregates

Million HUF

	2011	2012	2013	2014	2015	2016	2017	2018
1.1 Insurance business written in the reporting country								
1.1.1 Insurance business, by ownership								
Gross premiums								
Domestic undertakings	815 038	760 249	801 210	833 664	835 428	885 781	956 006	1 017 779
Foreign controlled undertakings	770 794	718 932	763 286	796 332	788 248	835 272	897 699	953 320
Foreign companies (branches)	..	..	..	..	..	..	..	..
All undertakings	815 038	760 249	801 210	833 664	835 428	885 781	956 006	1 017 779
Premiums ceded								
Domestic undertakings	131 231	127 261	111 755	116 117	115 801	118 081	120 524	126 479
Foreign controlled undertakings	120 088	118 373	104 254	108 557	104 464	107 021	106 729	113 942
Foreign companies (branches)	..	..	..	..	..	..	..	..
All undertakings	131 231	127 261	111 755	116 117	115 801	118 081	120 524	126 479
Net written premiums								
Domestic undertakings	683 807	632 989	689 455	717 547	719 627	767 700	835 482	891 300
Foreign controlled undertakings	650 706	600 559	659 032	687 774	683 784	728 251	790 970	839 379
Foreign companies (branches)	..	..	..	..	..	..	..	..
All undertakings	683 807	632 989	689 455	717 547	719 627	767 700	835 482	891 300
1.1.2 Insurance business on foreign risks, gross premiums								
Life	30 145	3 284	3 358	3 533	4 234	4 317	4 630	5 116
Non-life	2 165	1 257	1 840	1 923	1 052	2 308	2 657	2 100
Composite	5 326	7 943	4 500	2 829	4 368	8 142	9 004	8 816
of which:								
Life	80	279	781	228	216	177	172	199
Non-life	5 246	7 665	3 719	2 602	4 152	7 965	8 832	8 617
Total	37 636	12 484	9 698	8 285	9 654	14 767	16 291	16 033
1.1.3 Life insurance payments, by class, gross premiums								
Annuities	4 247	3 529	2 975	3 147	3 479	..	..	..
Unit linked	298 106	261 098	286 919	282 059	266 857	..	..	..
Other life insurance	142 599	138 251	146 439	171 738	156 617	..	..	..
Total life insurance	444 952	402 878	436 333	456 944	426 953	438 718	460 791	470 685
***of which:** Pension contracts*	37	..	19	..	10	..	..	..
1.1.4 Non-life insurance payments, by class, gross premiums								
Motor vehicle insurance	164 432	147 428	144 515	152 283	175 045	203 396	232 622	263 731
Marine, aviation and other transport insurance	933	663	661	793	879	142	172	201
Freight insurance	3 082	2 405	2 552	2 856	3 165	5 733	6 143	6 313
Fire and other property damage insurance	147 551	152 904	159 562	158 219	161 160	168 736	179 697	188 516
Pecuniary loss insurance	4 922	2 930	3 739	3 672	4 822	5 430	5 027	6 051
General liability insurance	17 956	18 856	20 074	21 904	23 585	21 274	24 525	26 379
Accident and health	22 596	23 361	25 922	28 358	29 859	22 389	24 898	31 241
***of which:** Health*	5 929	7 128	8 559	9 558	8 668	4 250	5 557	8 909
Other non-life insurance	8 811	8 758	7 781	8 557	9 909	19 916	22 112	24 662
Treaty reinsurance	..	..	..	..	..	..	..	..
Total non-life insurance	370 284	357 305	364 806	376 641	408 424	447 017	495 197	547 094
1.2 Gross claims payments								
Life								
Domestic undertakings	170 016	153 649	139 994	130 633	150 198	155 047	172 359	156 899
Foreign controlled undertakings	158 484	150 320	129 594	121 318	139 595	147 047	160 787	146 733
Foreign companies (branches)	..	..	..	..	..	..	..	..
All undertakings	170 016	153 649	139 994	130 633	150 198	155 047	172 359	156 899
Non-life								
Domestic undertakings	18 824	22 516	25 692	27 416	30 571	34 112	32 258	34 114
Foreign controlled undertakings	11 865	11 387	12 611	13 973	14 605	16 056	12 917	12 308
Foreign companies (branches)	..	..	..	..	..	..	..	..
All undertakings	18 824	22 516	25 692	27 416	30 571	34 112	32 258	34 114
Composite								
Domestic undertakings	411 093	413 298	422 789	379 879	356 926	361 448	389 622	413 120
Foreign controlled undertakings	411 093	413 298	422 789	379 879	356 926	361 448	389 622	413 120
Foreign companies (branches)	..	..	..	..	..	..	..	..
All undertakings	411 093	413 298	422 789	379 879	356 926	361 448	389 622	413 120
of which:								
Life	236 953	240 059	242 802	212 244	180 098	176 820	185 216	205 734
Domestic undertakings	236 953	240 059	242 802	212 244	180 098	176 820	185 216	205 734
Foreign controlled undertakings	236 953	240 059	242 802	212 244	180 098	176 820	185 216	205 734
Foreign companies (branches)	..	..	..	..	..	..	..	..
All undertakings	236 953	240 059	242 802	212 244	180 098	176 820	185 216	205 734
Non-life	174 139	173 240	179 988	167 635	176 829	184 628	204 406	207 386
Domestic undertakings	174 139	173 240	179 988	167 635	176 829	184 628	204 406	207 386
Foreign controlled undertakings	174 139	173 240	179 988	167 635	176 829	184 628	204 406	207 386
Foreign companies (branches)	..	..	..	..	..	..	..	..
All undertakings	174 139	173 240	179 988	167 635	176 829	184 628	204 406	207 386
Total								
Domestic undertakings	599 932	589 464	588 475	537 928	537 695	550 607	594 239	604 133
Foreign controlled undertakings	581 441	575 006	564 995	515 171	511 127	524 551	563 326	572 162
Foreign companies (branches)	..	..	..	..	..	..	..	..
All undertakings	599 932	589 464	588 475	537 928	537 695	550 607	594 239	604 133

Table 1. Selected aggregates *(cont.)*

Million HUF

	2011	2012	2013	2014	2015	2016	2017	2018
1.3 Commissions								
Life								
Domestic undertakings	23 907	20 760	14 900	14 024	13 526	16 531	17 513	15 243
Foreign controlled undertakings	13 391	14 215	11 559	11 559	11 089	14 360	15 017	12 599
Foreign companies (branches)	..	..	..	..	..	..	..	..
All undertakings	23 907	20 760	14 900	14 024	13 526	16 531	17 513	15 243
Non-life								
Domestic undertakings	6 479	6 319	7 349	7 243	9 161	10 325	13 383	14 338
Foreign controlled undertakings	5 335	4 457	4 813	4 948	5 986	5 650	6 550	6 809
Foreign companies (branches)	..	..	..	..	..	..	..	..
All undertakings	6 479	6 319	7 349	7 243	9 161	10 325	13 383	14 338
Composite								
Domestic undertakings	74 891	69 058	75 007	72 592	79 086	108 207	114 286	123 934
Foreign controlled undertakings	74 891	69 058	75 007	72 592	79 086	108 207	114 286	123 934
Foreign companies (branches)	..	..	..	..	..	..	..	..
All undertakings	74 891	69 058	75 007	72 592	79 086	108 207	114 286	123 934
of which:								
Life	30 426	26 909	29 847	30 235	29 116	39 083	38 017	36 194
Domestic undertakings	30 426	26 909	29 847	30 235	29 116	39 083	38 017	36 194
Foreign controlled undertakings	30 426	26 909	29 847	30 235	29 116	39 083	38 017	36 194
Foreign companies (branches)	..	..	..	..	..	..	..	..
All undertakings	30 426	26 909	29 847	30 235	29 116	39 083	38 017	36 194
Non-life	44 465	42 148	45 160	42 357	49 970	69 124	76 269	87 740
Domestic undertakings	44 465	42 148	45 160	42 357	49 970	69 124	76 269	87 740
Foreign controlled undertakings	44 465	42 148	45 160	42 357	49 970	69 124	76 269	87 740
Foreign companies (branches)	..	..	..	..	..	..	..	..
All undertakings	44 465	42 148	45 160	42 357	49 970	69 124	76 269	87 740
Total								
Domestic undertakings	105 277	96 136	97 256	93 859	101 773	135 063	145 182	153 515
Foreign controlled undertakings	93 617	87 729	91 380	89 099	96 162	128 218	135 853	143 341
Foreign companies (branches)	..	..	..	..	..	..	..	..
All undertakings	105 277	96 136	97 256	93 859	101 773	135 063	145 182	153 515
1.4 Gross operating expenses								
Life								
Domestic undertakings	52 633	37 846	32 595	35 399	32 897	34 946	34 955	32 702
Foreign controlled undertakings	36 587	32 963	27 473	30 053	29 279	31 818	30 865	28 684
Foreign companies (branches)	..	..	..	..	..	..	..	..
All undertakings	52 633	37 846	32 595	35 399	32 897	34 946	34 955	32 702
Non-life								
Domestic undertakings	17 229	16 277	17 413	17 638	20 337	21 977	21 528	19 122
Foreign controlled undertakings	12 859	10 465	11 126	11 890	14 690	13 298	10 965	11 520
Foreign companies (branches)	..	..	..	..	..	..	..	..
All undertakings	17 229	16 277	17 413	17 638	20 337	21 977	21 528	19 122
Composite								
Domestic undertakings	170 062	155 577	172 680	181 142	167 842	176 431	185 944	203 460
Foreign controlled undertakings	170 062	155 577	172 680	181 142	167 842	176 431	185 944	203 460
Foreign companies (branches)	..	..	..	..	..	..	..	..
All undertakings	170 062	155 577	172 680	181 142	167 842	176 431	185 944	203 460
of which:								
Life	68 791	55 125	56 633	70 675	55 349	56 859	50 779	55 001
Domestic undertakings	68 791	55 125	56 633	70 675	55 349	56 859	50 779	55 001
Foreign controlled undertakings	68 791	55 125	56 633	70 675	55 349	56 859	50 779	55 001
Foreign companies (branches)	..	..	..	..	..	..	..	..
All undertakings	68 791	55 125	56 633	70 675	55 349	56 859	50 779	55 001
Non-life	101 271	100 451	116 047	110 467	112 493	119 571	135 165	148 459
Domestic undertakings	101 271	100 451	116 047	110 467	112 493	119 571	135 165	148 459
Foreign controlled undertakings	101 271	100 451	116 047	110 467	112 493	119 571	135 165	148 459
Foreign companies (branches)	..	..	..	..	..	..	..	..
All undertakings	101 271	100 451	116 047	110 467	112 493	119 571	135 165	148 459
Total								
Domestic undertakings	239 924	209 699	222 687	234 179	221 076	233 354	242 427	255 284
Foreign controlled undertakings	219 509	199 004	211 279	223 085	211 811	221 547	227 774	243 664
Foreign companies (branches)	..	..	..	..	..	..	..	..
All undertakings	239 924	209 699	222 687	234 179	221 076	233 354	242 427	255 284

HUNGARY

Table 1. Selected aggregates *(cont.)*

Million HUF

	2011	2012	2013	2014	2015	2016	2017	2018
1.5 Insurance business written abroad by branches, gross premiums								
Life								
Branches and agencies	..	..	..	..	..	..	..	..
Subsidaries	..	..	..	..	..	..	..	..
Total	..	..	..	..	..	..	..	..
Non-life								
Branches and agencies	..	..	..	..	..	..	..	..
Subsidaries	..	..	..	..	..	..	..	..
Total	..	..	..	..	..	..	..	..
Composite								
Branches and agencies	..	..	..	..	..	..	..	..
Subsidaries	..	..	..	..	..	..	..	..
Total	..	..	..	..	..	..	..	..
of which:								
Life	..	..	..	..	..	..	..	..
Branches and agencies	..	..	..	..	..	..	..	..
Subsidaries	..	..	..	..	..	..	..	..
Total	..	..	..	..	..	..	..	..
Non-life	..	..	..	..	..	..	..	..
Branches and agencies	..	..	..	..	..	..	..	..
Subsidaries	..	..	..	..	..	..	..	..
Total	..	..	..	..	..	..	..	..
Total								
Branches and agencies	..	..	..	..	..	..	..	..
Subsidaries	..	..	..	..	..	..	..	..
Total	..	..	..	..	..	..	..	..

.. Not available

Note: Detailed metadata at: *http://metalinks.oecd.org/ins/20200312/5e3a.*

Source: *OECD Insurance Statistics (database)*

Table 2. Number of companies and employees

	2011	2012	2013	2014	2015	2016	2017	2018
2.1 Number of companies								
Life								
Domestic undertakings	12	12	10	10	10	8	7	6
Foreign controlled undertakings	9	9	7	7	7	7	6	5
Foreign companies (branches)	..	..	..	..	0	0	0	0
All undertakings	12	12	10	10	10	8	7	6
Non-life								
Domestic undertakings	15	13	12	12	11	10	9	9
Foreign controlled undertakings	9	7	6	6	6	6	5	5
Foreign companies (branches)	12	14	14	14	13	14	13	12
All undertakings	27	27	26	26	24	24	22	21
Composite								
Domestic undertakings	10	10	10	10	9	9	9	8
Foreign controlled undertakings	10	10	10	10	9	9	9	8
Foreign companies (branches)	1	1	1	1	2	2	2	2
All undertakings	11	11	11	11	11	11	11	10
Reinsurance								
Domestic undertakings	..	..	..	..	..	..	..	..
Foreign controlled undertakings	..	..	..	..	..	..	..	..
Foreign companies (branches)	..	..	..	..	..	..	..	..
All undertakings	..	..	..	..	..	..	..	..
Total								
Domestic undertakings	37	35	32	32	30	27	25	23
Foreign controlled undertakings	28	26	23	23	22	22	20	18
Foreign companies (branches)	13	15	15	15	15	16	15	14
All undertakings	50	50	47	47	45	43	40	37
2.2 Number of employees								
Insurance undertakings	9 580	9 701	9 363	9 229	8 728	8 542	8 133	11 116
Intermediaries	16 950	13 572	13 083	12 768	11 392	9 822	12 287	7 791
Total	26 530	23 273	22 445	21 997	20 121	18 364	20 420	18 907

.. Not available

Note: Detailed metadata at: *http://metalinks.oecd.org/ins/20200312/5e3a.*

Source: OECD Insurance Statistics (database)

Table 1. Selected aggregates

Million ISK

	2011	2012	2013	2014	2015	2016	2017	2018
1.1 Insurance business written in the reporting country								
1.1.1 Insurance business, by ownership								
Gross premiums								
Domestic undertakings	48 117	50 490	51 142	51 849	55 346	58 777	65 274	70 561
Foreign controlled undertakings	4 464	4 788	5 088	5 401	6 010	..	..	..
Foreign companies (branches)	0	..	..	..	..	..	..	..
All undertakings	48 117	50 490	51 142	51 849	55 346	58 777	65 274	70 561
Premiums ceded								
Domestic undertakings	3 425	3 371	3 136	2 918	2 882	2 725	2 613	2 869
Foreign controlled undertakings	328	318	310	310	272	..	..	..
Foreign companies (branches)	0	..	..	..	..	..	..	..
All undertakings	3 425	3 371	3 136	2 918	2 882	2 725	2 613	2 869
Net written premiums								
Domestic undertakings	44 692	47 118	48 005	48 931	52 465	56 052	62 662	67 693
Foreign controlled undertakings	4 136	4 470	4 779	5 091	5 737	..	..	..
Foreign companies (branches)	0	..	..	..	..	..	..	..
All undertakings	44 692	47 118	48 005	48 931	52 465	56 052	62 662	67 693
1.1.2 Insurance business on foreign risks, gross premiums								
Life	0	0	0	0	0	0	0	0
Non-life	2 528	2 632	2 156	2 563	3 018	1 010	1 737	3 444
Composite total	..	..	..	..	..	..	..	..
Total	2 528	2 632	2 156	2 563	3 018	1 010	1 737	3 444
1.1.3 Life insurance payments, by class, gross premiums								
Annuities	57	61	61	111	473	..	..	..
Unit linked	110	87	86	87	91	20	32	23
Other life insurance	3 227	3 532	3 913	4 042	4 087	5 141	5 789	5 815
Total life insurance	3 395	3 680	4 061	4 240	4 651	5 161	5 821	5 837
***of which:** Pension contracts*	0	0	0	0	0	0	0	0
1.1.4 Non-life insurance payments, by class, gross premiums								
Motor vehicle insurance	20 205	21 226	21 522	22 084	23 952	28 398	33 127	35 842
Marine, aviation and other transport insurance	2 629	2 746	3 372	3 419	3 690	3 631	3 139	3 251
Freight insurance	632	667	638	646	751	0	0	0
Fire and other property damage insurance	12 838	14 028	13 816	13 903	13 911	12 484	13 048	14 472
Pecuniary loss insurance	100	77	45	23	27	33	26	59
General liability insurance	2 782	2 932	2 556	2 565	2 672	3 078	3 561	3 974
Accident and health	5 318	5 108	5 102	4 947	5 646	5 960	6 509	7 093
***of which:** Health*	..	..	..	..	..	..	..	..
Other non-life insurance	27	27	30	22	42	32	42	33
Treaty reinsurance	0	0	0	0	0	0	0	0
Total non-life insurance	44 530	46 809	47 081	47 608	50 690	53 616	59 453	64 724
1.2 Gross claims payments								
Life								
Domestic undertakings	1 139	1 434	1 381	1 529	1 325	1 690	1 755	1 752
Foreign controlled undertakings	21	56	47	30	58	..	..	..
Foreign companies (branches)	..	..	..	..	..	..	..	..
All undertakings	1 139	1 434	1 381	1 529	1 325	1 690	1 755	1 752
Non-life								
Domestic undertakings	28 721	30 190	31 417	32 554	36 082	41 655	43 781	51 533
Foreign controlled undertakings	3 132	2 931	3 412	3 520	4 169	..	..	..
Foreign companies (branches)	..	..	..	..	..	..	..	..
All undertakings	28 721	30 190	31 417	32 554	36 082	41 655	43 781	51 533
Composite, all undertakings	..	..	..	..	..	..	..	..
Total								
Domestic undertakings	29 861	31 624	32 798	34 083	37 407	43 345	45 536	53 285
Foreign controlled undertakings	3 152	2 987	3 459	3 550	4 227	..	..	..
Foreign companies (branches)	..	..	..	..	..	..	..	..
All undertakings	29 861	31 624	32 798	34 083	37 407	43 345	45 536	53 285
1.3 Commissions								
Life								
Domestic undertakings	74	71	66	118	90	..	..	..
Foreign controlled undertakings	4	12	20	42	3	..	..	..
Foreign companies (branches)	..	..	..	..	..	..	..	..
All undertakings	74	71	66	118	90	..	..	..
Non-life								
Domestic undertakings	101	122	102	39	36	..	..	..
Foreign controlled undertakings	0	0	0	0	0	..	..	..
Foreign companies (branches)	..	..	..	..	..	..	..	..
All undertakings	101	122	102	39	36	..	..	..
Composite, all undertakings	..	..	..	..	..	..	..	..
Total								
Domestic undertakings	175	193	168	157	126	..	..	..
Foreign controlled undertakings	4	12	20	42	3	..	..	..
Foreign companies (branches)	..	..	..	..	..	..	..	..
All undertakings	175	193	168	157	126	..	..	..

Table 1. Selected aggregates *(cont.)*

Million ISK

	2011	2012	2013	2014	2015	2016	2017	2018
1.4 Gross operating expenses								
Life								
Domestic undertakings	945	1 119	1 384	1 098	1 498	1 231	1 528	1 394
Foreign controlled undertakings	57	77	90	18	161	..	..	..
Foreign companies (branches)	..	..	..	..	..	..	..	..
All undertakings	945	1 119	1 384	1 098	1 498	1 231	1 528	1 394
Non-life								
Domestic undertakings	9 081	9 987	9 860	9 680	4 314	6 931	7 422	11 994
Foreign controlled undertakings	965	996	1 084	1 086	1 225	..	..	..
Foreign companies (branches)	..	..	..	..	..	..	..	..
All undertakings	9 081	9 987	9 860	9 680	4 314	6 931	7 422	12 026
Composite, all undertakings	..	..	..	..	..	..	..	..
Total								
Domestic undertakings	10 027	11 106	11 244	10 778	5 812	8 162	8 950	13 389
Foreign controlled undertakings	1 022	1 072	1 173	1 104	1 387	..	..	..
Foreign companies (branches)	..	..	..	..	..	..	..	..
All undertakings	10 027	11 106	11 244	10 778	5 812	8 162	8 950	13 421
1.5 Insurance business written abroad by branches, gross premiums								
Life								
Branches and agencies	0	0	..	..	..	..	..	..
Subsidaries	0	0	..	..	..	..	..	..
Total	0	0	..	..	..	..	..	..
Non-life								
Branches and agencies	551	914	..	..	..	..	..	..
Subsidaries	0	0	..	..	..	..	..	..
Total	551	914	..	..	..	..	..	..
Composite total	..	..	..	..	..	..	..	..
Total								
Branches and agencies	551	914	..	..	..	..	..	..
Subsidaries	0	0	..	..	..	..	..	..
Total	551	914	..	..	..	..	..	..

.. Not available

Note: Detailed metadata at: *http://metalinks.oecd.org/ins/20200312/75bc.*

Source: OECD Insurance Statistics (database)

Table 2. Number of companies and employees

	2011	2012	2013	2014	2015	2016	2017	2018
2.1 Number of companies								
Life								
Domestic undertakings	5	5	5	5	5	4	4	4
Foreign controlled undertakings	1	1	1	1	1	..	..	..
Foreign companies (branches)	0	1	1	1	1	..	..	..
All undertakings	5	6	6	6	6	4	4	4
Non-life								
Domestic undertakings	6	6	5	5	5	4	4	4
Foreign controlled undertakings	1	1	1	1	1	..	..	..
Foreign companies (branches)	0	1	1	1	1	..	..	..
All undertakings	6	7	6	6	6	4	4	4
Composite, all undertakings	**0**	**0**	**0**	**0**	**0**	**0**	**0**	**0**
Reinsurance								
Domestic undertakings	2	2	2	2	2	0	0	0
Foreign controlled undertakings	0	0	..	..	..	..	..	..
Foreign companies (branches)	0	0	..	..	..	..	..	..
All undertakings	2	2	2	2	2	0	0	0
Total								
Domestic undertakings	13	13	12	12	12	8	8	8
Foreign controlled undertakings	2	2	2	2	2	0	0	0
Foreign companies (branches)	0	2	2	2	2	0	0	0
All undertakings	13	15	14	14	14	8	8	8
2.2 Number of employees								
Insurance undertakings	652	641	614	..	582	..	..	..
Intermediaries	0	..	..	592	..	..	..	..
Total	652	..	614	592	582	..	..	..

.. Not available

Note: Detailed metadata at: *http://metalinks.oecd.org/ins/20200312/75bc.*

Source: OECD Insurance Statistics (database)

Table 1. Selected aggregates

Million EUR

	2011	2012	2013	2014	2015	2016	2017	2018
1.1 Insurance business written in the reporting country								
1.1.1 Insurance business, by ownership								
Gross premiums								
Domestic undertakings	30 304	33 133	31 818	36 377	40 340	48 949	40 281	36 998
Foreign controlled undertakings	..	..	..	..	..	..	..	..
Foreign companies (branches)	1 731	2 348	2 301	3 184	3 645	..	3 821	3 756
All undertakings	32 035	35 481	34 119	39 561	43 985	48 949	44 102	40 754
Premiums ceded								
Domestic undertakings	3 478	3 755	3 908	3 891	4 933	9 985	..	..
Foreign controlled undertakings	..	..	..	..	..	..	..	..
Foreign companies (branches)	772	356	268	371	359	..	..	..
All undertakings	4 250	4 111	4 176	4 262	5 292	9 985	..	..
Net written premiums								
Domestic undertakings	26 826	29 379	27 910	32 486	35 407	38 964	..	..
Foreign controlled undertakings	..	..	..	..	..	..	..	..
Foreign companies (branches)	960	1 992	2 033	2 813	3 286	..	..	..
All undertakings	27 786	31 371	29 943	35 299	38 693	38 964	..	..
1.1.2 Insurance business on foreign risks, gross premiums								
Life	15 627	15 038	16 125	21 410	23 192	..	19 774	16 644
Non-life	3 195	3 676	3 826	3 960	4 263	..	2 277	2 671
Composite	..	..	..	..	..	..	6	191
of which:								
Life	..	..	..	..	..	..	..	..
Non-life	..	..	..	..	..	..	..	..
Total	18 821	18 714	19 951	25 370	27 455	..	22 057	19 506
1.1.3 Life insurance payments, by class, gross premiums								
Annuities	..	..	..	..	..	0	0	0
Unit linked	..	..	..	..	..	28 838	30 737	26 568
Other life insurance	..	..	..	..	..	4 477	4 279	4 102
Total life insurance	..	28 140	27 207	32 171	34 587	33 315	35 016	30 670
***of which:** Pension contracts*	..	..	..	..	..	..	..	..
1.1.4 Non-life insurance payments, by class, gross premiums								
Motor vehicle insurance	1 423	1 486	1 435	1 599	1 795	3 905	2 086	2 067
Marine, aviation and other transport insurance	237	243	183	143	163	421	144	219
Freight insurance	0	..	..	..	..	0	0	..
Fire and other property damage insurance	1 728	1 906	1 763	1 758	1 768	4 023	1 401	1 503
Pecuniary loss insurance	67	..	105	124	92	332	830	848
General liability insurance	1 072	1 147	1 127	1 301	1 400	2 887	1 288	1 296
Accident and health	1 432	1 288	1 171	1 235	2 750	1 935	2 396	2 323
***of which:** Health*	..	..	..	..	..	..	..	..
Other non-life insurance	485	563	504	494	585	1 159	158	217
Treaty reinsurance	284	374	330	373	414	746	217	..
Total non-life insurance	6 729	7 007	6 618	7 027	8 967	15 408	8 520	8 473
1.2 Gross claims payments								
Life								
Domestic undertakings	..	27 921	28 263	27 434	28 474	32 280	26 726	25 196
Foreign controlled undertakings	..	..	..	..	..	..	..	..
Foreign companies (branches)	..	..	1 235	1 114	1 356	..	2 435	2 052
All undertakings	..	27 921	29 498	28 548	29 830	32 280	29 161	27 248
Non-life								
Domestic undertakings	4 938	4 842	4 369	3 853	5 343	15 941	8 482	8 283
Foreign controlled undertakings	..	..	..	..	..	..	..	..
Foreign companies (branches)	1 023	983	677	1 177	1 179	..	725	871
All undertakings	5 961	5 825	5 046	5 030	6 522	15 941	9 207	9 154
Composite								
Domestic undertakings	..	..	..	..	..	..	..	..
Foreign controlled undertakings	..	..	..	..	..	..	..	..
Foreign companies (branches)	..	..	..	..	..	..	357	983
All undertakings	..	..	..	..	..	..	357	983
of which:								
Life	..	..	..	..	..	..	..	..
Domestic undertakings	..	..	..	..	..	..	..	..
Foreign controlled undertakings	..	..	..	..	..	..	..	..
Foreign companies (branches)	..	..	..	..	..	..	..	..
All undertakings	..	..	..	..	..	..	..	..
Non-life	..	..	..	..	..	..	..	..
Domestic undertakings	..	..	..	..	..	..	..	..
Foreign controlled undertakings	..	..	..	..	..	..	..	..
Foreign companies (branches)	..	..	..	..	..	..	..	..
All undertakings	..	..	..	..	..	..	..	..
Total								
Domestic undertakings	4 938	32 763	32 632	31 287	33 817	48 221	35 208	33 479
Foreign controlled undertakings	..	..	..	..	..	..	..	..
Foreign companies (branches)	1 023	983	1 912	2 291	2 535	..	3 517	3 906
All undertakings	5 961	33 746	34 544	33 578	36 352	48 221	38 725	37 385

IRELAND

Table 1. Selected aggregates *(cont.)*

Million EUR

	2011	2012	2013	2014	2015	2016	2017	2018
1.3 Commissions								
Life								
Domestic undertakings	..	1 593	1 844	2 051	2 281	2 198	1 517	1 625
Foreign controlled undertakings	..	..	..	..	..	..	..	..
Foreign companies (branches)	..	..	43	64	59	..	94	44
All undertakings	..	1 593	1 887	2 115	2 340	2 198	1 611	1 669
Non-life								
Domestic undertakings	764	657	737	764	896	2 292	957	1 012
Foreign controlled undertakings	..	..	..	..	..	..	..	..
Foreign companies (branches)	104	171	130	248	299	..	194	221
All undertakings	868	828	867	1 012	1 195	2 292	1 511	1 233
Composite								
Domestic undertakings	..	..	..	..	..	..	..	..
Foreign controlled undertakings	..	..	..	..	..	..	..	..
Foreign companies (branches)	..	..	..	..	..	..	80	110
All undertakings	..	..	..	..	..	..	80	110
of which:								
Life	..	..	..	..	..	..	..	..
Domestic undertakings	..	..	..	..	..	..	..	..
Foreign controlled undertakings	..	..	..	..	..	..	..	..
Foreign companies (branches)	..	..	..	..	..	..	..	..
All undertakings	..	..	..	..	..	..	..	..
Non-life	..	..	..	..	..	..	..	..
Domestic undertakings	..	..	..	..	..	..	..	..
Foreign controlled undertakings	..	..	..	..	..	..	..	..
Foreign companies (branches)	..	..	..	..	..	..	..	..
All undertakings	..	..	..	..	..	..	..	..
Total								
Domestic undertakings	764	2 250	2 581	2 815	3 177	4 490	2 474	2 637
Foreign controlled undertakings	..	..	..	..	..	..	..	..
Foreign companies (branches)	104	171	173	312	358	..	368	375
All undertakings	868	2 420	2 754	3 127	3 535	4 490	3 202	3 012
1.4 Gross operating expenses								
Life								
Domestic undertakings	..	1 268	1 346	1 429	1 437	1 319	444	..
Foreign controlled undertakings	..	..	..	..	..	..	..	..
Foreign companies (branches)	..	..	154	657	158	..	..	..
All undertakings	..	1 268	1 500	2 086	1 595	1 319	444	..
Non-life								
Domestic undertakings	688	622	650	589	484	1 873	932	..
Foreign controlled undertakings	..	..	..	..	..	..	..	..
Foreign companies (branches)	186	295	159	223	224	..	..	..
All undertakings	874	917	809	812	708	1 873	932	..
Composite								
Domestic undertakings	..	..	..	..	..	..	..	..
Foreign controlled undertakings	..	..	..	..	..	..	..	..
Foreign companies (branches)	..	..	..	..	..	..	..	..
All undertakings	..	..	..	..	..	..	..	..
of which:								
Life	..	..	..	..	..	..	..	..
Domestic undertakings	..	..	..	..	..	..	..	..
Foreign controlled undertakings	..	..	..	..	..	..	..	..
Foreign companies (branches)	..	..	..	..	..	..	..	..
All undertakings	..	..	..	..	..	..	..	..
Non-life	..	..	..	..	..	..	..	..
Domestic undertakings	..	..	..	..	..	..	..	..
Foreign controlled undertakings	..	..	..	..	..	..	..	..
Foreign companies (branches)	..	..	..	..	..	..	..	..
All undertakings	..	..	..	..	..	..	..	..
Total								
Domestic undertakings	688	1 891	1 996	2 018	1 921	3 192	1 376	..
Foreign controlled undertakings	..	..	..	..	..	..	..	..
Foreign companies (branches)	186	295	313	880	382	..	..	..
All undertakings	874	2 185	2 309	2 898	2 303	3 192	1 376	..

Table 1. Selected aggregates *(cont.)*

Million EUR

	2011	2012	2013	2014	2015	2016	2017	2018
1.5 Insurance business written abroad by branches, gross premiums								
Life								
Branches and agencies	2 434	3 422	5 563	5 970	6 234	..	6 438	5 266
Subsidaries	..	..	..	..	..	..	..	..
Total	2 434	3 422	5 563	5 970	6 234	..	6 438	5 266
Non-life								
Branches and agencies	9 626	9 599	9 228	9 640	9 835	..	8 739	9 029
Subsidaries	..	..	..	..	..	..	..	..
Total	9 626	9 599	9 228	9 640	9 835	..	8 739	9 029
Composite								
Branches and agencies	..	..	..	..	..	..	..	..
Subsidaries	..	..	..	..	..	..	..	..
Total	..	..	..	..	..	..	..	..
of which:								
Life	..	..	..	..	..	..	..	..
Branches and agencies	..	..	..	..	..	..	..	..
Subsidaries	..	..	..	..	..	..	..	..
Total	..	..	..	..	..	..	..	..
Non-life	..	..	..	..	..	..	..	..
Branches and agencies	..	..	..	..	..	..	..	..
Subsidaries	..	..	..	..	..	..	..	..
Total	..	..	..	..	..	..	..	..
Total								
Branches and agencies	12 060	13 021	14 791	15 610	16 069	..	15 177	14 295
Subsidaries	..	..	..	..	..	..	..	..
Total	12 060	13 021	14 791	15 610	16 069	..	15 177	14 295

.. Not available

Note: Detailed metadata at: *http://metalinks.oecd.org/ins/20200312/a0dc.*

Source: *OECD Insurance Statistics (database)*

Table 2. Number of companies and employees

	2011	2012	2013	2014	2015	2016	2017	2018
2.1 Number of companies								
Life								
Domestic undertakings	62	55	53	51	48	44	45	42
Foreign controlled undertakings	0	0	..	..	..	0	0	..
Foreign companies (branches)	9	8	8	8	11	11	12	13
All undertakings	71	63	61	59	59	55	57	55
Non-life								
Domestic undertakings	121	111	104	102	101	90	99	95
Foreign controlled undertakings	0	0	..	..	..	0	0	..
Foreign companies (branches)	28	28	27	30	32	31	30	38
All undertakings	149	139	131	132	133	121	129	133
Composite								
Domestic undertakings	0	0	0	0	0	0	1	0
Foreign controlled undertakings	0	0	0	0	0	0	0	..
Foreign companies (branches)	0	0	0	0	0	0	0	0
All undertakings	0	0	0	0	0	0	1	0
Reinsurance								
Domestic undertakings	102	87	77	75	67	61	64	63
Foreign controlled undertakings	0	0	..	..	..	0	0	..
Foreign companies (branches)	0	0	0	0	0	0	0	0
All undertakings	102	87	77	75	67	61	64	63
Total								
Domestic undertakings	285	253	234	228	216	196	209	200
Foreign controlled undertakings	..	..	..	..	..	0	0	..
Foreign companies (branches)	37	36	35	38	43	42	42	51
All undertakings	322	289	269	266	259	238	251	251
2.2 Number of employees								
Insurance undertakings	9 696	8 682	8 887	8 095	9 404	..	..	..
Intermediaries	..	..	..	..	..	..	..	..
Total	9 696	8 682	8 887	..	..	..	..	..

.. Not available

Note: Detailed metadata at: *http://metalinks.oecd.org/ins/20200312/a0dc.*

Source: OECD Insurance Statistics (database)

ISRAEL

Table 1. Selected aggregates

Million ILS

	2011	2012	2013	2014	2015	2016	2017	2018
1.1 Insurance business written in the reporting country								
1.1.1 Insurance business, by ownership								
Gross premiums								
Domestic undertakings	45 317	48 086	50 339	51 400	54 869	58 153	62 730	66 640
Foreign controlled undertakings	9 663	840	889	953	1 135	1 165	1 234	1 296
Foreign companies (branches)	..	..	..	..	..	..	..	..
All undertakings	45 317	48 086	50 339	51 400	54 869	58 153	62 730	66 640
Premiums ceded								
Domestic undertakings	6 529	6 877	6 418	5 934	6 356	8 756	8 468	9 454
Foreign controlled undertakings	894	185	164	162	232	225	228	249
Foreign companies (branches)	..	..	..	..	..	..	..	..
All undertakings	6 529	6 877	6 418	5 934	6 356	8 756	8 468	9 454
Net written premiums								
Domestic undertakings	38 788	41 209	43 921	45 466	48 512	49 398	54 263	57 186
Foreign controlled undertakings	8 769	656	726	791	903	940	1 006	1 047
Foreign companies (branches)	..	..	..	..	..	..	..	..
All undertakings	38 788	41 209	43 921	45 466	48 512	49 398	54 263	57 186
1.1.2 Insurance business on foreign risks, gross premiums								
Life	..	..	..	..	..	..	..	..
Non-life	..	..	..	..	..	..	..	..
Composite	3	..	..	..	..	..	..	..
of which:								
Life	..	..	..	..	..	..	..	..
Non-life	3	..	..	..	..	..	..	..
Total	3	..	..	..	..	..	..	..
1.1.3 Life insurance payments, by class, gross premiums								
Annuities	1 593	1 542	1 361	1 194	1 084	1 273	1 125	1 118
Unit linked	16 662	17 673	18 557	18 236	20 266	20 897	23 867	25 433
Other life insurance	5 654	6 242	6 709	7 141	8 066	8 492	8 730	9 412
Total life insurance	23 909	25 458	26 627	26 571	29 416	30 662	33 722	35 963
***of which:** Pension contracts*	..	..	..	..	..	..	..	..
1.1.4 Non-life insurance payments, by class, gross premiums								
Motor vehicle insurance	10 358	10 673	11 040	11 439	11 775	13 053	13 396	14 129
Marine, aviation and other transport insurance	41	41	38	38	39	38	36	40
Freight insurance	173	180	169	170	174	176	187	174
Fire and other property damage insurance	3 475	4 082	4 283	4 292	4 238	4 375	4 481	4 549
Pecuniary loss insurance	0	277	284	278	307	335	348	480
General liability insurance	2 354	2 487	2 575	2 697	2 814	2 917	3 094	3 250
Accident and health	3 950	4 396	4 869	5 425	5 678	6 086	6 961	7 548
***of which:** Health*	..	3 580	3 859	4 189	4 203	4 448	5 144	5 614
Other non-life insurance	1 056	492	452	492	426	502	506	506
Treaty reinsurance	..	..	..	0	0	0	..	0
Total non-life insurance	21 408	22 628	23 712	24 830	25 452	27 483	29 009	30 676
1.2 Gross claims payments								
Life								
Domestic undertakings	..	..	0	3	6	8	.. c	..
Foreign controlled undertakings	..	..	..	..	..	0	..	..
Foreign companies (branches)	..	..	..	..	..	..	..	..
All undertakings	..	..	0	3	6	8	.. c	..
Non-life								
Domestic undertakings	1 303	1 395	2 013	2 470	2 589	2 180	2 124	2 189
Foreign controlled undertakings	..	..	..	..	39	72	22	30
Foreign companies (branches)	..	..	..	..	..	..	..	..
All undertakings	1 303	1 395	2 013	2 470	2 589	2 180	2 124	2 189
Composite								
Domestic undertakings	24 636	25 830	24 594	27 644	30 828	31 879	35 461	36 580
Foreign controlled undertakings	5 004	393	280	462	640	538	0	578
Foreign companies (branches)	..	..	..	..	..	..	..	..
All undertakings	24 636	25 830	24 594	27 644	30 828	31 879	35 461	36 580
of which:								
Life	11 651	12 472	12 644	13 825	15 363	16 243	18 411	19 489
Domestic undertakings	11 651	12 472	12 644	13 825	15 363	16 243	18 411	19 489
Foreign controlled undertakings	3 564	27	18	26	39	36	42	50
Foreign companies (branches)	..	..	..	..	..	..	..	..
All undertakings	11 651	12 472	12 644	13 825	15 363	16 243	18 411	19 489
Non-life	12 985	13 358	11 949	13 819	15 465	15 636	17 051	17 091
Domestic undertakings	12 985	13 358	11 949	13 819	15 465	15 636	17 051	17 091
Foreign controlled undertakings	1 440	366	262	436	600	502	575	528
Foreign companies (branches)	..	..	..	..	..	..	..	..
All undertakings	12 985	13 358	11 949	13 819	15 465	15 636	17 051	17 091
Total								
Domestic undertakings	25 939	27 225	26 607	30 117	33 422	34 067	37 598	38 769
Foreign controlled undertakings	5 004	393	280	462	679	609	22	608
Foreign companies (branches)	..	..	..	..	..	..	..	..
All undertakings	25 939	27 225	26 607	30 117	33 422	34 067	37 598	38 769

Table 1. Selected aggregates *(cont.)*

Million ILS

	2011	2012	2013	2014	2015	2016	2017	2018
1.3 Commissions								
Life								
Domestic undertakings	..	..	0	6	15	19	.. c	..
Foreign controlled undertakings	..	..	..	..	..	0	..	..
Foreign companies (branches)	..	..	..	..	..	..	..	..
All undertakings	..	..	0	6	15	19	.. c	..
Non-life								
Domestic undertakings	159	175	248	281	317	291	341	358
Foreign controlled undertakings	..	..	..	..	0	0	0	0
Foreign companies (branches)	..	..	..	..	..	..	..	..
All undertakings	159	175	248	281	317	291	341	358
Composite								
Domestic undertakings	5 070	5 512	5 688	5 940	6 296	6 709	7 109	7 592
Foreign controlled undertakings	947	41	39	..	42	40	..	38
Foreign companies (branches)	..	..	..	..	..	..	..	..
All undertakings	5 070	5 512	5 688	5 940	6 296	6 709	7 109	7 592
of which:								
Life	2 328	2 577	2 571	2 639	2 912	3 097	3 215	3 531
Domestic undertakings	2 328	2 577	2 571	2 639	2 912	3 097	3 215	3 531
Foreign controlled undertakings	635	1	1	1	1	1	1	1
Foreign companies (branches)	..	..	..	..	..	..	..	..
All undertakings	2 328	2 577	2 571	2 639	2 912	3 097	3 215	3 531
Non-life	2 742	2 936	3 118	3 300	3 384	3 612	3 893	4 061
Domestic undertakings	2 742	2 936	3 118	3 300	3 384	3 612	3 893	4 061
Foreign controlled undertakings	312	40	38	38	41	39	37	37
Foreign companies (branches)	..	..	..	..	..	..	..	..
All undertakings	2 742	2 936	3 118	3 300	3 384	3 612	3 893	4 061
Total								
Domestic undertakings	5 229	5 688	5 936	6 226	6 628	7 019	7 464	7 950
Foreign controlled undertakings	947	41	39	..	42	40	0	38
Foreign companies (branches)	..	..	..	..	..	..	..	..
All undertakings	5 229	5 688	5 936	6 226	6 628	7 019	7 464	7 950
1.4 Gross operating expenses								
Life								
Domestic undertakings	..	..	1	10	32	32	.. c	..
Foreign controlled undertakings	..	..	..	..	..	0	..	..
Foreign companies (branches)	..	..	..	..	..	..	..	..
All undertakings	..	..	1	10	32	32	.. c	..
Non-life								
Domestic undertakings	306	305	449	322	402	380	417	32
Foreign controlled undertakings	..	..	..	..	30	29	33	36
Foreign companies (branches)	..	..	..	..	..	..	..	..
All undertakings	306	305	449	322	402	380	417	32
Composite								
Domestic undertakings	5 198	5 270	5 285	5 169	5 719	6 033	6 504	13 992
Foreign controlled undertakings	1 158	260	272	276	282	275	278	289
Foreign companies (branches)	..	..	..	..	..	..	..	..
All undertakings	5 198	5 270	5 285	5 169	5 719	6 033	6 504	13 992
of which:								
Life	2 104	2 323	2 542	2 608	2 790	2 707	2 849	2 946
Domestic undertakings	2 104	2 323	2 542	2 608	2 790	2 707	2 849	2 946
Foreign controlled undertakings	565	53	61	56	54	55	51	51
Foreign companies (branches)	..	..	..	..	..	..	..	..
All undertakings	2 104	2 323	2 542	2 608	2 790	2 707	2 849	2 946
Non-life	2 445	2 373	2 502	2 561	2 721	2 785	3 002	3 185
Domestic undertakings	2 445	2 373	2 502	2 561	2 721	2 785	3 002	3 185
Foreign controlled undertakings	368	208	212	220	228	220	227	239
Foreign companies (branches)	..	..	..	..	..	..	..	..
All undertakings	2 445	2 373	2 502	2 561	2 721	2 785	3 002	3 185
Total								
Domestic undertakings	5 504	5 574	5 736	5 501	6 153	6 445	6 940	14 024
Foreign controlled undertakings	1 158	260	272	276	312	304	311	325
Foreign companies (branches)	..	..	..	..	..	..	..	..
All undertakings	5 504	5 574	5 736	5 501	6 153	6 445	6 940	14 024

Table 1. Selected aggregates *(cont.)*

Million ILS

	2011	2012	2013	2014	2015	2016	2017	2018
1.5 Insurance business written abroad by branches, gross premiums								
Life								
Branches and agencies	..	..	..	..	..	..	..	..
Subsidaries	..	..	..	..	..	..	..	..
Total	..	..	..	..	..	..	..	..
Non-life								
Branches and agencies	..	..	..	..	..	..	..	..
Subsidaries	..	..	..	..	..	..	..	..
Total	..	..	..	..	..	..	..	..
Composite								
Branches and agencies	..	..	..	..	..	..	..	..
Subsidaries	..	..	..	..	..	..	..	..
Total	..	..	..	..	..	..	..	..
of which:								
Life	..	..	..	..	..	..	..	..
Branches and agencies	..	..	..	..	..	..	..	..
Subsidaries	..	..	..	..	..	..	..	..
Total	..	..	..	..	..	..	..	..
Non-life	..	..	..	..	..	..	..	..
Branches and agencies	..	..	..	..	..	..	..	..
Subsidaries	..	..	..	..	..	..	..	..
Total	..	..	..	..	..	..	..	..
Total								
Branches and agencies	..	..	..	..	..	..	..	..
Subsidaries	..	..	..	..	..	..	..	..
Total	..	..	..	..	..	..	..	..

.. Not available; c Confidential data

Note: Detailed metadata at: *http://metalinks.oecd.org/ins/20200312/294b*.

The statistical data for Israel are supplied by and under the responsibility of the relevant Israeli authorities. The use of such data by the OECD is without prejudice to the status of the Golan Heights, East Jerusalem and Israeli settlements in the West Bank under the terms of international law.

Source: OECD Insurance Statistics (database)

ISRAEL

Table 2. Number of companies and employees

	2011	2012	2013	2014	2015	2016	2017	2018
2.1 Number of companies								
Life								
Domestic undertakings	..	..	1	1	2	2	1	0
Foreign controlled undertakings	..	..	..	..	0	..	..	0
Foreign companies (branches)	..	..	..	..	0	..	..	0
All undertakings	..	..	1	1	2	2	1	0
Non-life								
Domestic undertakings	10	10	12	12	10	10	10	12
Foreign controlled undertakings	..	..	..	..	1	1	1	1
Foreign companies (branches)	..	2	2	3	3	3	3	3
All undertakings	10	12	14	15	13	13	13	15
Composite								
Domestic undertakings	13	13	10	10	11	10	10	10
Foreign controlled undertakings	2	1	1	1	1	1	1	1
Foreign companies (branches)	2	..	..	..	0	..	..	0
All undertakings	15	13	10	10	11	10	10	10
Reinsurance								
Domestic undertakings	..	..	..	..	0	..	..	0
Foreign controlled undertakings	..	..	..	..	0	..	..	0
Foreign companies (branches)	..	..	..	..	0	..	..	0
All undertakings	..	..	..	0	0	0	..	0
Total								
Domestic undertakings	23	23	23	23	23	22	21	22
Foreign controlled undertakings	2	1	1	1	2	..	2	2
Foreign companies (branches)	2	2	2	3	3	3	3	3
All undertakings	25	25	25	26	26	25	24	25
2.2 Number of employees								
Insurance undertakings	..	..	..	..	..	..	..	..
Intermediaries	..	..	..	..	..	..	..	..
Total	..	..	..	..	..	..	..	..

.. Not available

Note: Detailed metadata at: *http://metalinks.oecd.org/ins/20200312/294b.*

The statistical data for Israel are supplied by and under the responsibility of the relevant Israeli authorities. The use of such data by the OECD is without prejudice to the status of the Golan Heights, East Jerusalem and Israeli settlements in the West Bank under the terms of international law.

Source: OECD Insurance Statistics (database)

ITALY

Table 1. Selected aggregates

Million EUR

	2011	2012	2013	2014	2015	2016	2017	2018
1.1 Insurance business written in the reporting country								
1.1.1 Insurance business, by ownership								
Gross premiums								
Domestic undertakings	112 362	107 192	120 973	145 244	149 011	136 278	132 924	138 120
Foreign controlled undertakings	32 577	29 138	34 302	44 419	45 694	44 287	41 990	48 367
Foreign companies (branches)	416	399	373	375	473	521	504	565
All undertakings	112 778	107 591	121 345	145 619	149 484	136 799	133 429	138 685
Premiums ceded								
Domestic undertakings	5 043	5 178	4 513	4 203	4 079	4 914	4 939	5 213
Foreign controlled undertakings	1 166	1 392	1 116	991	983	1 822	1 829	1 867
Foreign companies (branches)	57	45	49	58	53	62	57	67
All undertakings	5 099	5 223	4 563	4 262	4 132	4 976	4 996	5 281
Net written premiums								
Domestic undertakings	107 319	102 014	116 459	141 041	144 932	131 364	127 986	132 907
Foreign controlled undertakings	31 411	27 746	33 186	43 428	44 711	42 465	40 160	46 500
Foreign companies (branches)	359	354	323	317	420	459	447	497
All undertakings	107 678	102 368	116 782	141 358	145 352	131 823	128 433	133 404
1.1.2 Insurance business on foreign risks, gross premiums								
Life	1	0	1	1	1	1	1	3
Non-life	60	50	53	59	54	59	57	72
Composite	1 608	1 935	2 044	1 904	2 016	2 070	2 037	2 008
of which:								
Life	1 213	1 327	1 232	1 073	1 166	1 255	1 252	1 215
Non-life	395	607	811	831	849	814	784	792
Total	1 670	1 984	2 098	1 963	2 071	2 130	2 095	2 082
1.1.3 Life insurance payments, by class, gross premiums								
Annuities	1 309	1 243	1 012	956	737	710	716	701
Unit linked	12 496	13 800	15 497	21 829	31 884	23 848	31 305	29 887
Other life insurance	60 064	54 597	68 501	87 639	82 220	77 596	66 709	71 545
Total life insurance	73 869	69 639	85 010	110 424	114 842	102 154	98 730	102 133
***of which:** Pension contracts*	4 116	4 296	3 825	4 873	5 492	5 848	6 308	6 631
1.1.4 Non-life insurance payments, by class, gross premiums								
Motor vehicle insurance	20 815	20 247	18 661	17 468	16 590	16 260	16 097	16 262
Marine, aviation and other transport insurance	432	366	327	334	326	417	387	288
Freight insurance	234	227	208	212	204	198	202	209
Fire and other property damage insurance	5 127	5 056	5 269	5 611	5 544	5 863	5 851	6 116
Pecuniary loss insurance	1 223	961	967	1 018	1 034	1 119	1 204	1 203
General liability insurance	2 979	2 972	2 905	2 879	2 952	3 073	3 094	3 198
Accident and health	5 306	5 151	5 144	5 221	5 415	5 868	6 200	6 471
***of which:** Health*	2 229	2 150	2 114	2 149	2 323	2 655	2 909	3 142
Other non-life insurance	944	698	1 163	988	1 082	1 217	1 293	1 373
Treaty reinsurance	275	417	0	0	0	0	0	0
Total non-life insurance	37 333	36 095	34 646	33 730	33 147	34 015	34 326	35 121
1.2 Gross claims payments								
Life								
Domestic undertakings	31 179	29 764	23 754	22 852	22 955	21 169	21 166	21 382
Foreign controlled undertakings	14 849	14 078	11 058	10 413	12 229	10 866	10 142	10 653
Foreign companies (branches)	0	0	0	0	0	0	0	0
All undertakings	31 179	29 764	23 754	22 852	22 955	21 169	21 166	21 382
Non-life								
Domestic undertakings	5 191	5 084	5 061	5 016	4 931	4 776	5 209	5 170
Foreign controlled undertakings	1 748	1 802	1 758	1 853	2 005	2 008	2 021	1 920
Foreign companies (branches)	249	257	231	257	308	369	364	357
All undertakings	5 440	5 341	5 292	5 273	5 240	5 144	5 574	5 527
Composite								
Domestic undertakings	66 523	67 451	64 138	61 204	65 892	59 690	68 163	69 576
Foreign controlled undertakings	17 536	16 282	16 899	14 972	16 842	16 097	17 146	17 740
Foreign companies (branches)	0	0	0	0	0	0	0	0
All undertakings	66 523	67 451	64 138	61 204	65 892	59 690	68 163	69 576
of which:								
Life	45 192	47 143	44 754	43 279	48 546	43 755	52 096	53 576
Domestic undertakings	45 192	47 143	44 754	43 279	48 546	43 755	52 096	53 576
Foreign controlled undertakings	12 633	11 858	12 685	11 217	12 693	12 061	13 358	13 790
Foreign companies (branches)	0	0	0	0	0	0	0	0
All undertakings	45 192	47 143	44 754	43 279	48 546	43 755	52 096	53 576
Non-life	21 330	20 308	19 384	17 925	17 346	15 935	16 067	16 000
Domestic undertakings	21 330	20 308	19 384	17 925	17 346	15 935	16 067	16 000
Foreign controlled undertakings	4 903	4 424	4 215	3 754	4 149	4 037	3 788	3 950
Foreign companies (branches)	0	0	0	0	0	0	0	0
All undertakings	21 330	20 308	19 384	17 925	17 346	15 935	16 067	16 000
Total								
Domestic undertakings	102 893	102 298	92 953	89 071	93 778	85 635	94 539	96 128
Foreign controlled undertakings	34 132	32 162	29 715	27 238	31 075	28 972	29 309	30 313
Foreign companies (branches)	249	257	231	257	308	369	364	357
All undertakings	103 141	102 555	93 185	89 328	94 087	86 003	94 904	96 485

ITALY

Table 1. Selected aggregates *(cont.)*

Million EUR

	2011	2012	2013	2014	2015	2016	2017	2018
1.3 Commissions								
Life								
Domestic undertakings	727	601	576	650	641	626	620	590
Foreign controlled undertakings	532	405	384	430	436	449	434	432
Foreign companies (branches)	0	0	0	0	0	0	0	..
All undertakings	727	601	576	650	641	626	620	590
Non-life								
Domestic undertakings	1 721	1 620	1 576	1 656	1 706	1 748	1 829	1 915
Foreign controlled undertakings	629	560	548	608	734	767	752	777
Foreign companies (branches)	82	78	73	72	93	107	108	123
All undertakings	1 803	1 698	1 649	1 729	1 799	1 855	1 937	2 038
Composite								
Domestic undertakings	7 516	7 101	7 278	7 573	7 699	7 571	7 600	7 673
Foreign controlled undertakings	1 916	1 778	1 830	1 978	2 106	2 006	2 073	2 139
Foreign companies (branches)	0	0	0	0	0	0	0	..
All undertakings	7 516	7 101	7 278	7 573	7 699	7 571	7 600	7 673
of which:								
Life	2 187	1 868	2 088	2 273	2 447	2 306	2 317	2 300
Domestic undertakings	2 187	1 868	2 088	2 273	2 447	2 306	2 317	2 300
Foreign controlled undertakings	560	413	450	510	542	504	550	608
Foreign companies (branches)	0	0	0	0	0	0	0	..
All undertakings	2 187	1 868	2 088	2 273	2 447	2 306	2 317	2 300
Non-life	5 329	5 232	5 190	5 300	5 251	5 265	5 283	5 372
Domestic undertakings	5 329	5 232	5 190	5 300	5 251	5 265	5 283	5 372
Foreign controlled undertakings	1 356	1 366	1 380	1 468	1 564	1 502	1 523	1 531
Foreign companies (branches)	0	0	0	0	0	0	0	..
All undertakings	5 329	5 232	5 190	5 300	5 251	5 265	5 283	5 372
Total								
Domestic undertakings	9 964	9 322	9 431	9 879	10 046	9 945	10 049	10 177
Foreign controlled undertakings	3 078	2 743	2 763	3 015	3 277	3 222	3 259	3 349
Foreign companies (branches)	82	78	73	72	93	107	108	123
All undertakings	10 046	9 399	9 504	9 952	10 139	10 052	10 157	10 300
1.4 Gross operating expenses								
Life								
Domestic undertakings	1 033	912	876	953	948	963	970	925
Foreign controlled undertakings	734	600	570	622	634	673	658	649
Foreign companies (branches)	0	0	0	0	0	0	0	..
All undertakings	1 033	912	876	953	948	963	970	925
Non-life								
Domestic undertakings	2 324	2 168	2 154	2 252	2 332	2 390	2 501	2 634
Foreign controlled undertakings	873	750	794	818	968	1 012	992	1 022
Foreign companies (branches)	119	115	112	110	144	176	174	183
All undertakings	2 442	2 283	2 266	2 362	2 476	2 565	2 676	2 817
Composite								
Domestic undertakings	9 381	9 321	9 490	9 686	9 829	9 860	9 929	10 069
Foreign controlled undertakings	2 363	2 304	2 294	2 443	2 632	2 566	2 658	2 742
Foreign companies (branches)	0	0	0	0	0	0	0	..
All undertakings	9 381	9 321	9 490	9 686	9 829	9 860	9 929	10 069
of which:								
Life	2 867	2 788	2 970	3 109	3 292	3 196	3 223	3 244
Domestic undertakings	2 867	2 788	2 970	3 109	3 292	3 196	3 223	3 244
Foreign controlled undertakings	724	635	628	696	743	708	773	833
Foreign companies (branches)	0	0	0	0	0	0	0	..
All undertakings	2 867	2 788	2 970	3 109	3 292	3 196	3 223	3 244
Non-life	6 514	6 532	6 520	6 577	6 537	6 664	6 706	6 825
Domestic undertakings	6 514	6 532	6 520	6 577	6 537	6 664	6 706	6 825
Foreign controlled undertakings	1 639	1 669	1 667	1 747	1 889	1 858	1 885	1 909
Foreign companies (branches)	0	0	0	0	0	0	0	..
All undertakings	6 514	6 532	6 520	6 577	6 537	6 664	6 706	6 825
Total								
Domestic undertakings	12 737	12 401	12 520	12 891	13 109	13 213	13 400	13 629
Foreign controlled undertakings	3 971	3 653	3 658	3 883	4 234	4 251	4 307	4 413
Foreign companies (branches)	119	115	112	110	144	176	174	183
All undertakings	12 856	12 516	12 633	13 001	13 253	13 388	13 574	13 812

Table 1. Selected aggregates *(cont.)*

Million EUR

	2011	2012	2013	2014	2015	2016	2017	2018
1.5 Insurance business written abroad by branches, gross premiums								
Life								
Branches and agencies	0	0	0	1	1	3	1	2
Subsidaries	1 938	2 813	3 333	3 469	4 224	1 339	1 712	1 403
Total	1 938	2 813	3 333	3 469	4 226	1 342	1 713	1 404
Non-life								
Branches and agencies	24	9	12	12	9	10	13	7
Subsidaries	0	0	0	0	0	0	0	..
Total	24	9	12	12	9	10	13	7
Composite								
Branches and agencies	717	762	823	892	868	1 376	1 114	1 138
Subsidaries	56 657	57 155	56 340	54 902	58 541	57 863	60 367	56 485
Total	57 375	57 917	57 163	55 795	59 409	59 239	61 482	57 623
of which:								
Life	38 781	39 265	39 445	39 878	42 059	41 554	43 469	40 058
Branches and agencies	106	127	154	175	235	477	215	208
Subsidaries	38 675	39 138	39 291	39 703	41 824	41 077	43 254	39 850
Total	38 781	39 265	39 445	39 878	42 059	41 554	43 469	40 058
Non-life	18 593	18 652	17 718	15 917	17 350	17 685	18 012	17 565
Branches and agencies	611	634	668	718	633	899	899	930
Subsidaries	17 982	18 018	17 049	15 199	16 717	16 785	17 113	16 635
Total	18 593	18 652	17 718	15 917	17 350	17 685	18 012	17 565
Total								
Branches and agencies	741	771	835	905	878	1 390	1 128	1 147
Subsidaries	58 596	59 968	59 673	58 371	62 765	59 202	62 079	57 887
Total	59 337	60 739	60 508	59 276	63 643	60 592	63 207	59 034

.. Not available
Note: Detailed metadata at: *http://metalinks.oecd.org/ins/20200312/a0b5*.
Source: OECD Insurance Statistics (database)

ITALY

Table 2. Number of companies and employees

	2011	2012	2013	2014	2015	2016	2017	2018
2.1 Number of companies								
Life								
Domestic undertakings	43	41	41	38	35	32	30	26
Foreign controlled undertakings	24	23	23	20	19	17	13	11
Foreign companies (branches)	21	20	17	19	20	22	19	20
All undertakings	64	61	58	57	55	54	49	46
Non-life								
Domestic undertakings	71	69	67	63	58	54	50	51
Foreign controlled undertakings	24	21	20	18	19	18	16	16
Foreign companies (branches)	59	61	65	60	65	65	73	81
All undertakings	130	130	132	123	123	119	123	132
Composite								
Domestic undertakings	28	25	23	21	21	21	20	20
Foreign controlled undertakings	11	9	8	8	9	10	9	9
Foreign companies (branches)	9	12	13	14	14	13	14	13
All undertakings	37	37	36	35	35	34	34	33
Reinsurance								
Domestic undertakings	0	0	0	0	0	0	0	..
Foreign controlled undertakings	0	0	0	0	0	0	0	..
Foreign companies (branches)	8	7	7	7	7	7	7	7
All undertakings	8	7	7	7	7	7	7	7
Total								
Domestic undertakings	142	135	131	122	114	107	100	97
Foreign controlled undertakings	59	53	51	46	47	45	38	36
Foreign companies (branches)	97	100	102	100	106	107	113	121
All undertakings	239	235	233	222	220	214	213	218
2.2 Number of employees								
Insurance undertakings	40 817	40 798	39 887	40 259	40 588	40 872	40 386	40 028
Intermediaries	226 235	220 130	227 444	220 288	220 850	212 596	..	..
Total	267 052	260 928	267 331	260 547	261 438	253 468	..	..

.. Not available

Note: Detailed metadata at: *http://metalinks.oecd.org/ins/20200312/a0b5.*

Source: OECD Insurance Statistics (database)

Table 1. Selected aggregates

Million JPY

	2011	2012	2013	2014	2015	2016	2017	2018
1.1 Insurance business written in the reporting country								
1.1.1 Insurance business, by ownership								
Gross premiums								
Domestic undertakings	41 906 428	44 184 695	42 971 395	46 031 579	46 908 456	42 615 488	41 452 663	44 740 881
Foreign controlled undertakings	4 089 357	6 746 278	6 184 716	6 724 592	7 046 820	6 617 836	6 432 494	8 315 056
Foreign companies (branches)	4 051 225	2 028 538	1 699 621	1 548 143	1 537 624	1 703 444	1 739 958	348 167
All undertakings	45 360 413	37 140 563	34 738 150	37 222 352	37 748 110	44 318 932	43 192 621	45 089 048
Premiums ceded								
Domestic undertakings	2 596 877	3 820 152	3 823 919	4 207 229	4 127 260	4 449 638	4 176 204	4 817 685
Foreign controlled undertakings	1 012 341	2 083 368	1 802 239	2 084 233	1 890 218	2 143 727	1 733 566	2 285 450
Foreign companies (branches)	554 339	20 507	38 391	47 768	75 917	214 477	239 041	223 967
All undertakings	3 041 779	2 188 965	1 780 848	2 129 106	2 022 086	4 664 115	4 415 245	5 041 652
Net written premiums								
Domestic undertakings	39 309 551	40 364 544	39 147 476	41 824 350	42 781 196	38 165 836	37 276 448	39 923 181
Foreign controlled undertakings	3 077 014	4 662 910	4 382 477	4 640 359	5 156 602	4 474 105	4 698 925	6 029 602
Foreign companies (branches)	3 500 605	2 008 031	1 661 230	1 500 375	1 461 707	1 488 976	1 499 865	124 190
All undertakings	42 322 354	34 951 598	32 957 302	35 093 246	35 726 024	39 654 812	38 776 313	40 047 371
1.1.2 Insurance business on foreign risks, gross premiums								
Life	..	..	..	..	..	..	..	..
Non-life	..	..	..	..	..	..	..	..
Composite total	..	..	..	..	..	..	..	..
Total	..	..	..	..	..	..	..	..
1.1.3 Life insurance payments, by class, gross premiums								
Annuities	..	4 374 166	4 312 468	5 154 122	4 729 892	4 340 846	3 607 407	3 875 104
Unit linked	..	..	..	..	..	..	..	..
Other life insurance	..	29 076 673	27 864 772	30 015 418	31 464 495	27 968 949	27 990 703	29 370 822
Total life insurance	35 863 385	33 450 839	32 177 240	35 169 540	36 194 387	32 309 795	31 598 110	33 245 926
***of which:** Pension contracts*	..	3 683 892	3 851 878	4 175 622	4 562 867	3 057 696	2 953 431	2 861 906
1.1.4 Non-life insurance payments, by class, gross premiums								
Motor vehicle insurance	3 650 671	5 268 338	5 632 807	5 786 949	5 916 489	6 026 253	5 814 388	5 905 312
Marine, aviation and other transport insurance	305 977	149 531	170 502	170 115	186 542	159 142	152 632	150 286
Freight insurance	67 288	217 090	242 939	248 817	242 488	230 397	239 546	253 139
Fire and other property damage insurance	1 762 054	1 787 943	1 983 049	2 104 111	2 228 178	..	..	..
Pecuniary loss insurance	..	216 797	266 835	299 082	342 570	..	..	..
General liability insurance	535 395	519 985	584 318	598 945	615 167	633 290	657 637	692 945
Accident and health	1 262 653	780 078	897 507	979 477	982 614	..	..	..
***of which:** Health*	..	-216	76	214	-152	..	..	..
Other non-life insurance	2 096 987	132 908	154 909	169 874	183 922	..	..	..
Treaty reinsurance	..	..	..	..	..	..	..	..
Total non-life insurance	9 730 581	9 072 670	9 932 866	10 357 370	10 697 970	10 859 799	10 750 127	11 173 102
1.2 Gross claims payments								
Life								
Domestic undertakings	29 178 265	31 012 138	33 069 327	34 214 304	31 685 988	28 227 418	28 115 903	28 748 864
Foreign controlled undertakings	2 738 842	5 218 820	6 584 738	6 428 288	5 559 928	5 107 453	5 198 975	5 980 013
Foreign companies (branches)	1 583 330	673 623	709 471	738 243	768 206	786 644	827 193	37 839
All undertakings	30 761 595	31 685 761	33 778 798	34 952 547	32 454 194	29 014 062	28 943 096	28 786 703
Non-life								
Domestic undertakings	9 249 885	6 215 207	5 904 278	5 953 809	5 917 050	6 694 135	5 856 017	7 585 094
Foreign controlled undertakings	400 264	251 245	341 353	373 601	366 795	383 518	237 359	480 088
Foreign companies (branches)	366 743	..	..	..	..	104 648	98 935	222 146
All undertakings	9 616 628	..	..	..	..	6 798 783	5 954 952	7 807 240
Composite, all undertakings	..	..	..	..	..	..	..	..
Total								
Domestic undertakings	38 428 150	37 227 345	38 973 605	40 168 113	37 603 038	34 921 553	33 971 920	36 333 958
Foreign controlled undertakings	3 139 106	5 470 065	6 926 091	6 801 889	5 926 723	5 490 971	5 436 334	6 460 101
Foreign companies (branches)	1 950 073	673 623	709 471	738 243	768 206	891 292	926 128	259 985
All undertakings	40 378 223	31 685 761	33 778 798	34 952 547	32 454 194	35 812 845	34 898 048	36 593 943
1.3 Commissions								
Life								
Domestic undertakings	..	..	..	..	..	..	..	..
Foreign controlled undertakings	..	..	..	..	..	..	..	..
Foreign companies (branches)	..	..	..	..	..	..	..	..
All undertakings	..	..	..	..	..	..	..	..
Non-life								
Domestic undertakings	1 241 891	1 141 653	1 149 357	1 229 205	1 273 631	1 240 454	1 221 324	1 241 826
Foreign controlled undertakings	71 775	48 003	25 883	33 975	37 223	20 067	-15 311	-19 855
Foreign companies (branches)	67 079	..	..	..	..	-19 897	-29 330	-33 799
All undertakings	1 308 970	..	..	..	..	1 220 557	1 191 994	1 208 027
Composite, all undertakings	..	..	..	..	..	..	..	..
Total								
Domestic undertakings	1 241 891	1 141 653	1 149 357	1 229 205	1 273 631	1 240 454	1 221 324	1 241 826
Foreign controlled undertakings	71 775	48 003	25 883	33 975	37 223	20 067	-15 311	-19 855
Foreign companies (branches)	67 079	..	..	..	..	-19 897	-29 330	-33 799
All undertakings	1 308 970	..	..	..	..	1 220 557	1 191 994	1 208 027

Table 1. Selected aggregates *(cont.)*

Million JPY

	2011	2012	2013	2014	2015	2016	2017	2018
1.4 Gross operating expenses								
Life								
Domestic undertakings	3 679 493	4 030 195	4 068 896	4 178 568	4 356 425	4 369 595	4 385 030	4 856 591
Foreign controlled undertakings	494 700	838 416	862 622	893 811	945 921	948 132	965 055	1 353 249
Foreign companies (branches)	565 754	319 261	320 576	320 518	349 858	357 069	366 406	22 814
All undertakings	4 245 247	4 349 456	4 389 472	4 499 086	4 706 283	4 726 664	4 751 436	4 879 405
Non-life								
Domestic undertakings	1 688 096	1 229 758	3 034 716	3 189 416	3 275 358	3 247 478	3 206 606	3 318 518
Foreign controlled undertakings	85 470	69 136	176 725	238 092	249 835	207 689	125 459	185 822
Foreign companies (branches)	124 057	..	..	..	..	34 405	37 023	34 772
All undertakings	1 812 153	..	..	..	..	3 281 883	3 243 629	3 353 290
Composite, all undertakings	..	..	..	..	..	..	..	..
Total								
Domestic undertakings	5 367 589	5 259 953	7 103 612	7 367 984	7 631 783	7 617 073	7 591 636	8 175 109
Foreign controlled undertakings	580 170	907 552	1 039 347	1 131 903	1 195 756	1 155 821	1 090 514	1 539 071
Foreign companies (branches)	689 811	319 261	320 576	320 518	349 858	391 474	403 429	57 586
All undertakings	6 057 400	4 349 456	4 389 472	4 499 086	4 706 283	8 008 547	7 995 065	8 232 695
1.5 Insurance business written abroad by branches, gross premiums								
Life								
Branches and agencies	..	..	..	..	..	..	..	..
Subsidaries	..	..	..	..	..	..	..	..
Total	..	..	..	..	..	..	..	..
Non-life								
Branches and agencies	..	..	..	..	..	..	..	..
Subsidaries	..	..	..	..	..	..	..	..
Total	..	..	..	..	..	..	..	..
Composite total	..	..	..	..	..	..	..	..
Total								
Branches and agencies	..	..	..	..	..	..	..	..
Subsidaries	..	..	..	..	..	..	..	..
Total	..	..	..	..	..	..	..	..

.. Not available

Note: Detailed metadata at: *http://metalinks.oecd.org/ins/20200312/eab3.*

Source: OECD Insurance Statistics (database)

JAPAN

Table 2. Number of companies and employees

	2011	2012	2013	2014	2015	2016	2017	2018
2.1 Number of companies								
Life								
Domestic undertakings	39	40	40	39	38	38	38	40
Foreign controlled undertakings	14	15	15	13	13	13	13	14
Foreign companies (branches)	4	3	3	3	3	3	3	1
All undertakings	43	43	43	42	41	41	41	41
Non-life								
Domestic undertakings	29	30	30	30	30	30	29	30
Foreign controlled undertakings	5	5	6	7	7	7	6	7
Foreign companies (branches)	23	23	22	22	22	21	23	21
All undertakings	52	53	52	52	52	51	52	51
Composite, all undertakings	**0**	**0**	**0**	**0**	**0**	**0**	..	..
Reinsurance								
Domestic undertakings	2	..	..	..	..	..	..	..
Foreign controlled undertakings	0	..	..	..	..	..	..	..
Foreign companies (branches)	5	..	..	..	..	..	..	..
All undertakings	7	..	..	..	..	..	..	..
Total								
Domestic undertakings	..	..	..	..	68	68	67	70
Foreign controlled undertakings	..	..	..	..	20	20	19	21
Foreign companies (branches)	..	..	..	..	25	24	26	22
All undertakings	..	..	..	..	93	92	93	92
2.2 Number of employees								
Insurance undertakings	..	447 435	221 675	226 043	120 353	..	..	..
Intermediaries	..	..	2 283 335	2 293 863	2 059 743	..	..	..
Total	..	..	2 505 010	2 519 906	2 080 096	..	345 582	..

.. Not available

Note: Detailed metadata at: *http://metalinks.oecd.org/ins/20200312/eab3.*

Source: OECD Insurance Statistics (database)

KOREA

Table 1. Selected aggregates

Million KRW

	2011	2012	2013	2014	2015	2016	2017	2018
1.1 Insurance business written in the reporting country								
1.1.1 Insurance business, by ownership								
Gross premiums								
Domestic undertakings	148 670 607	179 792 881	180 479 019	192 380 611	205 460 047	210 800 275	209 464 937	206 866 894
Foreign controlled undertakings	15 090 753	16 543 211	15 928 630	13 324 532	15 765 302	16 670 208	17 513 911	14 930 441
Foreign companies (branches)	4 083 506	3 894 692	4 755 050	4 594 745	2 267 929	4 629 847	4 849 409	5 320 101
All undertakings	152 754 113	183 687 573	185 234 069	196 975 356	207 727 976	215 430 122	214 314 346	212 186 995
Premiums ceded								
Domestic undertakings	7 618 035	8 770 133	9 411 425	9 694 294	10 255 858	10 505 959	11 215 981	11 733 647
Foreign controlled undertakings	322 429	581 696	538 227	478 174	638 961	599 183	611 390	584 975
Foreign companies (branches)	614 890	448 135	456 049	651 726	732 347	817 712	990 510	1 035 820
All undertakings	8 232 925	9 218 268	9 867 474	10 346 020	10 988 205	11 323 671	12 206 491	12 769 467
Net written premiums								
Domestic undertakings	141 052 572	171 022 748	171 067 594	182 686 317	195 204 189	200 294 316	198 248 956	195 133 247
Foreign controlled undertakings	14 768 324	15 961 515	15 390 403	12 846 358	15 126 341	16 071 025	16 902 521	14 345 466
Foreign companies (branches)	3 468 616	3 446 557	4 299 001	3 943 019	1 535 582	3 812 135	3 858 899	4 284 281
All undertakings	144 521 188	174 469 305	175 366 595	186 629 336	196 739 771	204 106 451	202 107 855	199 417 528
1.1.2 Insurance business on foreign risks, gross premiums								
Life	..	..	..	..	..	..	..	..
Non-life	..	..	..	..	..	..	..	..
Composite total	..	..	..	..	..	..	..	..
Total	..	..	..	..	..	..	..	..
1.1.3 Life insurance payments, by class, gross premiums								
Annuities	17 029 899	29 118 668	25 867 249	23 905 884	24 586 649	21 347 503	19 558 128	17 605 227
Unit linked	21 278 374	21 003 522	21 073 957	20 670 949	20 643 073	19 406 180	19 623 687	18 834 528
Other life insurance	48 349 089	57 004 710	61 618 265	65 998 453	71 983 930	79 057 566	74 791 666	74 403 374
Total life insurance	86 657 362	107 126 900	108 559 471	110 575 286	117 213 652	119 811 249	113 973 481	110 843 129
***of which:** Pension contracts*	7 039 411	6 187 541	8 103 216	11 817 288	13 694 337	16 718 996	14 905 838	16 869 826
1.1.4 Non-life insurance payments, by class, gross premiums								
Motor vehicle insurance	13 714 894	13 667 642	13 692 186	14 188 378	15 635 198	16 975 333	17 426 917	17 276 192
Marine, aviation and other transport insurance	1 173 162	1 249 845	1 062 919	1 006 367	971 854	854 536	917 229	832 470
Freight insurance	..	..	0	0	..	..	..	..
Fire and other property damage insurance	433 977	509 590	515 217	484 799	472 624	471 017	428 560	373 175
Pecuniary loss insurance	1 551 994	1 697 064	1 637 782	1 601 517	1 672 799	1 693 861	1 858 689	2 133 544
General liability insurance	828 088	870 395	947 583	910 341	967 362	1 100 438	1 182 101	1 233 606
Accident and health	16 518 450	18 558 162	49 501 658	24 196 315	39 104 233	30 297 640	33 024 528	36 093 627
***of which:** Health*	6 537 864	7 171 480	83 983	10 090 810	11 740 294	13 406 917	14 799 985	16 444 106
Other non-life insurance	30 630 990	38 774 054	8 105 434	32 685 216	30 357 048	42 702 138	43 864 781	41 435 506
Treaty reinsurance	..	..	0	0	..	..	..	..
Total non-life insurance	64 851 555	75 326 752	75 462 779	85 163 744	89 181 118	94 094 963	98 702 805	99 378 120
1.2 Gross claims payments								
Life								
Domestic undertakings	50 774 694	50 571 293	51 098 146	61 070 702	65 751 692	77 155 805	78 055 802	77 155 805
Foreign controlled undertakings	7 803 732	7 981 965	8 103 569	69 035 817	6 945 034	9 505 582	10 803 105	9 505 582
Foreign companies (branches)	1 295 108	1 251 467	1 252 924	1 292 842	1 333 124	1 410 493	1 457 100	1 410 493
All undertakings	52 069 802	51 822 760	52 351 070	62 363 544	67 084 816	78 566 298	79 512 902	78 566 298
Non-life								
Domestic undertakings	23 980 095	26 319 367	22 119 519	30 233 735	30 895 053	32 747 964	35 060 020	40 091 995
Foreign controlled undertakings	620 798	833 963	516 770	844 722	843 763	802 729	767 651	824 571
Foreign companies (branches)	919 952	914 946	7 033 799	1 098 087	1 264 227	1 282 459	1 285 551	1 554 862
All undertakings	24 900 047	27 234 313	29 153 318	31 331 823	32 159 280	34 030 423	36 345 571	41 646 857
Composite, all undertakings	..	..	..	..	..	..	..	..
Total								
Domestic undertakings	74 754 789	76 890 660	73 217 665	91 304 438	96 646 745	109 903 769	113 115 822	117 247 800
Foreign controlled undertakings	8 424 530	8 815 928	8 620 339	69 880 539	7 788 797	10 308 311	11 570 756	10 330 153
Foreign companies (branches)	2 215 060	2 166 413	8 286 723	2 390 929	2 597 351	2 692 952	2 742 651	2 965 355
All undertakings	76 969 849	79 057 073	81 504 388	93 695 367	99 244 096	112 596 721	115 858 473	120 213 155
1.3 Commissions								
Life								
Domestic undertakings	..	..	..	..	..	..	..	..
Foreign controlled undertakings	..	..	..	..	..	..	..	..
Foreign companies (branches)	..	..	..	..	..	..	..	..
All undertakings	..	..	..	..	..	..	..	..
Non-life								
Domestic undertakings	..	..	..	..	..	..	..	..
Foreign controlled undertakings	..	..	..	..	..	..	..	..
Foreign companies (branches)	..	..	..	..	..	..	..	..
All undertakings	..	..	..	..	..	..	..	..
Composite, all undertakings	..	..	..	..	..	..	..	..
Total								
Domestic undertakings	..	..	..	..	..	..	..	..
Foreign controlled undertakings	..	..	..	..	..	..	..	..
Foreign companies (branches)	..	..	..	..	..	..	..	..
All undertakings	..	..	..	..	..	..	..	..

Table 1. Selected aggregates *(cont.)*

Million KRW

	2011	2012	2013	2014	2015	2016	2017	2018
1.4 Gross operating expenses								
Life								
Domestic undertakings	27 793 931	23 307 641	25 608 456	27 511 983	28 987 407	28 236 989	28 574 504	36 539 562
Foreign controlled undertakings	7 229 266	5 189 114	5 278 175	806 034	756 903	5 074 779	5 675 330	5 878 573
Foreign companies (branches)	1 024 103	734 416	770 753	4 595 483	5 009 714	760 976	619 584	790 806
All undertakings	28 818 034	24 042 057	26 379 209	32 107 466	33 997 121	28 997 965	29 194 088	37 330 368
Non-life								
Domestic undertakings	9 820 687	11 569 785	11 294 192	16 760 436	13 511 865	14 238 364	15 685 551	16 637 805
Foreign controlled undertakings	121 666	320 770	129 781	245 017	182 669	163 724	225 860	254 141
Foreign companies (branches)	428 369	331 833	1 592 503	1 116 586	405 386	411 714	434 676	510 688
All undertakings	10 249 056	11 901 618	12 886 695	17 877 022	13 917 251	14 650 078	16 120 227	17 148 493
Composite, all undertakings	..	..	..	..	..	..	..	..
Total								
Domestic undertakings	37 614 618	34 877 426	36 902 648	44 272 419	42 499 272	42 475 353	44 260 055	53 177 367
Foreign controlled undertakings	7 350 932	5 509 884	5 407 956	1 051 051	939 572	5 238 503	5 901 190	6 132 714
Foreign companies (branches)	1 452 472	1 066 249	2 363 256	5 712 069	5 415 100	1 172 690	1 054 260	1 301 494
All undertakings	39 067 090	35 943 675	39 265 904	49 984 488	47 914 372	43 648 043	45 314 315	54 478 861
1.5 Insurance business written abroad by branches, gross premiums								
Life								
Branches and agencies	..	..	..	..	..	..	..	..
Subsidaries	..	..	..	..	..	..	..	..
Total	..	..	..	..	..	..	..	..
Non-life								
Branches and agencies	..	..	..	..	..	..	..	..
Subsidaries	..	..	..	..	..	..	..	..
Total	..	..	..	..	..	..	..	..
Composite total	..	..	..	..	..	..	..	..
Total								
Branches and agencies	..	..	..	..	..	..	..	..
Subsidaries	..	..	..	..	..	..	..	..
Total	..	..	..	..	..	..	..	..

.. Not available

Note: Detailed metadata at: *http://metalinks.oecd.org/ins/20200312/281a*.

Source: OECD Insurance Statistics (database)

KOREA

Table 2. Number of companies and employees

	2011	2012	2013	2014	2015	2016	2017	2018
2.1 Number of companies								
Life								
Domestic undertakings	22	23	24	24	24	24	24	24
Foreign controlled undertakings	8	8	8	7	7	8	8	8
Foreign companies (branches)	1	1	1	1	1	1	1	1
All undertakings	23	24	25	25	25	25	25	25
Non-life								
Domestic undertakings	15	16	16	17	17	17	18	17
Foreign controlled undertakings	6	6	3	4	4	4	5	4
Foreign companies (branches)	8	8	8	5	5	5	6	5
All undertakings	23	24	24	22	22	22	24	22
Composite, all undertakings	**0**	**0**	**0**	**0**	**0**	**0**	..	..
Reinsurance								
Domestic undertakings	1	1	1	1	1	1	1	1
Foreign controlled undertakings	0	..	..	0	0	0	0	0
Foreign companies (branches)	6	6	6	8	8	9	9	9
All undertakings	7	7	7	9	9	10	10	10
Total								
Domestic undertakings	38	40	41	42	42	42	43	42
Foreign controlled undertakings	14	14	11	11	11	12	13	12
Foreign companies (branches)	15	15	15	14	14	15	16	15
All undertakings	53	55	56	56	56	57	59	57
2.2 Number of employees								
Insurance undertakings	57 861	62 155	63 859	61 158	59 685	58 833	57 854	58 833
Intermediaries	278 594	288 362	280 087	245 127	235 319	229 292	222 411	229 292
Total	336 455	350 517	343 946	306 285	295 004	288 125	280 265	288 125

.. Not available

Note: Detailed metadata at: *http://metalinks.oecd.org/ins/20200312/281a.*

Source: OECD Insurance Statistics (database)

Table 1. Selected aggregates

Million EUR

	2011	2012	2013	2014	2015	2016	2017	2018
1.1 Insurance business written in the reporting country								
1.1.1 Insurance business, by ownership								
Gross premiums								
Domestic undertakings	326	354	350	371	379	364	419	489
Foreign controlled undertakings	137	155	150	151	188	267	293	352
Foreign companies (branches)	73	93	121	146	152	168	227	267
All undertakings	399	447	471	517	531	532	646	756
Premiums ceded								
Domestic undertakings	24	26	17	19	22	25	44	77
Foreign controlled undertakings	6	5	4	4	7	18	27	54
Foreign companies (branches)	..	..	..	..	..	..	..	..
All undertakings	24	26	17	19	22	25	44	77
Net written premiums								
Domestic undertakings	302	328	333	352	357	339	375	412
Foreign controlled undertakings	131	150	146	147	182	249	266	298
Foreign companies (branches)	73	93	121	146	152	168	227	267
All undertakings	375	421	454	498	509	507	602	679
1.1.2 Insurance business on foreign risks, gross premiums								
Life	..	..	..	..	..	0	0	..
Non-life	..	..	..	..	..	160	204	234
Composite	..	..	..	..	..	0	0	0
of which:								
Life	..	..	..	..	..	0	0	0
Non-life	..	..	..	..	..	..	0	..
Total	..	..	..	..	..	160	204	234
1.1.3 Life insurance payments, by class, gross premiums								
Annuities	0	0	0	0	0	11	18	25
Unit linked	23	21	23	34	43	45	57	55
Other life insurance	50	57	66	73	72	68	70	65
Total life insurance	74	79	89	107	115	124	145	145
***of which:** Pension contracts*	0	0	0	0	0	..	..	..
1.1.4 Non-life insurance payments, by class, gross premiums								
Motor vehicle insurance	184	204	221	222	221	229	301	381
Marine, aviation and other transport insurance	3	3	2	2	2	2	5	4
Freight insurance	5	6	5	3	3	3	1	3
Fire and other property damage insurance	55	63	67	86	84	76	84	90
Pecuniary loss insurance	12	12	11	13	14	12	11	16
General liability insurance	15	21	17	21	21	19	19	21
Accident and health	41	50	46	52	58	55	63	78
***of which:** Health*	34	42	38	42	48	45	54	64
Other non-life insurance	9	10	12	12	13	13	16	18
Treaty reinsurance	0	0	0	0	0	0	0	0
Total non-life insurance	325	368	382	411	416	409	501	611
1.2 Gross claims payments								
Life								
Domestic undertakings	15	19	31	26	29	0	0	..
Foreign controlled undertakings	15	18	26	24	27	0	0	0
Foreign companies (branches)	26	27	31	31	34	0	0	..
All undertakings	41	46	62	57	63	0	0	..
Non-life								
Domestic undertakings	164	169	165	184	198	180	193	229
Foreign controlled undertakings	78	75	68	77	92	139	126	170
Foreign companies (branches)	18	25	38	43	50	60	78	86
All undertakings	182	194	204	226	248	240	271	315
Composite								
Domestic undertakings	..	..	..	..	..	33	43	43
Foreign controlled undertakings	..	..	..	..	..	27	31	34
Foreign companies (branches)	..	..	..	..	..	40	47	48
All undertakings	..	..	..	..	..	72	90	91
of which:								
Life	..	..	..	..	..	72	90	91
Domestic undertakings	..	..	..	..	..	33	43	43
Foreign controlled undertakings	..	..	..	..	..	27	31	34
Foreign companies (branches)	..	..	..	..	..	40	47	48
All undertakings	..	..	..	..	..	72	90	91
Non-life	..	..	..	..	..	..	0	..
Domestic undertakings	..	..	..	..	..	..	0	..
Foreign controlled undertakings	..	..	..	..	..	..	0	..
Foreign companies (branches)	..	..	..	..	..	..	0	..
All undertakings	..	..	..	..	..	..	0	..
Total								
Domestic undertakings	179	188	196	209	227	213	236	272
Foreign controlled undertakings	92	93	94	102	119	166	158	203
Foreign companies (branches)	44	52	69	73	83	99	125	134
All undertakings	223	240	265	283	311	312	361	406

Table 1. Selected aggregates *(cont.)*

Million EUR

	2011	2012	2013	2014	2015	2016	2017	2018
1.3 Commissions								
Life								
Domestic undertakings	0	1	1	1	0	0	0	0
Foreign controlled undertakings	0	1	1	1	1	0	0	0
Foreign companies (branches)	4	4	5	5	6	..	..	..
All undertakings	4	5	5	6	6	0	0	0
Non-life								
Domestic undertakings	33	38	32	45	34	32	40	65
Foreign controlled undertakings	2	5	..	7	11	16	13	37
Foreign companies (branches)	2	4	10	12	13	..	..	..
All undertakings	35	41	42	58	47	32	40	65
Composite								
Domestic undertakings	..	..	..	..	..	0	1	1
Foreign controlled undertakings	..	..	..	..	..	0	0	1
Foreign companies (branches)	..	..	..	..	..	..	..	..
All undertakings	..	..	..	..	..	0	1	1
of which:								
Life	..	..	..	..	..	0	1	1
Domestic undertakings	..	..	..	..	..	0	1	1
Foreign controlled undertakings	..	..	..	..	..	0	0	1
Foreign companies (branches)	..	..	..	..	..	..	..	..
All undertakings	..	..	..	..	..	0	1	1
Non-life	..	..	..	..	..	..	0	..
Domestic undertakings	..	..	..	..	..	..	0	..
Foreign controlled undertakings	..	..	..	..	..	..	0	..
Foreign companies (branches)	..	..	..	..	..	..	..	..
All undertakings	..	..	..	..	..	..	0	..
Total								
Domestic undertakings	33	38	33	46	34	33	41	65
Foreign controlled undertakings	2	6	1	8	11	16	14	37
Foreign companies (branches)	6	8	15	17	19	..	..	..
All undertakings	39	46	48	64	53	33	41	65
1.4 Gross operating expenses								
Life								
Domestic undertakings	5	4	4	4	4	0	0	0
Foreign controlled undertakings	4	4	4	4	4	0	0	0
Foreign companies (branches)	..	..	..	..	..	..	..	..
All undertakings	5	4	4	4	4	0	0	0
Non-life								
Domestic undertakings	100	110	102	108	109	56	87	119
Foreign controlled undertakings	43	45	40	40	51	30	51	81
Foreign companies (branches)	..	..	..	..	..	..	..	..
All undertakings	100	110	102	108	109	56	87	119
Composite								
Domestic undertakings	..	..	..	..	..	4	5	5
Foreign controlled undertakings	..	..	..	..	..	4	4	5
Foreign companies (branches)	..	..	..	..	..	..	..	..
All undertakings	..	..	..	..	..	4	5	5
of which:								
Life	..	..	..	..	..	4	5	5
Domestic undertakings	..	..	..	..	..	4	5	5
Foreign controlled undertakings	..	..	..	..	..	4	4	5
Foreign companies (branches)	..	..	..	..	..	..	..	..
All undertakings	..	..	..	..	..	4	5	5
Non-life	..	..	..	..	..	..	0	..
Domestic undertakings	..	..	..	..	..	..	0	..
Foreign controlled undertakings	..	..	..	..	..	..	0	..
Foreign companies (branches)	..	..	..	..	..	..	..	..
All undertakings	..	..	..	..	..	..	0	..
Total								
Domestic undertakings	104	115	106	112	113	60	92	124
Foreign controlled undertakings	47	49	44	44	55	34	55	86
Foreign companies (branches)	..	..	..	..	..	..	..	..
All undertakings	104	115	106	112	113	60	92	124

Table 1. Selected aggregates *(cont.)*

Million EUR

	2011	2012	2013	2014	2015	2016	2017	2018
1.5 Insurance business written abroad by branches, gross premiums								
Life								
Branches and agencies	0	0	0	0	0	0	0	..
Subsidaries	..	..	..	..	..	..	..	..
Total	0	0	0	0	0	0	0	..
Non-life								
Branches and agencies	126	143	158	168	157	158	203	233
Subsidaries	..	..	..	..	..	..	..	..
Total	126	143	158	168	157	158	203	233
Composite								
Branches and agencies	..	..	..	..	..	0	0	..
Subsidaries	..	..	..	..	..	..	..	..
Total	..	..	..	..	..	0	0	..
of which:								
Life	..	..	..	..	..	0	0	..
Branches and agencies	..	..	..	..	..	0	0	..
Subsidaries	..	..	..	..	..	..	..	..
Total	..	..	..	..	..	0	0	..
Non-life	..	..	..	..	..	..	0	..
Branches and agencies	..	..	..	..	..	..	0	..
Subsidaries	..	..	..	..	..	..	..	..
Total	..	..	..	..	..	..	0	..
Total								
Branches and agencies	126	143	158	168	157	158	203	233
Subsidaries	..	..	..	..	..	..	..	..
Total	126	143	158	168	157	158	203	233

.. Not available

Note: Detailed metadata at: *http://metalinks.oecd.org/ins/20200312/782c.*

Source: OECD Insurance Statistics (database)

LATVIA

Table 2. Number of companies and employees

	2011	2012	2013	2014	2015	2016	2017	2018
2.1 Number of companies								
Life								
Domestic undertakings	3	2	2	2	2	..	0	0
Foreign controlled undertakings	1	1	1	1	1	..	0	0
Foreign companies (branches)	5	5	5	5	4	..	0	0
All undertakings	8	7	7	7	6	..	0	0
Non-life								
Domestic undertakings	9	7	5	5	6	5	4	4
Foreign controlled undertakings	4	3	2	2	3	3	2	2
Foreign companies (branches)	5	8	7	9	10	8	7	7
All undertakings	14	15	12	14	16	13	11	11
Composite								
Domestic undertakings	0	0	0	0	0	2	2	2
Foreign controlled undertakings	0	0	0	0	0	1	1	1
Foreign companies (branches)	0	0	0	0	0	4	4	4
All undertakings	0	0	0	0	0	6	6	6
Reinsurance								
Domestic undertakings	0	0	0	0	0	..	0	..
Foreign controlled undertakings	0	0	0	0	0	..	0	..
Foreign companies (branches)	0	0	0	0	0	..	0	..
All undertakings	0	0	0	0	0	..	0	..
Total								
Domestic undertakings	12	9	7	7	8	7	6	6
Foreign controlled undertakings	5	4	3	3	4	4	3	3
Foreign companies (branches)	10	13	12	14	14	12	11	11
All undertakings	22	22	19	21	22	19	17	17
2.2 Number of employees								
Insurance undertakings	2 873	2 749	2 300	2 121	1 047	..	..	..
Intermediaries	1 195	1 168	846	773	905	..	..	..
Total	4 068	3 917	3 146	2 894	1 952	..	..	..

.. Not available

Note: Detailed metadata at: *http://metalinks.oecd.org/ins/20200312/782c.*

Source: OECD Insurance Statistics (database)

LITHUANIA

Table 1. Selected aggregates

Million EUR

	2011	2012	2013	2014	2015	2016	2017	2018
1.1 Insurance business written in the reporting country								
1.1.1 Insurance business, by ownership								
Gross premiums								
Domestic undertakings	283	309	288	303	326	393	425	447
Foreign controlled undertakings	272	299	278	294	316	383	416	437
Foreign companies (branches)	209	208	280	298	319	317	367	432
All undertakings	493	518	567	601	645	710	793	878
Premiums ceded								
Domestic undertakings	14	14	10	8	8	21	27	29
Foreign controlled undertakings	14	13	10	8	8	21	27	29
Foreign companies (branches)	..	..	..	21	24	15	40	55
All undertakings	..	..	..	29	32	36	68	84
Net written premiums								
Domestic undertakings	269	296	277	295	318	372	398	418
Foreign controlled undertakings	258	285	268	285	308	362	388	408
Foreign companies (branches)	..	..	..	277	295	302	327	376
All undertakings	..	..	..	572	613	674	725	794
1.1.2 Insurance business on foreign risks, gross premiums								
Life	..	..	..	..	..	..	..	..
Non-life	..	..	..	..	..	..	..	..
Composite	..	..	..	..	..	..	..	..
of which:								
Life	..	..	..	..	..	..	..	..
Non-life	..	..	..	..	..	..	..	..
Total	..	..	..	..	..	..	..	..
1.1.3 Life insurance payments, by class, gross premiums								
Annuities	2	3	3	4	5	6	7	7
Unit linked	114	115	126	152	170	157	137	151
Other life insurance	46	48	52	59	60	84	88	90
Total life insurance	162	166	181	215	236	247	231	248
***of which:** Pension contracts*	..	..	..	..	..	1	..	..
1.1.4 Non-life insurance payments, by class, gross premiums								
Motor vehicle insurance	190	209	228	227	236	273	353	403
Marine, aviation and other transport insurance	1	2	2	2	2	2	2	2
Freight insurance	2	2	2	2	2	2	3	3
Fire and other property damage insurance	71	68	74	79	89	98	103	109
Pecuniary loss insurance	19	20	20	18	17	17	20	23
General liability insurance	15	16	19	20	20	20	21	22
Accident and health	31	34	40	37	42	49	56	65
***of which:** Health*	18	21	25	21	24	30	35	42
Other non-life insurance	1	1	1	1	1	2	3	3
Treaty reinsurance	..	..	..	..	..	..	0	0
Total non-life insurance	330	352	386	386	409	463	561	630
1.2 Gross claims payments								
Life								
Domestic undertakings	10	10	15	13	15	26	29	32
Foreign controlled undertakings	10	10	15	13	15	23	26	29
Foreign companies (branches)	59	60	41	47	42	45	56	48
All undertakings	70	70	57	60	57	71	85	80
Non-life								
Domestic undertakings	121	126	105	105	116	134	169	153
Foreign controlled undertakings	104	106	85	92	102	134	169	153
Foreign companies (branches)	93	74	104	111	113	117	126	158
All undertakings	214	200	209	216	229	251	295	311
Composite								
Domestic undertakings	28	43	40	35	40	43	65	46
Foreign controlled undertakings	27	41	38	33	38	43	65	46
Foreign companies (branches)	2	3	4	4	6	8	11	15
All undertakings	30	46	44	40	46	51	75	62
of which:								
Life	24	41	39	35	40	43	66	49
Domestic undertakings	23	39	37	32	36	39	60	42
Foreign controlled undertakings	22	37	35	30	34	39	60	42
Foreign companies (branches)	1	2	2	2	3	4	6	7
All undertakings	24	41	39	35	40	43	66	49
Non-life	6	5	5	5	6	8	9	13
Domestic undertakings	5	4	3	3	4	4	4	4
Foreign controlled undertakings	5	4	3	3	4	4	4	4
Foreign companies (branches)	1	1	2	2	2	4	5	9
All undertakings	6	5	5	5	6	8	9	13
Total								
Domestic undertakings	159	179	161	154	171	203	263	231
Foreign controlled undertakings	141	157	138	138	155	200	260	228
Foreign companies (branches)	154	137	149	163	161	170	193	221
All undertakings	314	316	310	316	332	373	456	453

Table 1. Selected aggregates *(cont.)*

Million EUR

	2011	2012	2013	2014	2015	2016	2017	2018
1.3 Commissions								
Life								
Domestic undertakings	0	0	0	0	0	0	0	0
Foreign controlled undertakings	0	0	0	0	0	0	0	0
Foreign companies (branches)	..	..	..	0	0	0	0	0
All undertakings	..	..	..	0	0	0	0	0
Non-life								
Domestic undertakings	1	1	0	1	0	2	5	7
Foreign controlled undertakings	1	1	0	1	0	2	5	7
Foreign companies (branches)	..	..	..	3	3	2	7	12
All undertakings	..	..	..	3	3	4	12	19
Composite								
Domestic undertakings	2	2	3	1	1	0	0	0
Foreign controlled undertakings	2	2	3	1	1	0	0	0
Foreign companies (branches)	..	..	..	0	1	1	1	1
All undertakings	..	..	..	1	1	1	1	2
of which:								
Life	..	..	..	..	1	1	1	2
Domestic undertakings	1	1	1	..	1	0	0	0
Foreign controlled undertakings	1	1	1	..	1	0	0	0
Foreign companies (branches)	..	..	..	..	1	1	1	1
All undertakings	..	..	..	..	1	1	1	2
Non-life	..	..	..	..	0	0	0	0
Domestic undertakings	1	1	2	..	0	0	0	0
Foreign controlled undertakings	1	1	2	..	0	0	0	0
Foreign companies (branches)	..	..	..	..	0	0	0	0
All undertakings	..	..	..	..	0	0	0	0
Total								
Domestic undertakings	3	3	3	1	1	3	5	7
Foreign controlled undertakings	3	3	3	1	1	3	5	7
Foreign companies (branches)	..	..	..	3	4	3	8	13
All undertakings	..	..	..	4	5	6	13	21
1.4 Gross operating expenses								
Life								
Domestic undertakings	8	8	9	9	12	16	16	16
Foreign controlled undertakings	8	8	9	9	12	14	14	15
Foreign companies (branches)	..	..	..	8	6	7	6	6
All undertakings	..	..	..	17	18	22	21	22
Non-life								
Domestic undertakings	73	79	72	71	97	87	90	94
Foreign controlled undertakings	69	75	68	68	94	85	89	92
Foreign companies (branches)	..	..	..	63	95	63	65	76
All undertakings	..	..	..	134	192	150	155	170
Composite								
Domestic undertakings	18	20	22	17	28	9	14	14
Foreign controlled undertakings	16	18	21	16	25	9	14	14
Foreign companies (branches)	..	..	..	9	29	12	13	14
All undertakings	..	..	..	27	56	22	26	28
of which:								
Life	..	..	..	26	55	20	24	25
Domestic undertakings	15	17	19	17	27	8	13	13
Foreign controlled undertakings	13	15	17	15	24	8	13	13
Foreign companies (branches)	..	..	..	9	28	12	11	12
All undertakings	..	..	..	26	55	20	24	25
Non-life	..	..	..	1	2	2	2	3
Domestic undertakings	3	3	3	1	1	1	1	1
Foreign controlled undertakings	3	3	3	1	1	1	1	1
Foreign companies (branches)	..	..	..	0	1	1	1	2
All undertakings	..	..	..	1	2	2	2	3
Total								
Domestic undertakings	99	107	102	97	137	111	120	124
Foreign controlled undertakings	93	101	98	93	131	108	116	121
Foreign companies (branches)	..	..	..	81	130	82	83	96
All undertakings	..	..	..	178	267	194	203	220

Table 1. Selected aggregates *(cont.)*

Million EUR

	2011	2012	2013	2014	2015	2016	2017	2018
1.5 Insurance business written abroad by branches, gross premiums								
Life								
Branches and agencies	0	0	0	0	0	0	0	0
Subsidaries	..	..	..	..	..	..	..	..
Total	0	0	0	0	0	0	0	0
Non-life								
Branches and agencies	0	0	1	17	40	65	115	142
Subsidaries	..	..	..	..	..	..	..	..
Total	0	0	1	17	40	65	115	142
Composite								
Branches and agencies	20	22	26	31	37	40	46	46
Subsidaries	..	..	..	..	..	..	..	..
Total	20	22	26	31	37	40	46	46
of which:								
Life	9	10	11	14	18	19	22	22
Branches and agencies	9	10	11	14	18	19	22	22
Subsidaries	..	..	..	..	..	..	..	..
Total	9	10	11	14	18	19	22	22
Non-life	11	12	15	17	20	21	24	24
Branches and agencies	11	12	15	17	20	21	24	24
Subsidaries	..	..	..	..	..	..	..	..
Total	11	12	15	17	20	21	24	24
Total								
Branches and agencies	20	22	27	48	77	105	161	188
Subsidaries	..	..	..	..	..	..	..	..
Total	20	22	27	48	77	105	161	188

.. Not available

Note: Detailed metadata at: *http://metalinks.oecd.org/ins/20200312/baca.*

Source: OECD Insurance Statistics (database)

LITHUANIA

Table 2. Number of companies and employees

	2011	2012	2013	2014	2015	2016	2017	2018
2.1 Number of companies								
Life								
Domestic undertakings	1	1	1	1	1	3	3	3
Foreign controlled undertakings	1	1	1	1	1	2	2	2
Foreign companies (branches)	4	4	3	3	3	2	2	2
All undertakings	5	5	4	4	4	5	5	5
Non-life								
Domestic undertakings	6	6	5	5	5	4	4	4
Foreign controlled undertakings	3	3	2	2	3	3	3	3
Foreign companies (branches)	9	9	10	10	10	9	9	8
All undertakings	15	15	15	15	15	13	13	12
Composite								
Domestic undertakings	4	4	4	4	4	2	2	2
Foreign controlled undertakings	3	3	3	3	3	2	2	2
Foreign companies (branches)	1	1	1	1	1	1	1	1
All undertakings	5	5	5	5	5	3	3	3
Reinsurance								
Domestic undertakings	..	..	..	..	..	..	..	..
Foreign controlled undertakings	..	..	..	..	..	..	..	..
Foreign companies (branches)	..	..	..	..	..	..	..	..
All undertakings	..	..	..	..	..	..	..	..
Total								
Domestic undertakings	11	11	10	10	10	9	9	9
Foreign controlled undertakings	7	7	6	6	7	7	7	7
Foreign companies (branches)	14	14	14	14	14	12	12	11
All undertakings	25	25	24	24	24	21	21	20
2.2 Number of employees								
Insurance undertakings	3 875	4 390	4 519	4 414	4 482	4 562	4 599	4 569
Intermediaries	1 325	1 320	1 320	1 433	1 441	1 480	1 463	1 459
Total	5 200	5 710	5 839	5 847	5 923	6 042	6 062	6 028

.. Not available

Note: Detailed metadata at: *http://metalinks.oecd.org/ins/20200312/baca*.

Source: OECD Insurance Statistics (database)

LUXEMBOURG

Table 1. Selected aggregates

Million EUR

	2011	2012	2013	2014	2015	2016	2017	2018
1.1 Insurance business written in the reporting country								
1.1.1 Insurance business, by ownership								
Gross premiums								
Domestic undertakings	13 626	19 445	18 410	21 712	19 100	18 259	21 446	20 702
Foreign controlled undertakings	12 583	17 930	17 036	20 356	17 075	13 690	18 728	18 360
Foreign companies (branches)	150	144	191	76	78	70	77	77
All undertakings	13 776	19 589	18 601	21 788	19 178	18 329	21 523	20 779
Premiums ceded								
Domestic undertakings	2 935	6 109	4 624	6 122	3 030	3 235	3 026	4 794
Foreign controlled undertakings	2 737	5 892	4 246	5 863	2 770	2 943	2 657	4 452
Foreign companies (branches)	37	40	37	33	26	31	27	33
All undertakings	2 973	6 149	4 661	6 155	3 056	3 267	3 053	4 827
Net written premiums								
Domestic undertakings	10 691	13 336	13 787	15 590	16 070	15 024	18 421	15 908
Foreign controlled undertakings	9 846	12 037	12 790	14 493	14 305	10 747	16 070	13 907
Foreign companies (branches)	113	104	153	43	52	39	50	44
All undertakings	10 804	13 440	13 940	15 633	16 122	15 063	18 470	15 952
1.1.2 Insurance business on foreign risks, gross premiums								
Life	11 564	17 115	15 837	18 455	16 383	15 071	18 182	17 356
Non-life	547	476	572	438	587	621	784	658
Composite	0	..	0	0	0	0	0	0
of which:								
Life	0	..	0	0	0	0	0	0
Non-life	0	..	0	0	0	0	0	0
Total	12 112	17 591	16 408	18 893	16 969	15 692	18 967	18 014
1.1.3 Life insurance payments, by class, gross premiums								
Annuities	..	..	..	..	..	..	..	..
Unit linked	8 836	11 224	10 516	11 086	12 874	11 949	15 426	12 966
Other life insurance	3 382	6 826	6 413	9 103	4 685	4 767	4 283	6 064
Total life insurance	12 218	18 050	16 929	20 190	17 559	16 716	19 709	19 030
of which: *Pension contracts*	..	..	..	..	..	..	..	..
1.1.4 Non-life insurance payments, by class, gross premiums								
Motor vehicle insurance	426	..	..	..	..	..	..	..
Marine, aviation and other transport insurance	0	..	..	..	..	..	..	..
Freight insurance	30	..	..	..	..	..	..	..
Fire and other property damage insurance	271	..	..	..	..	..	..	..
Pecuniary loss insurance	321	..	..	..	..	..	..	..
General liability insurance	106	..	..	..	..	..	..	..
Accident and health	90	..	..	..	..	..	..	..
of which: *Health*	59	..	..	..	..	..	..	..
Other non-life insurance	53	..	..	..	..	..	..	..
Treaty reinsurance	27	..	..	..	..	..	..	..
Total non-life insurance	1 325	1 300	1 501	1 339	1 476	1 554	1 767	1 707
1.2 Gross claims payments								
Life								
Domestic undertakings	7 091	11 111	11 696	10 597	9 995	11 802	12 002	11 103
Foreign controlled undertakings	6 863	10 823	11 179	10 214	9 032	11 035	11 291	10 262
Foreign companies (branches)	34	10	25	25	27	28	27	26
All undertakings	7 125	11 122	11 721	10 622	10 023	11 829	12 029	11 129
Non-life								
Domestic undertakings	606	623	1 105	809	900	860	961	987
Foreign controlled undertakings	315	348	691	428	512	766	500	488
Foreign companies (branches)	31	27	39	36	18	31	37	26
All undertakings	637	650	1 143	845	918	891	999	1 014
Composite								
Domestic undertakings	0	..	0	0	0	0	0	0
Foreign controlled undertakings	0	..	0	0	0	0	0	0
Foreign companies (branches)	39	38	27	133	17	8	8	9
All undertakings	39	38	27	133	17	8	8	9
of which:								
Life	19	20	15	130	17	8	8	9
Domestic undertakings	0	..	0	0	0	0	0	0
Foreign controlled undertakings	0	..	0	0	0	0	0	0
Foreign companies (branches)	19	20	15	130	17	8	8	9
All undertakings	19	20	15	130	17	8	8	9
Non-life	20	18	12	3	0	0	0	0
Domestic undertakings	0	..	0	0	0	0	0	0
Foreign controlled undertakings	0	..	0	0	0	0	0	0
Foreign companies (branches)	20	18	12	3	0	0	0	0
All undertakings	20	18	12	3	0	0	0	0
Total								
Domestic undertakings	7 697	11 734	12 801	11 406	10 896	12 661	12 964	12 091
Foreign controlled undertakings	7 178	11 171	11 869	10 642	9 544	11 802	11 791	10 751
Foreign companies (branches)	104	76	90	195	62	66	72	61
All undertakings	7 800	11 810	12 891	11 600	10 958	12 728	13 036	12 152

Table 1. Selected aggregates *(cont.)*

Million EUR

	2011	2012	2013	2014	2015	2016	2017	2018
1.3 Commissions								
Life								
Domestic undertakings	353	328	327	317	326	291	320	312
Foreign controlled undertakings	..	328	309	297	289	186	283	276
Foreign companies (branches)	0	0	0	0	0	0	0	0
All undertakings	353	328	328	317	326	292	320	312
Non-life								
Domestic undertakings	217	205	217	211	237	251	284	283
Foreign controlled undertakings	..	205	119	109	122	143	151	140
Foreign companies (branches)	12	11	12	9	9	9	8	7
All undertakings	229	217	229	221	246	260	292	290
Composite								
Domestic undertakings	0	..	0	0	0	0	0	0
Foreign controlled undertakings	..	..	0	0	0	0	0	0
Foreign companies (branches)	11	12	12	3	4	4	3	0
All undertakings	11	12	12	3	4	4	3	0
of which:								
Life	5	5	5	3	4	4	3	0
Domestic undertakings	0	..	0	0	0	0	0	0
Foreign controlled undertakings	..	..	0	0	0	0	0	0
Foreign companies (branches)	5	5	5	3	4	4	3	0
All undertakings	5	5	5	3	4	4	3	0
Non-life	7	7	7	0	0	0	0	0
Domestic undertakings	0	..	0	0	0	0	0	0
Foreign controlled undertakings	..	..	0	0	0	0	0	0
Foreign companies (branches)	7	7	7	0	0	0	0	0
All undertakings	7	7	7	0	0	0	0	0
Total								
Domestic undertakings	570	533	544	528	563	542	604	595
Foreign controlled undertakings	..	533	428	406	411	329	435	416
Foreign companies (branches)	23	24	25	13	14	14	11	7
All undertakings	593	557	569	541	576	556	615	602
1.4 Gross operating expenses								
Life								
Domestic undertakings	288	656	362	376	406	417	433	450
Foreign controlled undertakings	274	622	347	358	374	352	392	411
Foreign companies (branches)	0	0	0	1	0	1	1	1
All undertakings	288	656	362	376	406	418	433	450
Non-life								
Domestic undertakings	53	270	66	72	82	81	96	59
Foreign controlled undertakings	27	270	34	41	46	78	58	17
Foreign companies (branches)	3	14	3	2	2	3	3	5
All undertakings	55	285	69	74	84	84	99	64
Composite								
Domestic undertakings	0	..	0	0	0	0	0	0
Foreign controlled undertakings	0	..	0	0	0	0	0	0
Foreign companies (branches)	6	18	7	1	1	1	1	1
All undertakings	6	18	7	1	1	1	1	1
of which:								
Life	2	7	3	1	1	1	1	1
Domestic undertakings	0	..	0	0	0	0	0	0
Foreign controlled undertakings	0	..	0	0	0	0	0	0
Foreign companies (branches)	2	7	3	1	1	1	1	1
All undertakings	2	7	3	1	1	1	1	1
Non-life	3	11	4	0	0	0	0	0
Domestic undertakings	0	..	0	0	0	0	0	0
Foreign controlled undertakings	0	..	0	0	0	0	0	0
Foreign companies (branches)	3	11	4	0	0	0	0	0
All undertakings	3	11	4	0	0	0	0	0
Total								
Domestic undertakings	341	926	429	448	488	498	529	509
Foreign controlled undertakings	302	892	381	399	421	430	450	428
Foreign companies (branches)	8	33	9	4	3	4	5	6
All undertakings	349	959	438	451	491	502	534	515

Table 1. Selected aggregates *(cont.)*

Million EUR

	2011	2012	2013	2014	2015	2016	2017	2018
1.5 Insurance business written abroad by branches, gross premiums								
Life								
Branches and agencies	2 161	2 619	2 648	3 250	3 552	4 622	3 492	4 746
Subsidaries	0	0	..	..	..	..	..	..
Total	2 161	2 619	2 648	3 250	3 552	4 622	3 492	4 746
Non-life								
Branches and agencies	1 088	1 417	1 546	1 831	1 965	2 022	1 957	2 847
Subsidaries	0	0	..	..	..	..	..	..
Total	1 088	1 417	1 546	1 831	1 965	2 022	1 957	2 847
Composite								
Branches and agencies	0	..	0	0	0	0	0	0
Subsidaries	0	..	..	..	..	..	..	..
Total	0	..	0	0	0	0	0	0
of which:								
Life	0	..	0	0	0	0	0	0
Branches and agencies	0	..	0	0	0	0	0	0
Subsidaries	0	..	..	..	..	..	..	..
Total	0	..	0	0	0	0	0	0
Non-life	0	..	0	0	0	0	0	0
Branches and agencies	0	..	0	0	0	0	0	0
Subsidaries	0	..	..	..	..	..	..	..
Total	0	..	0	0	0	0	0	0
Total								
Branches and agencies	3 250	4 036	4 194	5 082	5 516	6 644	5 449	7 593
Subsidaries	0	0	..	..	..	..	..	..
Total	3 250	4 036	4 194	5 082	5 516	6 644	5 449	7 593

.. Not available

Note: Detailed metadata at: *http://metalinks.oecd.org/ins/20200312/ae65.*

Source: OECD *Insurance Statistics (database)*

Table 2. Number of companies and employees

	2011	2012	2013	2014	2015	2016	2017	2018
2.1 Number of companies								
Life								
Domestic undertakings	45	43	42	44	43	40	39	38
Foreign controlled undertakings	41	39	34	39	38	34	35	30
Foreign companies (branches)	2	1	2	2	2	3	3	3
All undertakings	47	44	44	46	45	43	42	41
Non-life								
Domestic undertakings	29	31	34	34	32	33	34	41
Foreign controlled undertakings	25	27	27	8	21	24	25	33
Foreign companies (branches)	10	11	10	10	10	10	9	8
All undertakings	39	42	44	44	42	43	43	49
Composite								
Domestic undertakings	0	0	0	0	0	0	0	0
Foreign controlled undertakings	0	0	0	0	0	0	0	0
Foreign companies (branches)	3	3	3	3	3	3	2	3
All undertakings	3	3	3	3	3	3	2	3
Reinsurance								
Domestic undertakings	242	238	226	224	217	208	204	198
Foreign controlled undertakings	222	219	207	205	204	191	187	181
Foreign companies (branches)	0	0	0	0	0	0	0	0
All undertakings	242	238	226	224	217	208	204	198
Total								
Domestic undertakings	316	312	302	302	292	281	277	277
Foreign controlled undertakings	288	285	268	252	263	249	247	244
Foreign companies (branches)	15	15	15	15	15	16	14	14
All undertakings	331	327	317	317	307	297	291	291
2.2 Number of employees								
Insurance undertakings	3 967	4 326	5 692	6 057	6 484	6 484	7 446	8 034
Intermediaries	9 375	9 659	10 030	550	561	522	586	637
Total	13 342	13 985	15 722	6 607	7 045	7 006	8 032	8 671

Note: Detailed metadata at: *http://metalinks.oecd.org/ins/20200312/ae65.*
Source: OECD Insurance Statistics (database)

MEXICO

Table 1. Selected aggregates

Million MXN

	2011	2012	2013	2014	2015	2016	2017	2018
1.1 Insurance business written in the reporting country								
1.1.1 Insurance business, by ownership								
Gross premiums								
Domestic undertakings	281 792	310 747	347 196	363 530	395 083	450 740	502 856	543 652
Foreign controlled undertakings	167 708	189 698	207 890	220 225	242 872	265 159	290 985	312 037
Foreign companies (branches)	..	..	..	..	..	..	..	..
All undertakings	281 792	310 747	347 196	363 530	395 083	450 740	502 856	543 652
Premiums ceded								
Domestic undertakings	49 771	50 188	60 551	58 378	67 135	70 420	93 577	91 472
Foreign controlled undertakings	21 903	24 728	26 822	29 932	40 217	40 674	58 977	51 768
Foreign companies (branches)	..	..	..	..	..	..	..	..
All undertakings	49 771	50 188	60 551	58 378	67 135	70 420	93 577	91 472
Net written premiums								
Domestic undertakings	232 021	260 559	286 645	305 152	327 947	380 320	409 279	452 180
Foreign controlled undertakings	145 805	164 970	181 068	190 293	202 655	224 485	232 008	260 270
Foreign companies (branches)	..	..	..	..	..	..	..	..
All undertakings	232 021	260 559	286 645	305 152	327 947	380 320	409 279	452 180
1.1.2 Insurance business on foreign risks, gross premiums								
Life	..	..	..	..	..	..	..	..
Non-life	349	425	402	..	..	..	..	..
Composite	1 553	1 787	1 692	..	..	..	..	..
of which:								
Life	..	..	..	..	..	..	..	..
Non-life	..	..	..	..	..	..	..	..
Total	1 902	2 212	2 093	..	..	..	..	..
1.1.3 Life insurance payments, by class, gross premiums								
Annuities	15 749	17 633	20 099	20 521	19 719	19 286	21 310	24 176
Unit linked	..	..	..	..	..	..	..	0
Other life insurance	109 511	125 175	138 959	148 624	162 199	189 860	193 587	218 641
Total life insurance	125 260	142 808	159 058	169 145	181 918	209 146	214 897	242 817
***of which:** Pension contracts*	..	..	..	..	..	..	..	..
1.1.4 Non-life insurance payments, by class, gross premiums								
Motor vehicle insurance	56 099	62 944	66 562	68 735	75 858	91 375	103 014	110 405
Marine, aviation and other transport insurance	7 049	7 691	7 851	9 356	11 007	11 312	16 558	12 811
Freight insurance	..	..	..	..	..	..	..	..
Fire and other property damage insurance	14 010	9 980	16 520	12 232	13 815	14 497	18 115	37 929
Pecuniary loss insurance	686	749	5 210	501	947	1 131	12 278	1 774
General liability insurance	5 914	6 920	7 341	7 201	9 099	9 668	12 005	11 757
Accident and health	41 814	45 526	51 189	56 686	59 550	66 512	76 720	85 417
***of which:** Health*	1 835	1 918	2 682	2 719	2 622	3 218	3 518	4 279
Other non-life insurance	30 214	33 390	32 581	38 511	42 081	45 976	48 006	39 687
Treaty reinsurance	..	..	..	..	..	..	..	..
Total non-life insurance	155 785	167 200	187 253	193 221	212 357	240 470	286 696	299 780
1.2 Gross claims payments								
Life								
Domestic undertakings	9 566	10 279	11 800	12 325	13 760	14 829	16 234	18 272
Foreign controlled undertakings	4 663	..	..	5 875	6 443	6 971	7 390	8 005
Foreign companies (branches)	..	..	..	..	..	..	..	..
All undertakings	9 566	10 279	11 800	12 325	13 760	14 829	16 234	18 272
Non-life								
Domestic undertakings	14 750	14 874	21 716	17 912	19 552	23 827	32 868	32 866
Foreign controlled undertakings	4 751	..	..	4 093	4 923	5 515	7 449	5 433
Foreign companies (branches)	..	..	..	..	..	..	..	..
All undertakings	14 750	14 874	21 716	17 912	19 552	23 827	32 868	32 866
Composite								
Domestic undertakings	109 005	115 041	159 315	148 932	162 803	185 481	204 354	224 193
Foreign controlled undertakings	70 654	..	..	104 822	109 465	125 575	136 316	151 138
Foreign companies (branches)	..	..	..	..	..	..	..	..
All undertakings	109 005	115 041	159 315	148 932	162 803	185 481	204 354	224 193
of which:								
Life	50 966	55 436	76 467	81 643	88 136	101 700	115 199	124 902
Domestic undertakings	50 966	55 436	76 467	81 643	88 136	101 700	115 199	124 902
Foreign controlled undertakings	38 918	..	..	67 855	70 802	81 029	89 726	97 155
Foreign companies (branches)	..	..	..	..	..	..	..	..
All undertakings	50 966	55 436	76 467	81 643	88 136	101 700	115 199	124 902
Non-life	58 039	59 605	82 848	67 289	74 667	83 781	89 154	99 291
Domestic undertakings	58 039	59 605	82 848	67 289	74 667	83 781	89 154	99 291
Foreign controlled undertakings	31 736	..	..	36 968	38 662	44 546	46 591	53 983
Foreign companies (branches)	..	..	..	..	..	..	..	..
All undertakings	58 039	59 605	82 848	67 289	74 667	83 781	89 154	99 291
Total								
Domestic undertakings	133 321	140 195	192 832	179 169	196 115	224 138	253 455	275 331
Foreign controlled undertakings	80 068	..	..	114 791	120 830	138 061	151 155	164 576
Foreign companies (branches)	..	..	..	..	..	..	..	..
All undertakings	133 321	140 195	192 832	179 169	196 115	224 138	253 455	275 331

Table 1. Selected aggregates *(cont.)*

Million MXN

	2011	2012	2013	2014	2015	2016	2017	2018
1.3 Commissions								
Life								
Domestic undertakings	1 257	1 133	1 075	749	1 045	1 155	..	..
Foreign controlled undertakings	268	277	251	74	192	247	..	..
Foreign companies (branches)	..	..	..	..	..	..	..	..
All undertakings	1 257	1 133	1 075	749	1 045	1 155	..	..
Non-life								
Domestic undertakings	5 935	6 911	8 410	9 458	7 257	9 473	..	..
Foreign controlled undertakings	2 373	2 721	3 523	3 808	1 888	1 618	..	..
Foreign companies (branches)	..	..	..	..	..	..	..	..
All undertakings	5 935	6 911	8 410	9 458	7 257	9 473	..	..
Composite								
Domestic undertakings	38 671	44 178	46 777	49 973	48 713	56 225	..	..
Foreign controlled undertakings	24 611	28 060	29 464	31 616	30 146	33 073	..	..
Foreign companies (branches)	..	..	..	..	..	..	..	..
All undertakings	38 671	44 178	46 777	49 973	48 713	56 225	..	..
of which:								
Life	15 773	18 508	19 316	21 023	22 507	26 955	..	..
Domestic undertakings	15 773	18 508	19 316	21 023	22 507	26 955	..	..
Foreign controlled undertakings	10 807	12 501	12 940	17 514	14 838	17 151	..	..
Foreign companies (branches)	..	..	..	..	..	..	..	..
All undertakings	15 773	18 508	19 316	21 023	22 507	26 955	..	..
Non-life	22 898	25 670	27 462	28 950	26 206	29 270	..	..
Domestic undertakings	22 898	25 670	27 462	28 950	26 206	29 270	..	..
Foreign controlled undertakings	13 803	15 559	16 524	14 103	15 308	15 922	..	..
Foreign companies (branches)	..	..	..	..	..	..	..	..
All undertakings	22 898	25 670	27 462	28 950	26 206	29 270	..	..
Total								
Domestic undertakings	45 863	52 222	56 263	60 180	57 016	66 853	..	..
Foreign controlled undertakings	27 251	31 058	33 239	35 498	32 226	34 937	..	..
Foreign companies (branches)	..	..	..	..	..	..	..	..
All undertakings	45 863	52 222	56 263	60 180	57 016	66 853	..	..
1.4 Gross operating expenses								
Life								
Domestic undertakings	1 095	1 313	1 486	1 156	1 336	1 705	1 617	1 480
Foreign controlled undertakings	675	..	..	570	661	723	759	734
Foreign companies (branches)	..	..	..	..	..	..	..	..
All undertakings	1 095	1 313	1 486	1 156	1 336	1 705	1 617	1 480
Non-life								
Domestic undertakings	2 337	2 968	3 545	4 198	4 924	5 852	7 490	8 280
Foreign controlled undertakings	1 402	..	..	2 010	3 137	3 249	4 041	3 412
Foreign companies (branches)	..	..	..	..	..	..	..	..
All undertakings	2 337	2 968	3 545	4 198	4 924	5 852	7 490	8 280
Composite								
Domestic undertakings	14 115	14 382	16 389	16 621	18 736	21 447	23 147	25 162
Foreign controlled undertakings	8 627	..	..	10 470	12 270	13 297	13 037	15 216
Foreign companies (branches)	..	..	..	..	..	..	..	..
All undertakings	14 115	14 382	16 389	16 621	18 736	21 447	23 147	25 162
of which:								
Life	6 838	7 085	8 530	8 486	9 990	11 792	11 674	12 701
Domestic undertakings	6 838	7 085	8 530	8 486	9 990	11 792	11 674	12 701
Foreign controlled undertakings	5 052	..	..	6 273	7 388	8 480	7 981	8 964
Foreign companies (branches)	..	..	..	..	..	..	..	..
All undertakings	6 838	7 085	8 530	8 486	9 990	11 792	11 674	12 701
Non-life	7 277	7 298	7 859	8 135	8 746	9 655	11 473	12 461
Domestic undertakings	7 277	7 298	7 859	8 135	8 746	9 655	11 473	12 461
Foreign controlled undertakings	3 575	..	..	4 198	4 882	4 818	5 055	6 252
Foreign companies (branches)	..	..	..	..	..	..	..	..
All undertakings	7 277	7 298	7 859	8 135	8 746	9 655	11 473	12 461
Total								
Domestic undertakings	17 548	18 662	21 420	21 974	24 996	29 004	32 254	34 923
Foreign controlled undertakings	10 704	..	..	13 050	16 068	17 270	17 837	19 363
Foreign companies (branches)	..	..	..	..	..	..	..	..
All undertakings	17 548	18 662	21 420	21 974	24 996	29 004	32 254	34 923

Table 1. Selected aggregates *(cont.)*

Million MXN

	2011	2012	2013	2014	2015	2016	2017	2018
1.5 Insurance business written abroad by branches, gross premiums								
Life								
Branches and agencies	..	..	..	..	..	..	..	..
Subsidaries	..	..	..	..	..	..	..	..
Total	..	..	..	..	..	..	..	..
Non-life								
Branches and agencies	..	..	..	..	..	..	..	..
Subsidaries	..	..	..	..	..	..	..	..
Total	..	..	..	..	..	..	..	..
Composite								
Branches and agencies	..	..	..	..	..	..	..	..
Subsidaries	..	..	..	..	..	..	..	..
Total	..	..	..	..	..	..	..	..
of which:								
Life	..	..	..	..	..	..	..	..
Branches and agencies	..	..	..	..	..	..	..	..
Subsidaries	..	..	..	..	..	..	..	..
Total	..	..	..	..	..	..	..	..
Non-life	..	..	..	..	..	..	..	..
Branches and agencies	..	..	..	..	..	..	..	..
Subsidaries	..	..	..	..	..	..	..	..
Total	..	..	..	..	..	..	..	..
Total								
Branches and agencies	..	..	..	..	..	..	..	..
Subsidaries	..	..	..	..	..	..	..	..
Total	..	..	..	..	..	..	..	..

.. Not available

Note: Detailed metadata at: *http://metalinks.oecd.org/ins/20200312/1c0b.*

Source: OECD Insurance Statistics (database)

Table 2. Number of companies and employees

	2011	2012	2013	2014	2015	2016	2017	2018
2.1 Number of companies								
Life								
Domestic undertakings	21	20	20	16	16	17	15	15
Foreign controlled undertakings	12	11	11	9	9	10	8	8
Foreign companies (branches)	..	..	..	..	..	..	..	..
All undertakings	21	20	20	16	16	17	15	15
Non-life								
Domestic undertakings	44	47	45	49	46	44	60	58
Foreign controlled undertakings	27	27	27	26	23	22	31	28
Foreign companies (branches)	..	..	..	..	..	..	..	..
All undertakings	44	47	45	49	46	44	60	58
Composite								
Domestic undertakings	35	35	37	38	37	37	38	36
Foreign controlled undertakings	20	21	21	22	21	20	21	20
Foreign companies (branches)	..	..	..	..	..	..	..	..
All undertakings	35	35	37	38	37	37	38	36
Reinsurance								
Domestic undertakings	2	2	2	2	3	2	2	2
Foreign controlled undertakings	..	0	0	0	0	0	0	..
Foreign companies (branches)	..	..	..	..	..	..	..	..
All undertakings	2	2	2	2	3	2	2	2
Total								
Domestic undertakings	102	104	104	105	102	100	115	111
Foreign controlled undertakings	59	59	59	57	53	52	60	56
Foreign companies (branches)	..	..	..	..	..	..	..	..
All undertakings	102	104	104	105	102	100	115	111
2.2 Number of employees								
Insurance undertakings	14 487	14 491	14 500	14 799	19 168	..	..	..
Intermediaries	35 173	36 190	46 712	51 780	55 005	57 900	61 695	..
Total	49 660	50 681	61 212	66 579	74 173	57 900	61 695	..

.. Not available

Note: Detailed metadata at: *http://metalinks.oecd.org/ins/20200312/1c0b.*

Source: OECD Insurance Statistics (database)

NETHERLANDS

Table 1. Selected aggregates

Million EUR

	2011	2012	2013	2014	2015	2016	2017	2018
1.1 Insurance business written in the reporting country								
1.1.1 Insurance business, by ownership								
Gross premiums								
Domestic undertakings	41 183	39 012	38 077	36 523	33 708	69 887	71 228	73 667
Foreign controlled undertakings	9 625	9 255	7 674	2 969	5 812	4 102	4 371	3 429
Foreign companies (branches)	955	891	430	62	0	..	..	..
All undertakings	42 138	39 903	38 507	36 585	33 708	69 887	71 228	73 667
Premiums ceded								
Domestic undertakings	5 720	3 109	2 951	3 880	2 814	1 198	1 698	1 460
Foreign controlled undertakings	1 701	1 706	1 484	1 615	1 365	287	353	84
Foreign companies (branches)	116	79	20	0	0	..	..	..
All undertakings	5 836	3 188	2 971	3 880	2 814	1 198	1 698	1 460
Net written premiums								
Domestic undertakings	35 463	35 903	35 126	32 643	30 894	68 689	69 530	72 207
Foreign controlled undertakings	7 923	7 549	6 190	1 354	4 447	3 815	4 018	3 345
Foreign companies (branches)	839	812	410	62	0	..	..	..
All undertakings	36 302	36 715	35 536	32 705	30 894	68 689	69 530	72 207
1.1.2 Insurance business on foreign risks, gross premiums								
Life	..	..	..	..	..	269	273	300
Non-life	..	..	..	..	..	534	452	1 102
Composite total	..	..	..	..	..	..	252	501
Total	..	..	..	..	..	803	977	1 903
1.1.3 Life insurance payments, by class, gross premiums								
Annuities	12 001	10 892	10 998	10 806	9 035	0	0	0
Unit linked	9 332	7 836	7 086	6 504	5 533	5 262	4 553	4 296
Other life insurance	329	247	188	150	122	8 465	8 411	7 674
Total life insurance	21 662	18 975	18 272	17 460	14 690	13 727	12 964	11 970
***of which:** Pension contracts*	6 887	6 034	5 810	5 552	5 208	334	157	38
1.1.4 Non-life insurance payments, by class, gross premiums								
Motor vehicle insurance	4 587	4 500	4 376	3 934	3 884	3 892	4 051	4 312
Marine, aviation and other transport insurance	563	596	525	435	404	361	283	273
Freight insurance	291	263	256	231	191	..	0	0
Fire and other property damage insurance	3 515	3 698	3 664	3 449	3 456	3 256	3 290	3 380
Pecuniary loss insurance	309	278	206	164	176	258	206	271
General liability insurance	1 045	1 116	1 125	1 064	1 033	882	883	919
Accident and health	8 585	8 560	8 167	7 867	7 851	46 459	47 499	50 393
***of which:** Health*	..	..	..	..	..	45 064	46 044	48 900
Other non-life insurance	2 027	1 907	1 919	1 976	2 016	1 049	1 165	1 099
Treaty reinsurance	..	..	..	..	..	..	0	0
Total non-life insurance	20 923	20 918	20 238	19 120	19 011	56 157	57 377	60 647
1.2 Gross claims payments								
Life								
Domestic undertakings	23 689	25 331	24 085	25 487	22 576	20 919	25 124	20 129
Foreign controlled undertakings	3 206	3 538	3 205	1 136	4 504	4 203	4 286	3 640
Foreign companies (branches)	378	401	420	0	0	..	..	..
All undertakings	24 067	25 732	24 505	25 487	22 576	20 919	25 124	20 129
Non-life								
Domestic undertakings	13 957	13 999	14 304	13 666	13 806	50 966	51 936	53 872
Foreign controlled undertakings	2 840	2 870	2 915	867	1 937	1 053	844	693
Foreign companies (branches)	42	41	41	149	0	..	..	..
All undertakings	13 999	14 040	14 345	13 815	13 806	50 966	51 936	53 872
Composite, all undertakings	**..**	**..**	**..**	**..**	**..**	**..**	**473**	**481**
Total								
Domestic undertakings	37 646	39 330	38 389	39 153	36 382	71 885	77 533	74 482
Foreign controlled undertakings	6 046	6 408	6 120	2 003	6 441	5 256	5 130	4 333
Foreign companies (branches)	420	442	461	149	0	..	..	..
All undertakings	38 066	39 772	38 850	39 302	36 382	71 885	77 533	74 482
1.3 Commissions								
Life								
Domestic undertakings	614	473	243	190	158	..	..	..
Foreign controlled undertakings	325	196	64	17	49	..	..	..
Foreign companies (branches)	14	17	12	0	0	..	..	..
All undertakings	628	490	255	190	158	..	..	..
Non-life								
Domestic undertakings	3 070	3 197	2 891	2 713	2 663	..	..	..
Foreign controlled undertakings	851	833	734	282	464	..	..	..
Foreign companies (branches)	23	22	22	21	0	..	..	..
All undertakings	3 093	3 219	2 913	2 734	2 663	..	..	..
Composite, all undertakings	**..**	**..**	**..**	**..**	**..**	**..**	**..**	**..**
Total								
Domestic undertakings	3 684	3 670	3 134	2 903	2 821	..	..	..
Foreign controlled undertakings	1 176	1 029	798	299	513	..	..	..
Foreign companies (branches)	37	39	34	21	0	..	..	..
All undertakings	3 721	3 709	3 168	2 924	2 821	..	..	..

Table 1. Selected aggregates *(cont.)*

Million EUR

	2011	2012	2013	2014	2015	2016	2017	2018
1.4 Gross operating expenses								
Life								
Domestic undertakings	2 768	2 827	2 266	2 497	2 072	2 183	2 002	1 839
Foreign controlled undertakings	349	342	297	113	378	417	356	274
Foreign companies (branches)	59	37	44	0	0	..	..	..
All undertakings	2 827	2 864	2 310	2 497	2 072	2 183	2 002	1 839
Non-life								
Domestic undertakings	4 863	4 933	4 809	4 635	4 485	6 219	6 156	6 235
Foreign controlled undertakings	1 244	1 181	1 136	373	771	525	550	461
Foreign companies (branches)	25	24	25	23	0	..	..	..
All undertakings	4 888	4 957	4 834	4 658	4 485	6 219	6 156	6 235
Composite, all undertakings	..	..	..	..	..	..	**115**	**71**
Total								
Domestic undertakings	7 631	7 759	7 075	7 132	6 557	8 402	8 273	8 145
Foreign controlled undertakings	1 593	1 523	1 433	486	1 149	942	906	735
Foreign companies (branches)	84	61	69	23	0	..	..	..
All undertakings	7 715	7 820	7 144	7 155	6 557	8 402	8 273	8 145
1.5 Insurance business written abroad by branches, gross premiums								
Life								
Branches and agencies	662	540	370	276	..	253	260	291
Subsidaries	..	..	..	..	..	..	..	..
Total	662	540	370	276	267	253	260	291
Non-life								
Branches and agencies	1 067	1 276	1 132	1 289	..	175	163	153
Subsidaries	..	..	..	..	..	..	..	..
Total	1 067	1 276	1 132	1 289	1 487	175	163	153
Composite total	..	..	..	..	..	..	**0**	**477**
Total								
Branches and agencies	1 729	1 816	1 502	1 565	..	428	423	921
Subsidaries	..	..	..	..	..	..	..	..
Total	1 729	1 816	1 502	1 565	1 754	428	423	921

.. Not available

Note: Detailed metadata at: *http://metalinks.oecd.org/ins/20200312/b3cf.*

Source: OECD Insurance Statistics (database)

NETHERLANDS

Table 2. Number of companies and employees

	2011	2012	2013	2014	2015	2016	2017	2018
2.1 Number of companies								
Life								
Domestic undertakings	52	41	36	38	..	31	30	27
Foreign controlled undertakings	8	6	6	7	..	11	10	6
Foreign companies (branches)	1	4	4	0	..	..	..	..
All undertakings	53	45	40	38	..	31	30	27
Non-life								
Domestic undertakings	174	158	316	136	..	107	101	96
Foreign controlled undertakings	5	15	14	8	..	9	8	7
Foreign companies (branches)	4	2	1	2	..	..	..	..
All undertakings	178	160	317	138	..	107	101	96
Composite, all undertakings	**0**	**0**	**0**	**0**	**0**	**0**	**0**	..
Reinsurance								
Domestic undertakings	16	15	11	10	..	9	9	8
Foreign controlled undertakings	1	1	0	0	..	0	0	0
Foreign companies (branches)	..	0	0	0	..	..	..	..
All undertakings	16	15	11	10	..	9	9	8
Total								
Domestic undertakings	242	214	363	184	..	147	140	131
Foreign controlled undertakings	14	22	20	15	..	20	18	13
Foreign companies (branches)	5	6	5	2	..	..	..	..
All undertakings	247	220	368	186	..	147	140	131
2.2 Number of employees								
Insurance undertakings	..	..	..	..	..	..	..	..
Intermediaries	..	..	..	..	..	..	..	..
Total	..	..	..	..	..	..	..	..

.. Not available

Note: Detailed metadata at: *http://metalinks.oecd.org/ins/20200312/b3cf.*

Source: OECD Insurance Statistics (database)

NEW ZEALAND

Table 1. Selected aggregates

Million NZD

	2011	2012	2013	2014	2015	2016	2017	2018
1.1 Insurance business written in the reporting country								
1.1.1 Insurance business, by ownership								
Gross premiums								
Domestic undertakings	..	..	..	..	..	..	..	..
Foreign controlled undertakings	..	..	..	..	..	..	..	..
Foreign companies (branches)	..	..	..	..	..	..	..	..
All undertakings	..	5 665	6 266	6 460	6 678	6 828	7 240	..
Premiums ceded								
Domestic undertakings	..	..	..	..	..	..	..	..
Foreign controlled undertakings	..	..	..	..	..	..	..	..
Foreign companies (branches)	..	..	..	..	..	..	..	..
All undertakings	..	1 207	1 412	1 292	1 305	1 789	1 852	..
Net written premiums								
Domestic undertakings	..	..	..	..	..	..	..	..
Foreign controlled undertakings	..	..	..	..	..	..	..	..
Foreign companies (branches)	..	..	..	..	..	..	..	..
All undertakings	..	6 365	6 758	7 186	7 523	7 303	7 729	..
1.1.2 Insurance business on foreign risks, gross premiums								
Life	..	..	..	..	..	..	..	..
Non-life	..	..	..	..	..	..	..	..
Composite	..	..	..	..	..	..	..	..
of which:								
Life	..	..	..	..	..	..	..	..
Non-life	..	..	..	..	..	..	..	..
Total	..	..	..	..	..	..	..	..
1.1.3 Life insurance payments, by class, gross premiums								
Annuities	..	..	..	..	..	..	..	..
Unit linked	..	..	..	..	..	..	..	..
Other life insurance	..	..	..	..	..	..	..	..
Total life insurance	..	..	..	..	..	..	..	..
of which: *Pension contracts*	..	..	..	..	..	..	..	..
1.1.4 Non-life insurance payments, by class, gross premiums								
Motor vehicle insurance	..	..	..	..	..	..	..	..
Marine, aviation and other transport insurance	..	..	..	..	..	..	..	..
Freight insurance	..	..	..	..	..	..	..	..
Fire and other property damage insurance	..	..	..	..	..	..	..	..
Pecuniary loss insurance	..	..	..	..	..	..	..	..
General liability insurance	..	..	..	..	..	..	..	..
Accident and health	..	..	..	..	..	..	..	..
of which: *Health*	..	..	..	..	..	..	..	..
Other non-life insurance	..	..	..	..	..	..	..	..
Treaty reinsurance	..	..	..	..	..	..	..	..
Total non-life insurance	..	5 665	6 266	6 460	6 678	6 828	7 240	..
1.2 Gross claims payments								
Life								
Domestic undertakings	..	..	..	..	..	..	..	..
Foreign controlled undertakings	..	..	..	..	..	..	..	..
Foreign companies (branches)	..	..	..	..	..	..	..	..
All undertakings	..	1 360	1 303	1 399	1 544	1 598	1 579	..
Non-life								
Domestic undertakings	..	..	..	..	..	..	..	..
Foreign controlled undertakings	..	..	..	..	..	..	..	..
Foreign companies (branches)	..	..	..	..	..	..	..	..
All undertakings	..	9 531	4 539	5 642	6 302	4 864	6 662	..
Composite								
Domestic undertakings	..	..	..	..	..	..	..	..
Foreign controlled undertakings	..	..	..	..	..	..	..	..
Foreign companies (branches)	..	..	..	..	..	..	..	..
All undertakings	..	..	..	..	..	..	..	..
of which:								
Life	..	..	..	..	..	..	..	..
Domestic undertakings	..	..	..	..	..	..	..	..
Foreign controlled undertakings	..	..	..	..	..	..	..	..
Foreign companies (branches)	..	..	..	..	..	..	..	..
All undertakings	..	..	..	..	..	..	..	..
Non-life	..	..	..	..	..	..	..	..
Domestic undertakings	..	..	..	..	..	..	..	..
Foreign controlled undertakings	..	..	..	..	..	..	..	..
Foreign companies (branches)	..	..	..	..	..	..	..	..
All undertakings	..	..	..	..	..	..	..	..
Total								
Domestic undertakings	..	..	..	..	..	..	..	..
Foreign controlled undertakings	..	..	..	..	..	..	..	..
Foreign companies (branches)	..	..	..	..	..	..	..	..
All undertakings	..	10 891	5 842	7 041	7 846	6 462	8 241	..

Table 1. Selected aggregates *(cont.)*

Million NZD

	2011	2012	2013	2014	2015	2016	2017	2018
1.3 Commissions								
Life								
Domestic undertakings	..	..	..	..	..	..	..	..
Foreign controlled undertakings	..	..	..	..	..	..	..	..
Foreign companies (branches)	..	..	..	..	..	..	..	..
All undertakings	..	..	..	..	..	..	..	..
Non-life								
Domestic undertakings	..	..	..	..	..	..	..	..
Foreign controlled undertakings	..	..	..	..	..	..	..	..
Foreign companies (branches)	..	..	..	..	..	..	..	..
All undertakings	..	..	..	..	..	..	..	..
Composite								
Domestic undertakings	..	..	..	..	..	..	..	..
Foreign controlled undertakings	..	..	..	..	..	..	..	..
Foreign companies (branches)	..	..	..	..	..	..	..	..
All undertakings	..	..	..	..	..	..	..	..
of which:								
Life	..	..	..	..	..	..	..	..
Domestic undertakings	..	..	..	..	..	..	..	..
Foreign controlled undertakings	..	..	..	..	..	..	..	..
Foreign companies (branches)	..	..	..	..	..	..	..	..
All undertakings	..	..	..	..	..	..	..	..
Non-life	..	..	..	..	..	..	..	..
Domestic undertakings	..	..	..	..	..	..	..	..
Foreign controlled undertakings	..	..	..	..	..	..	..	..
Foreign companies (branches)	..	..	..	..	..	..	..	..
All undertakings	..	..	..	..	..	..	..	..
Total								
Domestic undertakings	..	..	..	..	..	..	..	..
Foreign controlled undertakings	..	..	..	..	..	..	..	..
Foreign companies (branches)	..	..	..	..	..	..	..	..
All undertakings	..	..	..	..	..	..	..	..
1.4 Gross operating expenses								
Life								
Domestic undertakings	..	..	..	..	..	..	..	..
Foreign controlled undertakings	..	..	..	..	..	..	..	..
Foreign companies (branches)	..	..	..	..	..	..	..	..
All undertakings	..	2 169	2 151	2 384	2 323	2 489	2 476	..
Non-life								
Domestic undertakings	..	..	..	..	..	..	..	..
Foreign controlled undertakings	..	..	..	..	..	..	..	..
Foreign companies (branches)	..	..	..	..	..	..	..	..
All undertakings	..	12 070	6 102	7 490	8 472	6 875	8 884	..
Composite								
Domestic undertakings	..	..	..	..	..	..	..	..
Foreign controlled undertakings	..	..	..	..	..	..	..	..
Foreign companies (branches)	..	..	..	..	..	..	..	..
All undertakings	..	..	..	..	..	..	..	..
of which:								
Life	..	..	..	..	..	..	..	..
Domestic undertakings	..	..	..	..	..	..	..	..
Foreign controlled undertakings	..	..	..	..	..	..	..	..
Foreign companies (branches)	..	..	..	..	..	..	..	..
All undertakings	..	..	..	..	..	..	..	..
Non-life	..	..	..	..	..	..	..	..
Domestic undertakings	..	..	..	..	..	..	..	..
Foreign controlled undertakings	..	..	..	..	..	..	..	..
Foreign companies (branches)	..	..	..	..	..	..	..	..
All undertakings	..	..	..	..	..	..	..	..
Total								
Domestic undertakings	..	..	..	..	..	..	..	..
Foreign controlled undertakings	..	..	..	..	..	..	..	..
Foreign companies (branches)	..	..	..	..	..	..	..	..
All undertakings	..	14 239	8 253	9 874	10 795	9 364	11 360	..

Table 1. Selected aggregates *(cont.)*

Million NZD

	2011	2012	2013	2014	2015	2016	2017	2018
1.5 Insurance business written abroad by branches, gross premiums								
Life								
Branches and agencies	..	..	..	..	..	..	..	..
Subsidaries	..	..	..	..	..	..	..	..
Total	..	..	..	..	..	..	..	..
Non-life								
Branches and agencies	..	..	..	..	..	..	..	..
Subsidaries	..	..	..	..	..	..	..	..
Total	..	..	..	..	..	..	..	..
Composite								
Branches and agencies	..	..	..	..	..	..	..	..
Subsidaries	..	..	..	..	..	..	..	..
Total	..	..	..	..	..	..	..	..
of which:								
Life	..	..	..	..	..	..	..	..
Branches and agencies	..	..	..	..	..	..	..	..
Subsidaries	..	..	..	..	..	..	..	..
Total	..	..	..	..	..	..	..	..
Non-life	..	..	..	..	..	..	..	..
Branches and agencies	..	..	..	..	..	..	..	..
Subsidaries	..	..	..	..	..	..	..	..
Total	..	..	..	..	..	..	..	..
Total								
Branches and agencies	..	..	..	..	..	..	..	..
Subsidaries	..	..	..	..	..	..	..	..
Total	..	..	..	..	..	..	..	..

.. Not available

Note: Detailed metadata at: *http://metalinks.oecd.org/ins/20200312/0583.*

Source: OECD *Insurance Statistics (database)*

Table 2. Number of companies and employees

	2011	2012	2013	2014	2015	2016	2017	2018
2.1 Number of companies								
Life								
Domestic undertakings	..	..	..	..	..	..	..	..
Foreign controlled undertakings	..	..	..	..	..	..	..	..
Foreign companies (branches)	..	..	..	..	..	..	..	..
All undertakings	..	43	37	43	30	30	30	..
Non-life								
Domestic undertakings	..	..	..	..	..	..	..	..
Foreign controlled undertakings	..	..	..	..	..	..	..	..
Foreign companies (branches)	..	..	..	..	..	..	..	..
All undertakings	..	142	130	145	102	90	87	..
Composite								
Domestic undertakings	..	..	..	..	..	..	..	..
Foreign controlled undertakings	..	..	..	..	..	..	..	..
Foreign companies (branches)	..	..	..	..	..	..	..	..
All undertakings	..	..	..	..	..	..	..	..
Reinsurance								
Domestic undertakings	..	..	..	..	..	..	..	..
Foreign controlled undertakings	..	..	..	..	..	..	..	..
Foreign companies (branches)	..	..	..	..	..	..	..	..
All undertakings	..	..	..	..	..	..	..	..
Total								
Domestic undertakings	..	..	..	..	..	..	..	..
Foreign controlled undertakings	..	..	..	..	..	..	..	..
Foreign companies (branches)	..	..	..	..	..	..	..	..
All undertakings	..	185	167	188	132	120	117	..
2.2 Number of employees								
Insurance undertakings	..	..	10 780	10 720	10 680	..	..	..
Intermediaries	..	..	..	..	..	..	..	..
Total	..	10 640	10 780	..	..	..	..	..

.. Not available

Note: Detailed metadata at: *http://metalinks.oecd.org/ins/20200312/0583.*

Source: OECD Insurance Statistics (database)

NORWAY

Table 1. Selected aggregates

Million NOK

	2011	2012	2013	2014	2015	2016	2017	2018
1.1 Insurance business written in the reporting country								
1.1.1 Insurance business, by ownership								
Gross premiums								
Domestic undertakings	106 973	119 751	119 149	134 884	135 864	138 612	139 748	148 945
Foreign controlled undertakings	6 388	8 589	8 948	11 029	13 195	..	..	..
Foreign companies (branches)	26 383	30 039	30 872	31 867	30 638	31 150	29 049	29 917
All undertakings	133 356	149 790	150 021	166 751	166 502	169 762	168 797	178 862
Premiums ceded								
Domestic undertakings	..	6 252	6 396	6 891	7 973	7 053	7 061	7 109
Foreign controlled undertakings	..	316	173	198	218	..	..	..
Foreign companies (branches)	..	4 290	4 219	4 653	4 976	5 362	4 814	4 868
All undertakings	..	10 542	10 614	11 544	12 950	12 415	11 876	11 976
Net written premiums								
Domestic undertakings	..	113 499	112 754	127 993	127 890	131 559	132 686	141 836
Foreign controlled undertakings	..	8 273	8 775	10 832	12 978	..	..	..
Foreign companies (branches)	..	25 749	26 653	27 213	25 662	25 788	24 235	25 049
All undertakings	..	139 248	139 407	155 206	153 552	157 347	156 921	166 885
1.1.2 Insurance business on foreign risks, gross premiums								
Life	..	31	..	..	9	7	6	4 144
Non-life	1 556	7 352	6 202	11 468	11 250	10 855	10 417	10 989
Composite total	..	..	..	..	..	..	..	..
Total	1 556	7 383	6 202	11 468	11 260	10 862	10 422	15 133
1.1.3 Life insurance payments, by class, gross premiums								
Annuities	..	..	..	..	..	..	..	..
Unit linked	..	..	..	..	..	..	..	..
Other life insurance	..	..	..	..	..	..	..	..
Total life insurance	71 577	81 742	81 299	92 185	91 794	94 093	93 577	99 961
of which: *Pension contracts*	..	69 652	66 873	..	..	..	..	..
1.1.4 Non-life insurance payments, by class, gross premiums								
Motor vehicle insurance	10 787	19 403	..	20 378	20 706	20 897	21 029	22 316
Marine, aviation and other transport insurance	4 009	9 581	..	6 574	5 201	15 291	5 292	5 203
Freight insurance	..	..	..	..	..	0	..	..
Fire and other property damage insurance	10 811	17 738	..	18 195	19 041	23 135	22 553	23 487
Pecuniary loss insurance	125	585	..	127	97	432	92	98
General liability insurance	686	1 755	..	1 695	1 637	2 000	1 774	1 980
Accident and health	3 229	6 111	..	5 608	5 553	10 526	10 288	11 075
of which: *Health*	..	..	..	..	..	0	..	..
Other non-life insurance	5 967	12 875	..	21 989	13 048	7 085	6 088	12 644
Treaty reinsurance	..	..	..	..	..	0	..	2 099
Total non-life insurance	35 615	68 048	..	74 566	65 283	79 366	67 116	78 901
1.2 Gross claims payments								
Life								
Domestic undertakings	40 252	45 033	45 143	45 742	49 007	51 548	54 419	58 887
Foreign controlled undertakings	2 723	3 120	3 186	3 150	4 796	.. c	..	..
Foreign companies (branches)	494	482	692	476	235	288	281	298
All undertakings	40 746	45 515	45 835	46 218	49 242	51 836	54 700	59 185
Non-life								
Domestic undertakings	26 292	28 356	23 486	30 742	34 587	32 537	31 896	34 370
Foreign controlled undertakings	342	542	.. c	.. c	.. c	.. c	..	..
Foreign companies (branches)	17 552	24 549	20 026	22 287	21 584	21 146	20 655	20 427
All undertakings	43 844	52 905	43 512	53 030	56 170	53 683	52 550	54 797
Composite, all undertakings	..	..	..	..	..	..	..	..
Total								
Domestic undertakings	66 544	73 389	68 629	76 485	83 593	84 085	86 315	93 257
Foreign controlled undertakings	3 065	3 662	3 186	3 150	4 796	..	..	..
Foreign companies (branches)	18 046	25 031	20 718	22 763	21 819	21 434	20 935	20 725
All undertakings	84 590	98 420	89 347	99 248	105 413	105 519	107 250	113 983
1.3 Commissions								
Life								
Domestic undertakings	..	692	774	839	916	890	783	737
Foreign controlled undertakings	..	152	179	202	227	.. c	.. c	.. c
Foreign companies (branches)	..	0	0	0	..	..	..	..
All undertakings	..	692	774	839	916	890	783	737
Non-life								
Domestic undertakings	..	1 507	1 536	2 204	2 119	1 956	2 105	2 309
Foreign controlled undertakings	..	35	.. c	.. c	..	.. c	.. c	.. c
Foreign companies (branches)	..	1 101	1 084	1 099	1 107	950	915	916
All undertakings	..	2 608	2 619	3 303	3 226	2 906	3 020	3 224
Composite, all undertakings	..	..	..	..	..	..	..	..
Total								
Domestic undertakings	..	2 199	2 310	3 043	3 035	2 846	2 889	3 046
Foreign controlled undertakings	..	187	179	202	227	..	..	..
Foreign companies (branches)	..	1 101	1 084	1 099	1 107	950	915	916
All undertakings	..	3 300	3 393	4 142	4 142	3 797	3 804	3 961

NORWAY

Table 1. Selected aggregates *(cont.)*

Million NOK

	2011	2012	2013	2014	2015	2016	2017	2018
1.4 Gross operating expenses								
Life								
Domestic undertakings	5 818	7 019	6 688	7 205	7 383	7 750	7 380	7 817
Foreign controlled undertakings	688	692	185	807	765	.. c	..	..
Foreign companies (branches)	144	0	126	162	..	157	143	126
All undertakings	5 962	7 019	6 814	7 367	7 383	7 907	7 523	7 943
Non-life								
Domestic undertakings	6 155	5 527	5 925	6 585	6 138	6 139	6 956	11 045
Foreign controlled undertakings	76	48	.. c	.. c	.. c	.. c	..	..
Foreign companies (branches)	5 121	4 765	4 203	5 318	5 574	5 465	4 732	5 207
All undertakings	11 276	10 292	10 128	11 903	11 712	11 605	11 688	16 252
Composite, all undertakings	..	..	..	..	..	..	..	..
Total								
Domestic undertakings	11 973	12 546	12 613	13 790	13 521	13 889	14 336	18 862
Foreign controlled undertakings	764	740	185	807	765	..	..	..
Foreign companies (branches)	5 265	4 765	4 329	5 480	5 574	5 623	4 875	5 333
All undertakings	17 238	17 311	16 942	19 270	19 095	19 512	19 211	24 195
1.5 Insurance business written abroad by branches, gross premiums								
Life								
Branches and agencies	..	..	.. c	..	..	..	..	..
Subsidaries	..	..	..	..	..	..	..	..
Total	..	..	.. c	..	..	..	..	..
Non-life								
Branches and agencies	2 476	2 454	1 134	4 636	1 569	7 141	2 493	2 431
Subsidaries	..	..	.. c	.. c	..	..	..	..
Total	2 476	2 454	1 134	4 636	1 569	7 141	2 493	2 431
Composite total	..	..	..	..	..	..	..	..
Total								
Branches and agencies	2 476	2 454	1 134	4 636	1 569	7 141	2 493	2 431
Subsidaries	..	..	..	..	..	..	..	..
Total	2 476	2 454	1 134	4 636	1 569	7 141	2 493	2 431

.. Not available; c Confidential data

Note: Detailed metadata at: *http://metalinks.oecd.org/ins/20200312/7bbf.*

Source: *OECD Insurance Statistics (database)*

Table 2. Number of companies and employees

	2011	2012	2013	2014	2015	2016	2017	2018
2.1 Number of companies								
Life								
Domestic undertakings	12	10	12	10	10	10	13	12
Foreign controlled undertakings	2	2	2	2	2	2	3	3
Foreign companies (branches)	10	9	9	7	7	7	6	6
All undertakings	22	19	21	17	17	17	19	18
Non-life								
Domestic undertakings	76	63	59	59	58	59	58	56
Foreign controlled undertakings	1	1	1	1	2	2	2	1
Foreign companies (branches)	21	25	25	22	21	23	23	21
All undertakings	97	88	84	81	79	82	81	77
Composite, all undertakings	**0**	**0**	**0**	**0**	**0**	..	..	..
Reinsurance								
Domestic undertakings	..	..	..	..	..	..	..	..
Foreign controlled undertakings	..	..	..	..	..	..	..	..
Foreign companies (branches)	..	..	..	..	..	..	..	..
All undertakings	..	..	..	..	..	..	..	..
Total								
Domestic undertakings	88	73	71	69	68	69	71	68
Foreign controlled undertakings	3	3	3	3	4	4	5	4
Foreign companies (branches)	31	34	34	29	28	30	29	27
All undertakings	119	107	105	98	96	99	100	95
2.2 Number of employees								
Insurance undertakings	..	..	..	..	..	..	..	..
Intermediaries	..	..	..	..	..	..	..	..
Total	..	..	..	..	..	..	..	..

.. Not available

Note: Detailed metadata at: *http://metalinks.oecd.org/ins/20200312/7bbf.*

Source: OECD Insurance Statistics (database)

POLAND

Table 1. Selected aggregates

Million PLN

	2011	2012	2013	2014	2015	2016	2017	2018
1.1 Insurance business written in the reporting country								
1.1.1 Insurance business, by ownership								
Gross premiums								
Domestic undertakings	57 151	62 627	57 863	54 927	54 804	56 039	62 339	62 161
Foreign controlled undertakings	31 683	35 100	31 562	30 425	30 801	31 961	33 189	33 452
Foreign companies (branches)	..	..	..	..	..	..	..	..
All undertakings	57 151	62 627	57 863	54 927	54 804	56 039	62 339	62 161
Premiums ceded								
Domestic undertakings	3 852	4 598	4 214	4 170	5 197	6 765	7 216	7 235
Foreign controlled undertakings	4 647	4 224	3 664	3 533	4 355	4 798	4 664	4 396
Foreign companies (branches)	..	..	..	..	..	..	..	..
All undertakings	3 852	4 598	4 214	4 170	5 197	6 765	7 216	7 235
Net written premiums								
Domestic undertakings	53 299	58 029	53 649	50 757	49 606	49 274	55 123	54 927
Foreign controlled undertakings	27 036	30 876	27 898	26 892	26 446	27 163	28 525	29 057
Foreign companies (branches)	..	..	..	..	..	..	..	..
All undertakings	53 299	58 029	53 649	50 757	49 606	49 274	55 123	54 927
1.1.2 Insurance business on foreign risks, gross premiums								
Life	..	..	..	..	..	..	118	100
Non-life	..	..	..	..	..	..	181	255
Composite total	..	..	..	..	..	..	..	..
Total	..	..	..	..	..	..	299	355
1.1.3 Life insurance payments, by class, gross premiums								
Annuities	98	99	107	114	131	138	0	0
Unit linked	10 307	12 046	13 052	12 600	12 996	10 325	10 955	7 487
Other life insurance	21 415	24 203	18 082	15 933	14 377	13 370	13 583	14 216
Total life insurance	31 820	36 348	31 241	28 646	27 505	23 833	24 539	21 702
***of which:** Pension contracts*	376	371	396	356	356	..	243	230
1.1.4 Non-life insurance payments, by class, gross premiums								
Motor vehicle insurance	14 543	14 780	13 945	13 397	13 910	18 744	23 249	24 295
Marine, aviation and other transport insurance	232	256	267	275	210	185	271	319
Freight insurance	107	119	117	126	116	120	..	..
Fire and other property damage insurance	5 056	5 441	5 973	5 715	5 938	6 246	6 877	7 618
Pecuniary loss insurance	1 631	1 526	1 858	2 149	1 893	1 805	1 713	1 812
General liability insurance	1 459	1 773	1 891	1 964	2 134	1 915	2 064	2 297
Accident and health	1 688	1 801	1 926	2 007	2 273	2 222	2 347	2 715
***of which:** Health*	1 245	513	612	656	613	618	561	872
Other non-life insurance	575	554	622	627	804	947	1 256	1 403
Treaty reinsurance	..	..	..	..	..	..	..	..
Total non-life insurance	25 291	26 250	26 599	26 260	27 278	32 182	37 777	40 459
1.2 Gross claims payments								
Life								
Domestic undertakings	26 069	25 917	23 087	20 360	19 358	18 284	20 315	21 401
Foreign controlled undertakings	12 116	13 331	10 927	9 783	8 795	9 543	9 295	10 029
Foreign companies (branches)	..	..	..	..	..	..	..	..
All undertakings	26 069	25 917	23 087	20 360	19 358	18 284	20 315	21 401
Non-life								
Domestic undertakings	13 738	14 046	13 711	13 811	15 488	18 393	19 931	21 011
Foreign controlled undertakings	8 128	8 890	8 434	8 579	9 515	10 911	11 453	12 435
Foreign companies (branches)	..	..	..	..	..	..	..	..
All undertakings	13 738	14 046	13 711	13 811	15 488	18 393	19 931	21 011
Composite, all undertakings	..	..	..	..	..	..	..	..
Total								
Domestic undertakings	39 807	39 963	36 798	34 171	34 846	36 677	40 246	42 412
Foreign controlled undertakings	20 244	22 221	19 362	18 363	18 310	20 454	20 748	22 464
Foreign companies (branches)	..	..	..	..	..	..	..	..
All undertakings	39 807	39 963	36 798	34 171	34 846	36 677	40 246	42 412
1.3 Commissions								
Life								
Domestic undertakings	3 245	70	93	203	231	222	183	133
Foreign controlled undertakings	2 591	69	70	191	223	218	179	127
Foreign companies (branches)	..	..	..	..	..	..	..	..
All undertakings	3 245	70	93	203	231	222	183	133
Non-life								
Domestic undertakings	4 015	657	740	651	719	1 115	1 545	1 795
Foreign controlled undertakings	2 659	648	606	594	657	929	1 122	1 222
Foreign companies (branches)	..	..	..	..	..	..	..	..
All undertakings	4 015	657	740	651	719	1 115	1 545	1 795
Composite, all undertakings	..	..	..	..	..	..	..	..
Total								
Domestic undertakings	7 260	727	833	854	950	1 337	1 727	1 928
Foreign controlled undertakings	5 250	717	676	785	880	1 147	1 301	1 350
Foreign companies (branches)	..	..	..	..	..	..	..	..
All undertakings	7 260	727	833	854	950	1 337	1 727	1 928

Table 1. Selected aggregates *(cont.)*

Million PLN

	2011	2012	2013	2014	2015	2016	2017	2018
1.4 Gross operating expenses								
Life								
Domestic undertakings	5 605	6 416	6 146	6 588	6 476	5 647	5 963	5 697
Foreign controlled undertakings	3 944	4 244	3 831	4 369	4 182	3 797	3 491	3 276
Foreign companies (branches)	..	..	..	..	..	..	..	..
All undertakings	5 605	6 416	6 146	6 588	6 476	5 647	5 963	5 697
Non-life								
Domestic undertakings	7 276	7 733	7 775	8 018	8 335	9 104	12 793	14 073
Foreign controlled undertakings	4 549	5 225	5 090	5 135	5 569	5 978	7 938	8 744
Foreign companies (branches)	..	..	..	..	..	..	..	..
All undertakings	7 276	7 733	7 775	8 018	8 335	9 104	12 793	14 073
Composite, all undertakings	..	..	..	..	..	..	..	..
Total								
Domestic undertakings	12 882	14 149	13 921	14 606	14 811	14 751	18 756	19 770
Foreign controlled undertakings	8 493	9 469	8 921	9 504	9 751	9 776	11 429	12 021
Foreign companies (branches)	..	..	..	..	..	..	..	..
All undertakings	12 882	14 149	13 921	14 606	14 811	14 751	18 756	19 770
1.5 Insurance business written abroad by branches, gross premiums								
Life								
Branches and agencies	19	26	..	79	92	..	95	80
Subsidaries	..	..	..	..	..	..	..	..
Total	19	26	..	79	92	..	95	80
Non-life								
Branches and agencies	62	53	..	98	116	..	..	..
Subsidaries	49	..	..	..	..	..	..	..
Total	111	53	..	98	116	..	..	..
Composite total	..	..	..	..	..	..	..	..
Total								
Branches and agencies	82	79	..	177	208	..	95	80
Subsidaries	49	..	..	..	..	..	..	..
Total	130	79	..	177	208	..	95	80

.. Not available

Note: Detailed metadata at: *http://metalinks.oecd.org/ins/20200312/23f2*.

Source: OECD Insurance Statistics (database)

Table 2. Number of companies and employees

	2011	2012	2013	2014	2015	2016	2017	2018
2.1 Number of companies								
Life								
Domestic undertakings	28	28	27	26	28	27	27	26
Foreign controlled undertakings	22	23	21	19	21	21	20	18
Foreign companies (branches)	2	..	..	..	..	..	..	..
All undertakings	30	28	27	26	28	27	27	26
Non-life								
Domestic undertakings	32	30	30	30	32	33	33	33
Foreign controlled undertakings	22	21	19	19	22	20	19	19
Foreign companies (branches)	11	..	..	..	..	..	..	..
All undertakings	43	30	30	30	32	33	33	33
Composite, all undertakings	**0**	**0**	**0**	**0**	**0**	**0**	..	..
Reinsurance								
Domestic undertakings	1	1	1	1	1	1	1	1
Foreign controlled undertakings	1	1	1	1	1	1	1	1
Foreign companies (branches)	..	..	..	..	..	..	..	..
All undertakings	1	1	1	1	1	1	1	1
Total								
Domestic undertakings	61	59	58	57	61	61	61	60
Foreign controlled undertakings	45	45	41	39	44	42	40	38
Foreign companies (branches)	13	..	..	..	..	..	..	..
All undertakings	74	59	58	57	61	61	61	38
2.2 Number of employees								
Insurance undertakings	37 239	37 205	37 187	35 922	35 282	..	..	..
Intermediaries	68 168	58 879	69 621	58 004	49 126	..	..	..
Total	105 407	96 083	106 808	93 926	84 408	..	..	..

.. Not available

Note: Detailed metadata at: *http://metalinks.oecd.org/ins/20200312/23f2.*

Source: OECD Insurance Statistics (database)

PORTUGAL

Table 1. Selected aggregates

Million EUR

	2011	2012	2013	2014	2015	2016	2017	2018
1.1 Insurance business written in the reporting country								
1.1.1 Insurance business, by ownership								
Gross premiums								
Domestic undertakings	11 165	10 553	12 802	14 051	12 568	10 913	11 455	12 590
Foreign controlled undertakings	1 676	1 553	1 617	8 737	8 890	9 048	10 640	11 441
Foreign companies (branches)	73	0	0	0	0	0	0	0
All undertakings	11 238	10 553	12 802	14 051	12 568	10 913	11 455	12 590
Premiums ceded								
Domestic undertakings	982	1 096	1 144	1 118	1 194	1 214	1 307	1 338
Foreign controlled undertakings	153	130	140	836	924	992	1 180	1 209
Foreign companies (branches)	23	0	0	0	0	0	0	0
All undertakings	1 005	1 096	1 144	1 118	1 194	1 214	1 307	1 338
Net written premiums								
Domestic undertakings	10 183	9 457	11 658	12 933	11 374	9 698	10 148	11 252
Foreign controlled undertakings	1 523	1 423	1 477	7 902	7 966	8 056	9 460	10 232
Foreign companies (branches)	50	0	0	0	0	0	0	0
All undertakings	10 232	9 457	11 658	12 933	11 374	9 698	10 148	11 252
1.1.2 Insurance business on foreign risks, gross premiums								
Life	0	2	3	13	8	11	8	0
Non-life	2	15	14	13	13	4	7	8
Composite	0	54	64	92	107	127	129	127
of which:								
Life	0	27	27	53	63	70	74	65
Non-life	0	27	38	39	44	57	55	63
Total	2	72	81	118	129	142	144	136
1.1.3 Life insurance payments, by class, gross premiums								
Annuities	19	46	79	64	109	142	183	142
Unit linked	1 954	1 999	1 851	1 966	2 119	1 655	2 077	1 703
Other life insurance	5 240	4 633	7 094	8 220	6 254	4 708	4 450	5 934
Total life insurance	7 213	6 678	9 023	10 249	8 481	6 504	6 710	7 779
***of which:** Pension contracts*	..	..	..	..	..	..	..	..
1.1.4 Non-life insurance payments, by class, gross premiums								
Motor vehicle insurance	1 447	1 353	1 277	1 256	1 316	1 399	1 482	1 429
Marine, aviation and other transport insurance	35	35	33	29	28	25	27	26
Freight insurance	26	25	25	24	23	22	22	0
Fire and other property damage insurance	686	702	700	699	745	771	795	764
Pecuniary loss insurance	54	63	69	70	73	84	83	47
General liability insurance	90	89	84	87	94	99	102	101
Accident and health	1 480	1 430	1 413	1 452	1 602	1 783	1 999	2 141
***of which:** Health*	820	838	862	896	973	1 084	1 208	1 307
Other non-life insurance	170	177	178	183	205	225	235	239
Treaty reinsurance	0	0	0	0	0	0	0	..
Total non-life insurance	3 988	3 874	3 778	3 802	4 086	4 408	4 745	4 747
1.2 Gross claims payments								
Life								
Domestic undertakings	6 935	4 875	4 518	5 254	6 133	6 568	3 940	3 306
Foreign controlled undertakings	505	461	374	2 667	2 724	2 252	2 853	2 749
Foreign companies (branches)	0	0	0	0	0	0	0	0
All undertakings	6 935	4 875	4 518	5 254	6 133	6 568	3 940	3 306
Non-life								
Domestic undertakings	1 588	1 471	1 446	1 407	1 520	1 336	1 413	1 530
Foreign controlled undertakings	424	385	376	1 174	1 278	1 070	1 130	1 200
Foreign companies (branches)	0	0	0	0	0	0	0	0
All undertakings	1 588	1 471	1 446	1 407	1 520	1 336	1 413	1 530
Composite								
Domestic undertakings	7 987	5 927	5 427	5 201	5 128	4 554	4 230	5 086
Foreign controlled undertakings	517	541	562	3 991	3 922	4 501	4 180	4 606
Foreign companies (branches)	43	0	0	0	0	0	0	0
All undertakings	8 030	5 927	5 427	5 201	5 128	4 554	4 230	5 086
of which:								
Life	6 661	4 616	4 067	3 895	3 840	2 867	2 479	3 320
Domestic undertakings	6 621	4 616	4 067	3 895	3 840	2 867	2 479	3 320
Foreign controlled undertakings	173	184	167	2 904	2 839	2 815	2 431	2 843
Foreign companies (branches)	41	0	0	0	0	0	0	0
All undertakings	6 661	4 616	4 067	3 895	3 840	2 867	2 479	3 320
Non-life	1 369	1 311	1 360	1 306	1 288	1 687	1 751	1 766
Domestic undertakings	1 367	1 311	1 360	1 306	1 288	1 687	1 751	1 766
Foreign controlled undertakings	344	357	395	1 087	1 083	1 686	1 749	1 763
Foreign companies (branches)	2	0	0	0	0	0	0	0
All undertakings	1 369	1 311	1 360	1 306	1 288	1 687	1 751	1 766
Total								
Domestic undertakings	16 510	12 274	11 391	11 861	12 782	12 458	9 582	9 922
Foreign controlled undertakings	1 446	1 387	1 312	7 832	7 923	7 822	8 163	8 555
Foreign companies (branches)	43	0	0	0	0	0	0	0
All undertakings	16 553	12 274	11 391	11 861	12 782	12 458	9 582	9 922

Table 1. Selected aggregates *(cont.)*

Million EUR

	2011	2012	2013	2014	2015	2016	2017	2018
1.3 Commissions								
Life								
Domestic undertakings	38	47	144	40	77	105	103	89
Foreign controlled undertakings	9	7	7	15	41	42	85	78
Foreign companies (branches)	0	0	0	0	0	0	0	0
All undertakings	38	47	144	40	77	105	103	89
Non-life								
Domestic undertakings	155	157	156	153	178	164	183	194
Foreign controlled undertakings	44	40	38	117	133	98	115	124
Foreign companies (branches)	0	0	0	0	0	0	0	0
All undertakings	155	157	156	153	178	164	183	194
Composite								
Domestic undertakings	273	272	291	301	295	286	351	350
Foreign controlled undertakings	76	81	99	208	222	283	344	333
Foreign companies (branches)	20	0	0	0	0	0	0	0
All undertakings	293	272	291	301	295	286	351	350
of which:								
Life	114	87	98	100	82	49	58	75
Domestic undertakings	96	87	98	100	82	49	58	75
Foreign controlled undertakings	20	21	28	42	44	47	52	58
Foreign companies (branches)	18	0	0	0	0	0	0	0
All undertakings	114	87	98	100	82	49	58	75
Non-life	179	185	193	201	214	237	293	275
Domestic undertakings	177	185	193	201	214	237	293	275
Foreign controlled undertakings	56	60	71	165	178	236	291	275
Foreign companies (branches)	2	0	0	0	0	0	0	0
All undertakings	179	185	193	201	214	237	293	275
Total								
Domestic undertakings	466	476	591	493	550	554	637	633
Foreign controlled undertakings	130	128	144	339	396	423	543	534
Foreign companies (branches)	20	0	0	0	0	0	0	0
All undertakings	486	476	591	493	550	554	637	633
1.4 Gross operating expenses								
Life								
Domestic undertakings	202	206	314	212	244	300	298	280
Foreign controlled undertakings	37	36	33	136	163	168	248	246
Foreign companies (branches)	0	0	0	0	0	0	0	0
All undertakings	202	206	314	212	244	300	298	280
Non-life								
Domestic undertakings	528	511	496	495	550	467	494	513
Foreign controlled undertakings	155	144	133	398	441	357	388	402
Foreign companies (branches)	0	0	0	0	0	0	0	0
All undertakings	528	511	496	495	550	467	494	513
Composite								
Domestic undertakings	710	723	715	717	720	711	851	823
Foreign controlled undertakings	190	200	198	541	571	702	839	790
Foreign companies (branches)	39	0	0	0	0	0	0	0
All undertakings	750	723	715	717	720	711	851	823
of which:								
Life	258	221	234	230	222	148	173	206
Domestic undertakings	226	221	234	230	222	148	173	206
Foreign controlled undertakings	48	49	48	125	145	140	162	175
Foreign companies (branches)	32	0	0	0	0	0	0	0
All undertakings	258	221	234	230	222	148	173	206
Non-life	492	502	481	487	497	562	678	617
Domestic undertakings	484	502	481	487	497	562	678	617
Foreign controlled undertakings	142	151	151	416	427	562	677	615
Foreign companies (branches)	7	0	0	0	0	0	0	0
All undertakings	492	502	481	487	497	562	678	617
Total								
Domestic undertakings	1 440	1 440	1 525	1 425	1 513	1 478	1 643	1 615
Foreign controlled undertakings	381	380	364	1 076	1 176	1 227	1 474	1 438
Foreign companies (branches)	39	0	0	0	0	0	0	0
All undertakings	1 480	1 440	1 525	1 425	1 513	1 478	1 643	1 615

Table 1. Selected aggregates *(cont.)*

Million EUR

	2011	2012	2013	2014	2015	2016	2017	2018
1.5 Insurance business written abroad by branches, gross premiums								
Life								
Branches and agencies	6	2	3	13	8	11	8	0
Subsidaries	0	0	0	0	0	0	0	0
Total	6	2	3	13	8	11	8	0
Non-life								
Branches and agencies	8	14	12	12	12	1	3	0
Subsidaries	0	0	0	0	0	0	0	0
Total	8	14	12	12	12	1	3	0
Composite								
Branches and agencies	55	54	64	92	107	127	129	195
Subsidaries	0	0	0	0	0	0	0	0
Total	55	54	64	92	107	127	129	195
of which:								
Life	28	27	27	53	63	70	74	132
Branches and agencies	28	27	27	53	63	70	74	132
Subsidaries	0	0	0	0	0	0	0	0
Total	28	27	27	53	63	70	74	132
Non-life	27	27	38	39	44	57	55	63
Branches and agencies	27	27	38	39	44	57	55	63
Subsidaries	0	0	0	0	0	0	0	0
Total	27	27	38	39	44	57	55	63
Total								
Branches and agencies	69	70	79	117	128	138	140	195
Subsidaries	0	0	0	0	0	0	0	0
Total	69	70	79	117	128	138	140	195

.. Not available

Note: Detailed metadata at: *http://metalinks.oecd.org/ins/20200312/045a*.

Source: OECD Insurance Statistics (database)

Table 2. Number of companies and employees

	2011	2012	2013	2014	2015	2016	2017	2018
2.1 Number of companies								
Life								
Domestic undertakings	14	14	14	16	16	14	13	12
Foreign controlled undertakings	5	5	5	10	10	9	9	10
Foreign companies (branches)	6	6	5	5	5	4	4	5
All undertakings	20	20	19	21	21	18	17	17
Non-life								
Domestic undertakings	21	21	21	21	24	23	23	23
Foreign controlled undertakings	5	4	4	15	16	15	15	16
Foreign companies (branches)	24	25	24	23	21	19	19	23
All undertakings	45	46	45	44	45	42	42	46
Composite								
Domestic undertakings	7	6	6	5	5	5	6	5
Foreign controlled undertakings	2	2	2	3	3	4	4	3
Foreign companies (branches)	5	5	6	6	7	7	7	9
All undertakings	12	11	12	11	12	12	13	14
Reinsurance								
Domestic undertakings	1	1	1	1	1	1	1	1
Foreign controlled undertakings	0	0	0	1	1	1	1	1
Foreign companies (branches)	0	0	0	0	0	0	0	0
All undertakings	1	1	1	1	1	1	1	1
Total								
Domestic undertakings	43	42	42	43	46	43	43	41
Foreign controlled undertakings	12	11	11	29	30	29	29	30
Foreign companies (branches)	35	36	35	34	33	30	30	37
All undertakings	78	78	77	77	79	73	73	78
2.2 Number of employees								
Insurance undertakings	10 937	8 807	9 224	9 252	9 441	9 387	9 381	8 781
Intermediaries	25 397	24 624	24 207	23 465	22 738	21 426	20 258	18 999
Total	36 334	33 431	33 431	32 717	32 179	30 813	29 639	27 780

Note: Detailed metadata at: *http://metalinks.oecd.org/ins/20200312/045a.*
Source: OECD Insurance Statistics (database)

SLOVAK REPUBLIC

Table 1. Selected aggregates

Million EUR

	2011	2012	2013	2014	2015	2016	2017	2018
1.1 Insurance business written in the reporting country								
1.1.1 Insurance business, by ownership								
Gross premiums								
Domestic undertakings	2 040	2 036	2 082	2 106	2 020	..	4 186	..
Foreign controlled undertakings	1 875	1 863	1 901	1 918	1 827	..	..	..
Foreign companies (branches)	114	121	146	142	143	..	282	..
All undertakings	2 154	2 157	2 228	2 248	2 163	..	4 468	..
Premiums ceded								
Domestic undertakings	294	294	298	314	319	..	319	..
Foreign controlled undertakings	268	267	268	283	287	..	..	..
Foreign companies (branches)	17	17	19	17	17	..	31	..
All undertakings	312	311	316	331	336	..	350	..
Net written premiums								
Domestic undertakings	1 746	1 742	1 785	1 792	1 701	..	3 868	..
Foreign controlled undertakings	1 606	1 596	1 633	1 635	1 540	..	..	..
Foreign companies (branches)	96	104	127	126	126	..	250	..
All undertakings	1 842	1 846	1 912	1 917	1 827	..	4 118	..
1.1.2 Insurance business on foreign risks, gross premiums								
Life	..	..	..	..	..	..	..	..
Non-life	..	..	..	..	..	..	..	..
Composite	..	..	..	..	..	..	..	..
of which:								
Life	..	..	..	..	..	..	..	..
Non-life	..	..	..	..	..	..	..	..
Total	..	..	..	..	..	..	..	..
1.1.3 Life insurance payments, by class, gross premiums								
Annuities	619	607	649	623	586	..	2	..
Unit linked	338	409	423	417	351	..	166	..
Other life insurance	137	146	164	180	171	..	950	..
Total life insurance	1 094	1 162	1 236	1 220	1 108	..	1 119	..
of which: *Pension contracts*	15	13	12	12	12	..	..	..
1.1.4 Non-life insurance payments, by class, gross premiums								
Motor vehicle insurance	568	548	528	532	547	..	309	..
Marine, aviation and other transport insurance	6	7	6	6	6	..	10	..
Freight insurance	8	8	8	8	8	..	..	..
Fire and other property damage insurance	248	247	250	257	257	..	276	..
Pecuniary loss insurance	25	24	27	33	34	..	11	..
General liability insurance	65	68	73	78	78	..	80	..
Accident and health	38	40	45	49	44	..	..	..
of which: *Health*	2	2	2	2	3	..	..	..
Other non-life insurance	31	32	34	35	39	..	397	..
Treaty reinsurance	19	21	21	32	42	..	..	..
Total non-life insurance	1 009	996	992	1 028	1 055	..	1 083	..
1.2 Gross claims payments								
Life								
Domestic undertakings	97	93	91	107	98	186	76	..
Foreign controlled undertakings	97	93	91	107	98	..	73	..
Foreign companies (branches)	0	0	0	0	2	..	117	..
All undertakings	97	93	91	108	100	..	193	..
Non-life								
Domestic undertakings	5	1	0	0	0	..	..	..
Foreign controlled undertakings	5	1	0	0	0	..	..	..
Foreign companies (branches)	24	44	27	29	32	..	21	..
All undertakings	29	45	27	29	32	..	..	..
Composite								
Domestic undertakings	1 075	1 083	1 117	1 084	1 057	2 291	..	..
Foreign controlled undertakings	945	948	979	948	911	1 909	76	..
Foreign companies (branches)	5	12	14	16	16	..	21	..
All undertakings	1 079	1 094	1 131	1 099	1 073	..	..	..
of which:								
Life	566	640	658	646	575	..	..	..
Domestic undertakings	562	632	647	634	563	1 794	..	..
Foreign controlled undertakings	463	527	544	533	457	1 459	72	..
Foreign companies (branches)	4	8	11	12	12	..	17	..
All undertakings	566	640	658	646	575	..	..	..
Non-life	513	455	473	453	497	..	..	..
Domestic undertakings	513	451	470	450	494	497	..	..
Foreign controlled undertakings	483	421	435	415	454	450	4	..
Foreign companies (branches)	0	4	4	3	3	..	5	..
All undertakings	513	455	473	453	497	..	..	..
Total								
Domestic undertakings	1 177	1 176	1 208	1 191	1 155	2 477	76	..
Foreign controlled undertakings	1 047	1 042	1 070	1 055	1 010	1 909	149	..
Foreign companies (branches)	30	55	42	44	49	..	159	..
All undertakings	1 206	1 232	1 249	1 236	1 205	..	193	..

Table 1. Selected aggregates *(cont.)*

Million EUR

	2011	2012	2013	2014	2015	2016	2017	2018
1.3 Commissions								
Life								
Domestic undertakings	26	28	29	33	37	..	..	..
Foreign controlled undertakings	26	28	29	33	37	..	..	..
Foreign companies (branches)	1	1	1	1	2	..	23	..
All undertakings	27	29	30	34	39	..	..	..
Non-life								
Domestic undertakings	2	1	0	0	0	..	..	..
Foreign controlled undertakings	2	1	0	0	0	..	..	..
Foreign companies (branches)	9	11	13	15	18	..	21	..
All undertakings	11	12	13	15	18	..	..	..
Composite								
Domestic undertakings	230	238	251	259	250	..	..	..
Foreign controlled undertakings	219	225	238	244	233	..	..	..
Foreign companies (branches)	17	17	18	4	16	..	20	..
All undertakings	247	255	269	264	266	..	..	..
of which:								
Life	97	102	107	95	89	..	..	..
Domestic undertakings	82	86	93	95	77	..	..	..
Foreign controlled undertakings	79	81	90	91	73	..	..	..
Foreign companies (branches)	16	16	14	0	12	..	13	..
All undertakings	97	102	107	95	89	..	..	..
Non-life	149	154	162	168	177	..	..	..
Domestic undertakings	149	152	158	164	173	..	..	..
Foreign controlled undertakings	141	143	149	153	160	..	..	..
Foreign companies (branches)	1	2	4	4	5	..	7	..
All undertakings	149	154	162	168	177	..	..	..
Total								
Domestic undertakings	258	266	279	292	287	..	..	..
Foreign controlled undertakings	247	253	267	277	270	..	..	..
Foreign companies (branches)	27	30	32	21	36	..	64	..
All undertakings	285	296	311	313	323	..	..	..
1.4 Gross operating expenses								
Life								
Domestic undertakings	58	58	57	63	72	..	55	..
Foreign controlled undertakings	58	58	57	63	72	..	..	..
Foreign companies (branches)	2	3	2	2	3	..	51	..
All undertakings	60	60	59	65	75	..	105	..
Non-life								
Domestic undertakings	6	2	0	0	0	..	..	..
Foreign controlled undertakings	6	2	0	0	0	..	..	..
Foreign companies (branches)	23	26	30	31	32	..	41	..
All undertakings	29	28	30	31	32	..	41	..
Composite								
Domestic undertakings	492	510	522	529	505	..	502	..
Foreign controlled undertakings	465	481	492	498	472	..	..	..
Foreign companies (branches)	23	29	28	7	25	..	29	..
All undertakings	515	539	549	536	531	..	531	..
of which:								
Life	212	231	228	212	187	..	179	..
Domestic undertakings	190	207	207	212	170	..	161	..
Foreign controlled undertakings	180	195	197	202	160	..	..	..
Foreign companies (branches)	22	24	21	1	17	..	19	..
All undertakings	212	231	228	212	187	..	179	..
Non-life	302	308	321	324	344	..	351	..
Domestic undertakings	301	303	314	317	336	..	341	..
Foreign controlled undertakings	285	286	295	295	312	..	..	..
Foreign companies (branches)	1	5	7	6	8	..	10	..
All undertakings	302	308	321	324	344	..	351	..
Total								
Domestic undertakings	555	569	578	592	578	..	556	..
Foreign controlled undertakings	529	541	549	561	544	..	..	..
Foreign companies (branches)	48	57	60	40	60	..	121	..
All undertakings	603	627	639	632	638	..	677	..

Table 1. Selected aggregates *(cont.)*

Million EUR

	2011	2012	2013	2014	2015	2016	2017	2018
1.5 Insurance business written abroad by branches, gross premiums								
Life								
Branches and agencies	0	0	0	0	1	..	..	..
Subsidaries	0	0	0	1	5	..	..	..
Total	0	0	0	1	6	..	..	..
Non-life								
Branches and agencies	0	0	0	0	0	..	..	..
Subsidaries	0	0	0	0	0	..	..	..
Total	0	0	0	0	0	..	..	..
Composite								
Branches and agencies	0	1	1	2	2	..	..	..
Subsidaries	4	3	3	4	6	..	..	..
Total	4	4	5	6	8	..	..	..
of which:								
Life	0	0	0	0	0	..	..	..
Branches and agencies	0	0	0	0	0	..	..	..
Subsidaries	0	0	0	0	0	..	..	..
Total	0	0	0	0	0	..	..	..
Non-life	4	4	5	6	8	..	..	..
Branches and agencies	0	1	1	2	2	..	..	..
Subsidaries	4	3	3	4	6	..	..	..
Total	4	4	5	6	8	..	..	..
Total								
Branches and agencies	0	1	1	2	3	..	..	..
Subsidaries	4	3	3	5	10	..	..	..
Total	4	4	5	7	14	..	..	..

.. Not available

Note: Detailed metadata at: *http://metalinks.oecd.org/ins/20200312/f91f.*

Source: OECD Insurance Statistics (database)

Table 2. Number of companies and employees

	2011	2012	2013	2014	2015	2016	2017	2018
2.1 Number of companies								
Life								
Domestic undertakings	6	5	5	5	5	3	3	..
Foreign controlled undertakings	6	5	5	5	5	3	2	..
Foreign companies (branches)	2	1	1	1	1	2	2	..
All undertakings	8	6	6	6	6	5	5	..
Non-life								
Domestic undertakings	2	1	0	0	0	0	0	..
Foreign controlled undertakings	2	1	0	0	0	0	0	..
Foreign companies (branches)	13	16	17	17	17	19	19	..
All undertakings	15	17	17	17	17	19	19	..
Composite								
Domestic undertakings	12	12	12	12	12	12	12	..
Foreign controlled undertakings	10	10	10	10	10	12	10	..
Foreign companies (branches)	2	2	2	2	2	18	2	..
All undertakings	14	14	14	14	14	30	14	..
Reinsurance								
Domestic undertakings	0	0	0	0	0	0	0	..
Foreign controlled undertakings	0	0	0	0	0	0	0	..
Foreign companies (branches)	1	1	1	1	1	0	0	..
All undertakings	1	1	1	1	1	0	0	..
Total								
Domestic undertakings	20	18	17	17	17	15	15	..
Foreign controlled undertakings	18	16	15	15	15	15	12	..
Foreign companies (branches)	18	20	21	21	21	39	23	..
All undertakings	38	38	38	38	38	54	38	..
2.2 Number of employees								
Insurance undertakings	6 087	5 878	5 778	5 937	..	..	..	..
Intermediaries	1 020	1 373	..	1 358	..	..	..	..
Total	7 107	7 251	..	7 295	..	..	..	..

.. Not available

Note: Detailed metadata at: *http://metalinks.oecd.org/ins/20200312/f91f.*

Source: OECD Insurance Statistics (database)

SLOVENIA

Table 1. Selected aggregates

Million EUR

	2011	2012	2013	2014	2015	2016	2017	2018
1.1 Insurance business written in the reporting country								
1.1.1 Insurance business, by ownership								
Gross premiums								
Domestic undertakings	2 184	2 192	2 114	2 095	2 150	2 182	2 298	2 424
Foreign controlled undertakings	169	166	166	166	172	180	186	191
Foreign companies (branches)	..	..	..	..	..	..	..	..
All undertakings	2 184	2 192	2 114	2 095	2 150	2 182	2 298	2 424
Premiums ceded								
Domestic undertakings	279	283	258	274	256	269	310	320
Foreign controlled undertakings	40	27	27	28	33	39	42	42
Foreign companies (branches)	..	..	..	..	..	..	..	..
All undertakings	279	283	258	274	256	269	310	320
Net written premiums								
Domestic undertakings	1 905	1 909	1 856	1 821	1 894	1 914	1 988	2 105
Foreign controlled undertakings	128	139	140	137	139	141	144	149
Foreign companies (branches)	..	..	..	..	..	..	..	..
All undertakings	1 905	1 909	1 856	1 821	1 894	1 914	1 988	2 105
1.1.2 Insurance business on foreign risks, gross premiums								
Life	0	0	..	..	..	..	..	..
Non-life	..	..	0	0	0	..	..	..
Composite	0	2	2	1	1	..	..	..
of which:								
Life	..	..	0	0	1	..	..	..
Non-life	0	2	1	1	0	..	..	..
Total	0	2	2	2	2	..	..	..
1.1.3 Life insurance payments, by class, gross premiums								
Annuities	..	..	..	..	..	..	..	..
Unit linked	228	219	201	195	215	213	223	225
Other life insurance	252	266	273	284	283	279	293	301
Total life insurance	479	485	473	479	498	492	516	526
of which: *Pension contracts*	51	65	45	37	37	39	41	41
1.1.4 Non-life insurance payments, by class, gross premiums								
Motor vehicle insurance	601	559	513	495	484	499	539	590
Marine, aviation and other transport insurance	15	18	15	16	18	18	19	21
Freight insurance	15	15	14	13	15	16	16	16
Fire and other property damage insurance	389	396	370	372	393	405	415	439
Pecuniary loss insurance	50	48	49	56	62	62	64	60
General liability insurance	58	61	63	65	64	72	73	79
Accident and health	544	580	585	574	591	591	623	661
of which: *Health*	428	467	480	470	484	489	522	556
Other non-life insurance	32	30	31	24	25	28	33	34
Treaty reinsurance	0	0	..	0	0	0	0	0
Total non-life insurance	1 704	1 706	1 641	1 616	1 652	1 690	1 782	1 898
1.2 Gross claims payments								
Life								
Domestic undertakings	35	40	31	36	52	50	46	..
Foreign controlled undertakings	0	0	0	1	0	2	..	..
Foreign companies (branches)	..	..	..	..	..	..	..	..
All undertakings	35	40	31	36	52	50	46	..
Non-life								
Domestic undertakings	443	463	482	449	499	491	532	556
Foreign controlled undertakings	0	..	..	..	1	0	..	0
Foreign companies (branches)	..	..	..	..	..	..	..	..
All undertakings	443	463	482	449	499	491	532	556
Composite								
Domestic undertakings	878	902	951	941	911	903	995	1 115
Foreign controlled undertakings	77	84	93	90	91	95	104	111
Foreign companies (branches)	..	..	..	..	..	..	..	..
All undertakings	878	902	951	941	911	903	995	1 115
of which:								
Life	229	259	299	304	305	314	347	402
Domestic undertakings	229	259	299	304	305	314	347	402
Foreign controlled undertakings	41	47	51	50	51	50	50	49
Foreign companies (branches)	..	..	..	..	..	..	..	..
All undertakings	229	259	299	304	305	314	347	402
Non-life	649	642	651	637	606	590	648	713
Domestic undertakings	649	642	651	637	606	590	648	713
Foreign controlled undertakings	36	38	42	41	40	45	54	62
Foreign companies (branches)	..	..	..	..	..	..	..	..
All undertakings	649	642	651	637	606	590	648	713
Total								
Domestic undertakings	1 355	1 404	1 464	1 426	1 461	1 445	1 573	1 670
Foreign controlled undertakings	78	85	93	91	91	97	104	111
Foreign companies (branches)	..	..	..	..	..	..	..	..
All undertakings	1 355	1 404	1 464	1 426	1 461	1 445	1 573	1 670

Table 1. Selected aggregates *(cont.)*

Million EUR

	2011	2012	2013	2014	2015	2016	2017	2018
1.3 Commissions								
Life								
Domestic undertakings	7	6	3	3	3	3	4	..
Foreign controlled undertakings	0	0	0	0	0	0	..	..
Foreign companies (branches)	..	..	..	..	..	..	..	..
All undertakings	7	6	3	3	3	3	4	..
Non-life								
Domestic undertakings	2	2	4	7	8	7	8	9
Foreign controlled undertakings	0	..	..	..	0	0	..	0
Foreign companies (branches)	..	..	..	..	..	..	..	..
All undertakings	2	2	4	7	8	7	8	9
Composite								
Domestic undertakings	90	80	84	86	89	86	92	104
Foreign controlled undertakings	19	19	19	20	21	28	22	23
Foreign companies (branches)	..	..	..	..	..	..	..	..
All undertakings	90	80	84	86	89	86	92	104
of which:								
Life	36	27	32	32	34	32	32	35
Domestic undertakings	36	27	32	32	34	32	32	35
Foreign controlled undertakings	9	10	10	10	10	15	9	9
Foreign companies (branches)	..	..	..	..	..	..	..	..
All undertakings	36	27	32	32	34	32	32	35
Non-life	53	53	52	54	56	54	60	68
Domestic undertakings	53	53	52	54	56	54	60	68
Foreign controlled undertakings	9	9	9	10	11	13	13	14
Foreign companies (branches)	..	..	..	..	..	..	..	..
All undertakings	53	53	52	54	56	54	60	68
Total								
Domestic undertakings	99	89	91	96	100	96	104	112
Foreign controlled undertakings	19	20	19	20	21	28	22	23
Foreign companies (branches)	..	..	..	..	..	..	..	..
All undertakings	99	89	91	96	100	96	104	112
1.4 Gross operating expenses								
Life								
Domestic undertakings	26	28	14	15	16	12	15	..
Foreign controlled undertakings	1	2	2	1	1	1	..	..
Foreign companies (branches)	..	..	..	..	..	..	..	..
All undertakings	26	28	14	15	16	12	15	..
Non-life								
Domestic undertakings	74	80	81	86	90	97	97	105
Foreign controlled undertakings	1	..	..	..	0	1	..	1
Foreign companies (branches)	..	..	..	..	..	..	..	..
All undertakings	74	80	81	86	90	97	97	105
Composite								
Domestic undertakings	356	361	366	362	368	378	388	418
Foreign controlled undertakings	52	56	47	57	60	60	66	68
Foreign companies (branches)	..	..	..	..	..	..	..	..
All undertakings	356	361	366	362	368	378	388	418
of which:								
Life	91	93	104	99	100	99	102	116
Domestic undertakings	91	93	104	99	100	99	102	116
Foreign controlled undertakings	26	28	26	27	28	26	27	27
Foreign companies (branches)	..	..	..	..	..	..	..	..
All undertakings	91	93	104	99	100	99	102	116
Non-life	265	269	263	263	268	279	286	302
Domestic undertakings	265	269	263	263	268	279	286	302
Foreign controlled undertakings	26	28	21	30	32	33	39	41
Foreign companies (branches)	..	..	..	..	..	..	..	..
All undertakings	265	269	263	263	268	279	286	302
Total								
Domestic undertakings	456	469	461	462	474	487	500	523
Foreign controlled undertakings	55	57	49	59	62	62	66	69
Foreign companies (branches)	..	..	..	..	..	..	..	..
All undertakings	456	469	461	462	474	487	500	523

Table 1. Selected aggregates *(cont.)*

Million EUR

	2011	2012	2013	2014	2015	2016	2017	2018
1.5 Insurance business written abroad by branches, gross premiums								
Life								
Branches and agencies	0	..	..	..	..	..	..	..
Subsidaries	..	..	..	..	..	..	..	..
Total	0	..	..	..	..	..	..	..
Non-life								
Branches and agencies	..	..	..	..	..	..	1	1
Subsidaries	..	..	..	..	..	..	..	..
Total	..	..	..	..	..	..	1	1
Composite								
Branches and agencies	0	..	..	..	2	..	31	44
Subsidaries	..	..	..	..	..	..	..	..
Total	0	..	..	..	2	..	31	44
of which:								
Life	..	..	..	..	2	..	6	7
Branches and agencies	..	..	..	..	2	..	6	7
Subsidaries	..	..	..	..	..	..	..	..
Total	..	..	..	..	2	..	6	7
Non-life	0	..	..	..	0	..	25	37
Branches and agencies	0	..	..	..	0	..	25	37
Subsidaries	..	..	..	..	..	..	..	..
Total	0	..	..	..	0	..	25	37
Total								
Branches and agencies	0	..	..	..	2	..	32	45
Subsidaries	..	..	..	..	..	..	..	..
Total	0	..	..	..	2	..	32	45

.. Not available

Note: Detailed metadata at: *http://metalinks.oecd.org/ins/20200312/f516.*

Source: OECD Insurance Statistics (database)

Table 2. Number of companies and employees

	2011	2012	2013	2014	2015	2016	2017	2018
2.1 Number of companies								
Life								
Domestic undertakings	4	4	3	3	3	3	2	0
Foreign controlled undertakings	1	1	1	1	1	1	0	0
Foreign companies (branches)	0	0	0	0	0	0	0	0
All undertakings	4	4	3	3	3	3	2	0
Non-life								
Domestic undertakings	4	3	3	3	4	4	4	4
Foreign controlled undertakings	1	0	0	0	0	0	0	1
Foreign companies (branches)	1	3	4	4	4	4	4	3
All undertakings	5	6	7	7	8	8	8	7
Composite								
Domestic undertakings	8	8	8	8	8	7	7	9
Foreign controlled undertakings	3	3	3	3	3	3	3	3
Foreign companies (branches)	2	2	2	2	2	2	2	4
All undertakings	10	10	10	10	10	9	9	13
Reinsurance								
Domestic undertakings	2	2	2	2	2	2	2	2
Foreign controlled undertakings	0	0	0	0	0	0	0	0
Foreign companies (branches)	0	0	0	0	0	0	0	0
All undertakings	2	2	2	2	2	2	2	2
Total								
Domestic undertakings	18	17	16	16	17	16	15	15
Foreign controlled undertakings	5	4	4	4	4	4	3	4
Foreign companies (branches)	3	5	6	6	6	6	6	7
All undertakings	21	22	22	22	23	22	21	22
2.2 Number of employees								
Insurance undertakings	..	..	..	..	..	..	..	..
Intermediaries	..	..	..	..	..	..	..	..
Total	..	..	..	..	..	..	..	..

.. Not available

Note: Detailed metadata at: *http://metalinks.oecd.org/ins/20200312/f516.*

Source: OECD Insurance Statistics (database)

SPAIN

Table 1. Selected aggregates

Million EUR

	2011	2012	2013	2014	2015	2016	2017	2018
1.1 Insurance business written in the reporting country								
1.1.1 Insurance business, by ownership								
Gross premiums								
Domestic undertakings	61 922	56 608	58 110	57 662	59 048	66 541	65 719	66 538
Foreign controlled undertakings	8 045	14 689	12 578	12 542	11 038	..	..	..
Foreign companies (branches)	133	117	0	0	0	..	..	..
All undertakings	62 055	56 725	58 110	57 662	59 048	66 541	65 719	66 538
Premiums ceded								
Domestic undertakings	4 305	4 235	5 831	5 019	5 161	6 014	6 206	6 020
Foreign controlled undertakings	793	1 094	1 058	923	736	..	..	..
Foreign companies (branches)	44	42	0	0	0	..	..	..
All undertakings	4 349	4 277	5 831	5 019	5 161	6 014	6 206	6 020
Net written premiums								
Domestic undertakings	57 617	52 373	52 279	52 643	53 886	60 527	59 513	60 518
Foreign controlled undertakings	7 252	13 594	11 520	11 620	10 301	..	..	..
Foreign companies (branches)	89	75	0	0	0	..	..	..
All undertakings	57 706	52 448	52 279	52 643	53 886	60 527	59 513	60 518
1.1.2 Insurance business on foreign risks, gross premiums								
Life	1	16	22	7	11	13	9	11
Non-life	73	138	79	73	59	45	20	3
Composite	79	54	52	44	61	49	26	147
of which:								
Life	42	39	42	34	46	35	2	28
Non-life	36	16	10	9	15	14	24	119
Total	153	209	153	123	130	107	55	160
1.1.3 Life insurance payments, by class, gross premiums								
Annuities	8 992	7 052	7 946	6 406	5 881	8 746	8 318	7 583
Unit linked	4 077	3 748	3 062	2 816	2 721	2 981	4 431	4 432
Other life insurance	16 704	15 828	14 865	16 021	17 128	19 330	16 270	16 559
Total life insurance	29 773	26 629	25 873	25 244	25 730	31 056	29 019	28 574
***of which:** Pension contracts*	..	..	..	..	..	..	..	..
1.1.4 Non-life insurance payments, by class, gross premiums								
Motor vehicle insurance	10 698	9 961	9 610	9 445	9 695	10 451	10 918	11 212
Marine, aviation and other transport insurance	480	329	390	361	369	369	367	389
Freight insurance	268	194	294	268	261	270	281	301
Fire and other property damage insurance	2 701	913	2 246	2 315	2 610	2 895	2 770	3 425
Pecuniary loss insurance	359	311	175	178	208	283	247	252
General liability insurance	1 274	1 096	1 077	1 009	1 011	1 049	1 100	1 181
Accident and health	7 630	7 629	7 888	8 227	8 449	8 879	9 329	9 744
***of which:** Health*	6 650	6 777	7 031	7 356	7 536	7 902	8 224	8 652
Other non-life insurance	10 410	10 502	10 531	10 558	10 729	11 001	11 264	11 029
Treaty reinsurance	0	0	0	0	0	0	..	..
Total non-life insurance	33 820	30 933	32 211	32 362	33 332	35 197	36 275	37 532
1.2 Gross claims payments								
Life								
Domestic undertakings	12 763	15 189	14 147	16 777	18 872	3 070	3 685	3 096
Foreign controlled undertakings	1 996	2 127	1 814	1 688	1 582	..	..	..
Foreign companies (branches)	0	0	0	0	0	..	..	..
All undertakings	12 763	15 189	14 147	16 777	18 872	3 070	3 685	3 096
Non-life								
Domestic undertakings	9 573	9 489	9 463	9 250	9 593	9 453	10 280	9 702
Foreign controlled undertakings	4 025	3 926	3 947	3 890	2 592	..	..	..
Foreign companies (branches)	0	0	0	0	0	..	..	..
All undertakings	9 573	9 489	9 463	9 250	9 593	9 453	10 280	9 702
Composite								
Domestic undertakings	23 611	22 204	21 477	21 596	20 659	32 425	35 292	35 464
Foreign controlled undertakings	5 663	6 495	5 208	5 230	5 136	..	..	..
Foreign companies (branches)	63	49	0	0	0	..	..	..
All undertakings	23 674	22 252	21 477	21 596	20 659	32 425	35 292	35 464
of which:								
Life	11 327	11 547	9 702	9 986	8 948	20 670	22 722	21 474
Domestic undertakings	11 288	11 511	9 702	9 986	8 948	20 670	22 722	21 474
Foreign controlled undertakings	2 437	3 836	2 320	2 497	2 292	..	..	..
Foreign companies (branches)	38	36	0	0	0	..	..	..
All undertakings	11 327	11 547	9 702	9 986	8 948	20 670	22 722	21 474
Non-life	12 347	10 705	11 775	11 610	11 711	11 755	12 571	13 989
Domestic undertakings	12 323	10 693	11 775	11 610	11 711	11 755	12 571	13 989
Foreign controlled undertakings	3 226	2 659	2 888	2 733	2 843	..	..	..
Foreign companies (branches)	24	12	0	0	0	..	..	..
All undertakings	12 347	10 705	11 775	11 610	11 711	11 755	12 571	13 989
Total								
Domestic undertakings	45 947	46 882	45 088	47 622	49 125	44 947	49 258	48 262
Foreign controlled undertakings	11 684	12 548	10 968	10 809	9 310	..	..	..
Foreign companies (branches)	63	49	0	0	0	..	..	..
All undertakings	46 009	46 930	45 088	47 622	49 125	44 947	49 258	48 262

Table 1. Selected aggregates *(cont.)*

Million EUR

	2011	2012	2013	2014	2015	2016	2017	2018
1.3 Commissions								
Life								
Domestic undertakings	..	..	..	660	712	234	257	273
Foreign controlled undertakings	..	..	..	86	71	..	..	..
Foreign companies (branches)	..	..	..	0	0	..	..	..
All undertakings	..	..	..	660	712	234	257	273
Non-life								
Domestic undertakings	..	..	..	1 472	1 436	1 433	1 522	1 524
Foreign controlled undertakings	..	..	..	642	517	..	..	..
Foreign companies (branches)	..	..	..	0	0	..	..	..
All undertakings	..	..	..	1 472	1 436	1 433	1 522	1 524
Composite								
Domestic undertakings	..	..	..	2 270	2 635	3 328	4 629	3 786
Foreign controlled undertakings	..	..	..	669	710	..	..	..
Foreign companies (branches)	..	..	..	0	0	..	..	..
All undertakings	..	..	..	2 270	2 635	3 328	4 629	3 786
of which:								
Life	..	..	..	418	379	979	1 185	1 114
Domestic undertakings	..	..	..	418	379	979	1 185	1 114
Foreign controlled undertakings	..	..	..	94	103	..	..	..
Foreign companies (branches)	..	..	..	0	0	..	..	..
All undertakings	..	..	..	418	379	979	1 185	1 114
Non-life	..	..	..	1 852	2 255	2 349	3 444	2 672
Domestic undertakings	..	..	..	1 852	2 255	2 349	3 444	2 672
Foreign controlled undertakings	..	..	..	576	607	..	..	..
Foreign companies (branches)	..	..	..	0	0	..	..	..
All undertakings	..	..	..	1 852	2 255	2 349	3 444	2 672
Total								
Domestic undertakings	..	..	..	4 403	4 782	4 995	6 408	5 583
Foreign controlled undertakings	..	..	..	1 398	1 298	..	..	..
Foreign companies (branches)	..	..	..	0	0	..	..	..
All undertakings	..	..	..	4 403	4 782	4 995	6 408	5 583
1.4 Gross operating expenses								
Life								
Domestic undertakings	171	220	968	994	1 075	425	455	484
Foreign controlled undertakings	42	39	201	190	192	..	..	..
Foreign companies (branches)	0	0	0	..	..	..	..	..
All undertakings	171	220	968	994	1 075	425	455	484
Non-life								
Domestic undertakings	487	491	3 046	2 880	2 832	2 876	3 081	3 065
Foreign controlled undertakings	254	242	1 272	1 289	947	..	..	..
Foreign companies (branches)	0	0	0	..	..	..	..	..
All undertakings	487	491	3 046	2 880	2 832	2 876	3 081	3 065
Composite								
Domestic undertakings	622	564	5 322	5 034	5 250	6 332	6 550	6 855
Foreign controlled undertakings	140	120	1 152	1 070	1 100	..	..	..
Foreign companies (branches)	6	5	1	..	4	..	..	..
All undertakings	628	569	5 323	5 034	5 254	6 332	6 550	6 855
of which:								
Life	119	87	809	797	729	1 489	1 546	1 677
Domestic undertakings	117	85	809	797	729	1 489	1 546	1 677
Foreign controlled undertakings	25	26	162	178	186	..	..	..
Foreign companies (branches)	2	2	0	..	..	..	..	..
All undertakings	119	87	809	797	729	1 489	1 546	1 677
Non-life	509	482	4 515	4 237	4 525	4 843	5 004	5 178
Domestic undertakings	506	479	4 514	4 237	4 521	4 843	5 004	5 178
Foreign controlled undertakings	116	94	990	892	913	..	..	..
Foreign companies (branches)	4	3	1	0	4	..	..	..
All undertakings	509	482	4 515	4 237	4 525	4 843	5 004	5 178
Total								
Domestic undertakings	1 280	1 275	9 337	8 907	9 157	9 633	10 087	10 405
Foreign controlled undertakings	436	401	2 625	2 549	2 239	..	..	..
Foreign companies (branches)	6	5	1	..	4	..	..	..
All undertakings	1 286	1 280	9 338	8 907	9 161	9 633	10 087	10 405

Table 1. Selected aggregates *(cont.)*

Million EUR

	2011	2012	2013	2014	2015	2016	2017	2018
1.5 Insurance business written abroad by branches, gross premiums								
Life								
Branches and agencies	938	323	274	0	0	0	0	1
Subsidaries	..	..	..	..	..	..	..	..
Total	..	..	..	..	..	0	0	1
Non-life								
Branches and agencies	296	419	592	654	701	1 694	1 841	1 537
Subsidaries	..	..	..	..	..	..	..	..
Total	..	..	..	..	..	1 694	1 841	1 537
Composite								
Branches and agencies	759	135	885	1 286	1 361	1 262	1 385	2 155
Subsidaries	..	..	..	..	..	..	..	..
Total	..	..	..	..	..	1 262	1 385	2 155
of which:								
Life	..	..	..	..	..	518	574	812
Branches and agencies	157	23	212	559	694	518	574	812
Subsidaries	..	..	..	..	..	..	..	..
Total	..	..	..	..	..	518	574	812
Non-life	..	..	..	..	..	744	812	1 344
Branches and agencies	602	113	673	728	667	744	812	1 344
Subsidaries	..	..	..	..	..	..	..	..
Total	..	..	..	..	..	744	812	1 344
Total								
Branches and agencies	1 994	878	1 751	1 940	2 062	2 955	3 226	3 693
Subsidaries	..	..	..	..	..	..	..	..
Total	..	..	..	..	..	2 955	3 226	3 693

.. Not available

Note: Detailed metadata at: *http://metalinks.oecd.org/ins/20200312/540f.*

Source: OECD Insurance Statistics (database)

Table 2. Number of companies and employees

	2011	2012	2013	2014	2015	2016	2017	2018
2.1 Number of companies								
Life								
Domestic undertakings	89	84	83	79	78	32	32	29
Foreign controlled undertakings	11	10	10	9	8	..	..	..
Foreign companies (branches)	0	0	0	0	0	..	..	..
All undertakings	89	84	83	79	78	32	32	29
Non-life								
Domestic undertakings	140	136	132	127	118	121	111	105
Foreign controlled undertakings	19	18	19	19	17	..	..	..
Foreign companies (branches)	0	0	0	0	1	..	..	..
All undertakings	140	136	132	127	119	121	111	105
Composite								
Domestic undertakings	47	46	47	45	41	75	74	74
Foreign controlled undertakings	10	10	8	8	8	..	..	..
Foreign companies (branches)	2	2	1	1	0	..	..	..
All undertakings	49	48	48	46	41	75	74	74
Reinsurance								
Domestic undertakings	2	2	2	3	3	3	3	3
Foreign controlled undertakings	..	0	0	0	0	..	..	..
Foreign companies (branches)	0	0	0	0	0	..	..	..
All undertakings	2	2	2	3	3	3	3	3
Total								
Domestic undertakings	278	268	264	254	240	231	220	211
Foreign controlled undertakings	40	38	37	36	33	..	..	..
Foreign companies (branches)	2	2	1	1	1	..	..	..
All undertakings	280	270	265	255	241	231	220	211
2.2 Number of employees								
Insurance undertakings	46 557	46 439	46 324	45 535	45 218	47 453	47 498	47 380
Intermediaries	..	..	121 427	129 549	..	..	..	..
Total	..	..	167 751	175 084	..	..	..	..

.. Not available

Note: Detailed metadata at: *http://metalinks.oecd.org/ins/20200312/540f.*

Source: OECD Insurance Statistics (database)

SWEDEN

Table 1. Selected aggregates

Million SEK

	2011	2012	2013	2014	2015	2016	2017	2018
1.1 Insurance business written in the reporting country								
1.1.1 Insurance business, by ownership								
Gross premiums								
Domestic undertakings	182 225	167 132	177 197	332 028	339 533	334 834	379 418	426 318
Foreign controlled undertakings	63 298	65 752	66 854	66 041	62 537	67 208	78 911	97 388
Foreign companies (branches)	..	..	..	10 260	..	..	..	..
All undertakings	182 225	167 132	177 197	342 288	339 533	334 834	379 418	426 318
Premiums ceded								
Domestic undertakings	12 870	13 068	12 967	15 157	10 306	9 139	10 693	11 095
Foreign controlled undertakings	4 583	5 428	4 727	3 870	4 441	4 296	5 538	6 138
Foreign companies (branches)	..	..	..	..	..	..	..	..
All undertakings	12 870	13 068	12 967	15 157	10 306	9 139	10 693	11 095
Net written premiums								
Domestic undertakings	169 355	154 064	164 230	316 871	329 227	325 695	368 725	415 223
Foreign controlled undertakings	58 715	60 324	62 127	62 171	58 096	62 912	73 373	91 250
Foreign companies (branches)	..	..	..	10 260	..	..	..	..
All undertakings	169 355	154 064	164 230	327 131	329 227	325 695	368 725	415 223
1.1.2 Insurance business on foreign risks, gross premiums								
Life	..	..	..	581	667	60	58	58
Non-life	..	..	..	28 134	27 121	26 941	30 482	40 549
Composite total	..	..	..	..	..	..	..	..
Total	..	..	..	28 715	27 788	27 001	30 540	40 607
1.1.3 Life insurance payments, by class, gross premiums								
Annuities	72 263	73 378	73 377	205 927	169 626	94 037	107 773	126 049
Unit linked	3 790	1 708	1 188	2 366	75 221	85 696	97 951	107 143
Other life insurance	13 615	13 229	13 591	29 900	3 957	71 084	82 841	89 138
Total life insurance	89 668	88 315	88 156	238 192	248 804	250 817	288 565	322 330
***of which:** Pension contracts*	..	..	..	..	..	..	..	..
1.1.4 Non-life insurance payments, by class, gross premiums								
Motor vehicle insurance	..	..	..	30 360	21 348	..	..	..
Marine, aviation and other transport insurance	..	..	..	2 627	749	..	..	..
Freight insurance	..	..	..	..	..	..	..	..
Fire and other property damage insurance	..	..	..	29 146	36 720	..	..	..
Pecuniary loss insurance	..	..	..	459	1 070	..	..	..
General liability insurance	..	..	..	4 045	4 119	..	..	..
Accident and health	..	..	..	5 674	5 155	..	..	..
***of which:** Health*	..	..	..	..	..	..	..	..
Other non-life insurance	..	..	..	9 165	21 483	..	..	..
Treaty reinsurance	..	..	..	13 811	..	..	..	..
Total non-life insurance	91 819	76 947	84 766	95 287	90 644	83 954	90 800	103 940
1.2 Gross claims payments								
Life								
Domestic undertakings	53 464	58 780	64 657	60 930	64 815	76 869	76 390	77 434
Foreign controlled undertakings	7 533	3 499	6 337	6 055	5 719	5 852	5 784	5 704
Foreign companies (branches)	..	..	..	5 999	..	..	..	..
All undertakings	53 464	58 780	64 657	66 929	64 815	76 869	76 390	77 434
Non-life								
Domestic undertakings	68 400	69 882	69 100	75 805	64 537	65 941	66 635	77 278
Foreign controlled undertakings	31 370	31 639	31 398	31 024	23 701	22 495	25 544	32 791
Foreign companies (branches)	..	..	..	5 328	..	..	..	..
All undertakings	68 400	69 882	69 100	81 133	64 537	65 941	66 635	77 278
Composite, all undertakings	..	..	..	..	..	..	..	..
Total								
Domestic undertakings	121 864	128 662	133 757	136 735	129 352	142 810	143 025	154 712
Foreign controlled undertakings	38 903	35 138	37 735	37 079	29 420	28 347	31 328	38 495
Foreign companies (branches)	..	..	..	11 327	..	..	..	..
All undertakings	121 864	128 662	133 757	148 062	129 352	142 810	143 025	154 712
1.3 Commissions								
Life								
Domestic undertakings	..	..	..	4 167	3 782	3 063	3 545	3 494
Foreign controlled undertakings	..	..	..	1 302	610	274	589	587
Foreign companies (branches)	..	..	..	121	..	..	..	..
All undertakings	..	..	..	4 288	3 782	3 063	3 545	3 494
Non-life								
Domestic undertakings	..	..	..	4 168	4 264	3 848	3 953	3 711
Foreign controlled undertakings	..	..	..	2 049	2 589	2 362	2 482	2 634
Foreign companies (branches)	..	..	..	786	..	..	..	..
All undertakings	..	..	..	4 954	4 264	3 848	3 953	3 711
Composite, all undertakings	..	..	..	..	..	..	..	..
Total								
Domestic undertakings	..	..	..	8 335	8 046	6 911	7 498	7 205
Foreign controlled undertakings	..	..	..	3 351	3 199	2 636	3 071	3 221
Foreign companies (branches)	..	..	..	907	..	..	..	..
All undertakings	..	..	..	9 242	8 046	6 911	7 498	7 205

Table 1. Selected aggregates *(cont.)*

Million SEK

	2011	2012	2013	2014	2015	2016	2017	2018
1.4 Gross operating expenses								
Life								
Domestic undertakings	10 785	11 509	12 115	12 738	13 573	12 617	13 248	15 095
Foreign controlled undertakings	3 488	3 557	3 630	3 639	2 122	1 297	1 918	1 901
Foreign companies (branches)	..	..	..	..	..	..	..	..
All undertakings	10 785	11 509	12 115	12 738	13 573	12 617	13 248	15 095
Non-life								
Domestic undertakings	14 468	14 989	15 004	16 878	16 854	15 781	15 863	18 250
Foreign controlled undertakings	7 262	7 138	7 248	8 238	7 704	7 205	7 691	9 496
Foreign companies (branches)	..	..	..	..	..	..	..	..
All undertakings	14 468	14 989	15 004	16 878	16 854	15 781	15 863	18 250
Composite, all undertakings	..	..	..	..	..	..	..	..
Total								
Domestic undertakings	25 253	26 498	27 119	29 616	30 427	28 398	29 111	33 345
Foreign controlled undertakings	10 750	10 695	10 878	11 877	9 826	8 502	9 609	11 397
Foreign companies (branches)	..	..	..	..	..	..	..	..
All undertakings	25 253	26 498	27 119	29 616	30 427	28 398	29 111	33 345
1.5 Insurance business written abroad by branches, gross premiums								
Life								
Branches and agencies	108	234	..	243	279	347	347	447
Subsidaries	..	..	..	..	..	..	..	..
Total	108	234	..	243	279	347	347	447
Non-life								
Branches and agencies	18 526	18 948	..	18 630	18 207	24 226	24 226	34 479
Subsidaries	..	..	..	..	..	..	..	..
Total	18 526	18 948	..	18 630	18 207	24 226	24 226	34 479
Composite total	..	..	..	..	..	..	..	..
Total								
Branches and agencies	18 634	19 182	..	18 873	18 486	24 573	24 573	34 926
Subsidaries	..	..	..	..	..	..	..	..
Total	18 634	19 182	..	18 873	18 486	24 573	24 573	34 926

.. Not available

Note: Detailed metadata at: *http://metalinks.oecd.org/ins/20200312/a0cf.*

Source: OECD Insurance Statistics (database)

Table 2. Number of companies and employees

	2011	2012	2013	2014	2015	2016	2017	2018
2.1 Number of companies								
Life								
Domestic undertakings	39	39	39	39	38	37	36	35
Foreign controlled undertakings	8	9	8	8	8	6	6	4
Foreign companies (branches)	5	5	5	6	8	6	4	4
All undertakings	44	44	44	45	46	43	46	39
Non-life								
Domestic undertakings	139	131	130	130	127	120	117	127
Foreign controlled undertakings	18	46	44	34	24	14	15	8
Foreign companies (branches)	31	32	32	28	33	31	25	9
All undertakings	170	163	162	158	160	151	157	136
Composite, all undertakings	**0**	**0**	**0**	**0**	**0**	**0**	..	..
Reinsurance								
Domestic undertakings	3	2	1	1	1	0	..	..
Foreign controlled undertakings	2	0	0	0	1	0	..	..
Foreign companies (branches)	..	0	..	0	0	..	..	..
All undertakings	3	2	1	1	1	..	..	..
Total								
Domestic undertakings	181	172	170	170	166	157	153	162
Foreign controlled undertakings	28	55	52	42	33	20	21	12
Foreign companies (branches)	36	37	37	34	41	37	29	13
All undertakings	217	209	207	204	207	194	203	175
2.2 Number of employees								
Insurance undertakings	18 848	19 158	19 059	19 573	18 792	20 600	21 900	20 865
Intermediaries	2 000	2 000	2 000	3 849	3 235	3 540	3 585	3 789
Total	20 848	21 158	21 059	23 422	22 027	..	25 485	24 654

.. Not available

Note: Detailed metadata at: *http://metalinks.oecd.org/ins/20200312/a0cf.*

Source: OECD Insurance Statistics (database)

SWITZERLAND

Table 1. Selected aggregates

Million CHF

	2011	2012	2013	2014	2015	2016	2017	2018
1.1 Insurance business written in the reporting country								
1.1.1 Insurance business, by ownership								
Gross premiums								
Domestic undertakings	61 417	63 507	66 569	66 312	65 628	63 975	63 967	65 722
Foreign controlled undertakings	13 600	14 322	15 423	14 214	13 846	12 578	11 699	12 241
Foreign companies (branches)	2 062	2 331	2 267	1 923	2 091	2 522	2 768	2 198
All undertakings	63 479	65 838	68 836	68 235	67 720	66 497	66 735	67 920
Premiums ceded								
Domestic undertakings	4 000	4 479	4 536	4 346	4 141	3 363	4 085	4 283
Foreign controlled undertakings	1 024	1 219	963	831	731	506	502	613
Foreign companies (branches)	467	487	532	533	553	813	874	776
All undertakings	4 467	4 965	5 068	4 879	4 694	4 176	4 959	5 059
Net written premiums								
Domestic undertakings	57 417	59 028	62 033	61 966	61 487	60 612	59 882	61 439
Foreign controlled undertakings	12 577	13 102	14 460	13 383	13 115	12 072	11 197	11 628
Foreign companies (branches)	1 595	1 845	1 735	1 390	1 539	1 709	1 894	1 422
All undertakings	59 012	60 873	63 768	63 356	63 026	62 321	61 776	62 861
1.1.2 Insurance business on foreign risks, gross premiums								
Life	..	..	..	..	..	..	..	..
Non-life	..	..	..	..	..	..	..	..
Composite total	..	..	..	..	..	..	..	..
Total	..	..	..	..	..	..	..	..
1.1.3 Life insurance payments, by class, gross premiums								
Annuities	737	677	564	441	495	428	317	246
Unit linked	2 423	2 637	2 403	1 730	1 755	1 738	1 861	1 947
Other life insurance	27 397	27 841	29 707	30 478	30 359	28 518	27 445	27 607
Total life insurance	30 557	31 155	32 675	32 649	32 609	30 684	29 623	29 800
***of which:** Pension contracts*	..	..	..	..	..	..	..	..
1.1.4 Non-life insurance payments, by class, gross premiums								
Motor vehicle insurance	6 382	6 526	6 556	6 580	6 595	6 598	6 742	6 804
Marine, aviation and other transport insurance	804	968	1 060	876	732	657	681	635
Freight insurance	..	..	..	..	..	..	..	..
Fire and other property damage insurance	7 457	8 150	8 206	8 123	7 909	7 411	7 397	7 804
Pecuniary loss insurance	832	932	1 042	1 096	897	1 095	1 108	1 055
General liability insurance	3 243	3 514	3 558	3 658	3 562	3 293	3 447	3 416
Accident and health	12 551	13 093	13 889	13 414	13 387	14 585	15 626	16 692
***of which:** Health*	9 383	9 656	9 911	9 934	10 266	10 606	11 361	11 901
Other non-life insurance	1 036	1 151	1 351	1 378	1 525	1 649	1 715	1 361
Treaty reinsurance	..	..	..	..	..	..	..	..
Total non-life insurance	32 306	34 334	35 661	35 125	34 607	35 288	36 716	37 767
1.2 Gross claims payments								
Life								
Domestic undertakings	27 182	25 817	27 624	27 943	27 794	29 083	29 352	44 908
Foreign controlled undertakings	7 354	7 060	8 854	7 917	8 123	8 578	8 159	11 255
Foreign companies (branches)	104	186	306	3	3	3	3	7
All undertakings	27 286	26 003	27 930	27 946	27 797	29 086	29 355	44 915
Non-life								
Domestic undertakings	15 548	20 279	19 735	20 149	20 621	20 498	20 716	42 021
Foreign controlled undertakings	1 974	2 292	2 171	2 281	2 671	2 471	2 299	4 534
Foreign companies (branches)	404	667	798	874	902	1 105	1 164	1 219
All undertakings	15 952	20 946	20 533	21 023	21 523	21 603	21 880	43 240
Composite, all undertakings	..	..	..	..	..	..	..	..
Total								
Domestic undertakings	42 730	46 096	47 359	48 092	48 415	49 581	50 068	86 929
Foreign controlled undertakings	9 328	9 352	11 025	10 198	10 794	11 049	10 458	15 789
Foreign companies (branches)	509	853	1 104	877	905	1 108	1 167	1 226
All undertakings	43 238	46 949	48 463	48 969	49 320	50 689	51 235	88 155
1.3 Commissions								
Life								
Domestic undertakings	848	875	904	920	856	856	836	829
Foreign controlled undertakings	107	103	148	114	169	169	163	163
Foreign companies (branches)	8	8	11	0	0	1	1	1
All undertakings	856	883	915	920	856	857	837	830
Non-life								
Domestic undertakings	1 886	1 955	2 067	1 597	2 188	2 289	2 078	1 403
Foreign controlled undertakings	450	442	372	381	441	450	453	458
Foreign companies (branches)	85	88	95	91	78	65	24	72
All undertakings	1 970	2 043	2 162	1 688	2 266	2 354	2 102	1 475
Composite, all undertakings	..	..	..	..	..	..	..	..
Total								
Domestic undertakings	2 734	2 830	2 971	2 517	3 044	3 145	2 914	2 232
Foreign controlled undertakings	557	545	520	495	610	619	616	621
Foreign companies (branches)	92	96	106	91	78	66	25	73
All undertakings	2 826	2 926	3 077	2 608	3 122	3 211	2 939	2 305

SWITZERLAND

Table 1. Selected aggregates *(cont.)*

Million CHF

	2011	2012	2013	2014	2015	2016	2017	2018
1.4 Gross operating expenses								
Life								
Domestic undertakings	2 444	1 390	1 289	1 364	1 078	1 085	1 091	1 117
Foreign controlled undertakings	450	239	176	209	156	156	160	186
Foreign companies (branches)	11	4	4	2	1	1	2	3
All undertakings	2 455	1 394	1 293	1 366	1 079	1 086	1 093	1 120
Non-life								
Domestic undertakings	7 179	3 835	3 745	5 520	2 975	2 981	3 185	3 388
Foreign controlled undertakings	1 039	371	416	420	341	310	316	353
Foreign companies (branches)	408	80	100	108	103	215	195	186
All undertakings	7 588	3 915	3 845	5 628	3 078	3 196	3 380	3 574
Composite, all undertakings	..	..	..	..	..	..	..	..
Total								
Domestic undertakings	9 624	5 225	5 034	6 884	4 053	4 066	4 276	4 505
Foreign controlled undertakings	1 489	610	592	629	497	466	476	539
Foreign companies (branches)	419	84	104	110	104	216	197	189
All undertakings	10 043	5 309	5 138	6 994	4 157	4 282	4 473	4 694
1.5 Insurance business written abroad by branches, gross premiums								
Life								
Branches and agencies	2 036	2 006	1 967	1 794	1 604	1 567	1 613	1 653
Subsidaries	..	..	..	..	..	..	..	..
Total	2 036	2 006	1 967	1 794	1 604	1 567	1 613	1 653
Non-life								
Branches and agencies	13 446	15 417	15 563	15 331	14 100	12 578	12 689	6 664
Subsidaries	..	..	..	..	..	..	..	..
Total	13 446	15 417	15 563	15 331	14 100	12 578	12 689	6 664
Composite total	..	..	..	..	..	..	..	..
Total								
Branches and agencies	15 482	17 423	17 531	17 125	15 704	14 145	14 302	8 317
Subsidaries	..	..	..	..	..	..	..	..
Total	15 482	17 423	17 531	17 125	15 704	14 145	14 302	8 317

.. Not available

Note: Detailed metadata at: *http://metalinks.oecd.org/ins/20200312/0b27.*

Source: OECD Insurance Statistics (database)

Table 2. Number of companies and employees

	2011	2012	2013	2014	2015	2016	2017	2018
2.1 Number of companies								
Life								
Domestic undertakings	20	19	19	18	17	16	16	16
Foreign controlled undertakings	1	1	1	1	1	1	1	1
Foreign companies (branches)	4	4	4	3	3	3	3	3
All undertakings	24	23	23	21	20	19	19	19
Non-life								
Domestic undertakings	79	81	80	79	76	74	73	70
Foreign controlled undertakings	6	6	6	6	6	5	5	5
Foreign companies (branches)	45	42	44	48	46	46	45	44
All undertakings	124	123	124	127	122	120	118	114
Composite, all undertakings	**0**	**0**	**0**	**0**	**0**	**0**	..	..
Reinsurance								
Domestic undertakings	62	61	62	62	59	55	55	54
Foreign controlled undertakings	7	7	7	7	7	7	6	6
Foreign companies (branches)	..	..	..	..	..	..	..	..
All undertakings	62	61	62	62	59	55	55	54
Total								
Domestic undertakings	161	161	161	159	152	145	144	140
Foreign controlled undertakings	14	14	14	14	14	13	12	12
Foreign companies (branches)	49	46	48	51	49	49	48	47
All undertakings	210	207	209	210	201	194	192	187
2.2 Number of employees								
Insurance undertakings	..	..	..	..	..	..	..	..
Intermediaries	..	..	..	..	..	..	..	..
Total	..	..	..	..	..	..	..	..

.. Not available

Note: Detailed metadata at: *http://metalinks.oecd.org/ins/20200312/0b27.*

Source: OECD Insurance Statistics (database)

TURKEY

Table 1. Selected aggregates

Million TRY

	2011	2012	2013	2014	2015	2016	2017	2018
1.1 Insurance business written in the reporting country								
1.1.1 Insurance business, by ownership								
Gross premiums								
Domestic undertakings	17 131	20 427	25 084	26 872	31 903	41 280	47 495	54 416
Foreign controlled undertakings	8 956	10 122	14 981	15 528	20 981	25 640	26 984	29 792
Foreign companies (branches)	32	46	68	77	126	152	201	304
All undertakings	17 164	20 473	25 152	26 949	32 029	41 431	47 696	54 720
Premiums ceded								
Domestic undertakings	4 287	4 483	6 077	6 686	7 984	9 816	13 268	15 814
Foreign controlled undertakings	2 229	2 192	3 458	3 510	4 773	5 482	6 672	7 850
Foreign companies (branches)	22	33	49	57	74	76	96	131
All undertakings	4 309	4 516	6 126	6 743	8 059	9 892	13 364	15 945
Net written premiums								
Domestic undertakings	12 845	15 944	19 006	20 186	23 919	31 464	34 227	38 601
Foreign controlled undertakings	6 728	7 931	11 522	12 018	16 208	20 158	20 312	21 942
Foreign companies (branches)	10	13	20	20	52	76	105	173
All undertakings	12 854	15 957	19 026	20 206	23 971	31 540	34 332	38 774
1.1.2 Insurance business on foreign risks, gross premiums								
Life	..	..	..	3 280	..	6 166	..	..
Non-life	..	..	..	22 711	..	34 322	..	..
Composite	..	..	..	958	..	943	..	..
of which:								
Life	..	..	..	24	..	19	..	..
Non-life	..	..	..	934	..	924	..	..
Total	..	..	..	26 948	..	41 431	..	..
1.1.3 Life insurance payments, by class, gross premiums								
Annuities	..	..	..	..	..	..	..	..
Unit linked	..	..	..	..	..	..	..	..
Other life insurance	..	..	..	..	..	..	..	..
Total life insurance	3 087	3 107	3 354	3 895	3 720	5 916	6 766	6 835
***of which:** Pension contracts*	..	..	..	..	..	..	..	..
1.1.4 Non-life insurance payments, by class, gross premiums								
Motor vehicle insurance	6 761	8 091	10 411	10 648	13 102	19 156	19 981	23 614
Marine, aviation and other transport insurance	268	263	253	321	423	455	490	706
Freight insurance	359	378	416	530	580	585	652	828
Fire and other property damage insurance	3 783	4 390	5 512	6 992	8 105	9 032	10 101	12 208
Pecuniary loss insurance	204	228	302	318	443	439	549	666
General liability insurance	386	420	508	679	811	863	1 028	1 389
Accident and health	2 657	2 897	3 352	4 010	4 685	4 582	6 708	8 051
***of which:** Health*	1 999	2 227	2 472	0	0	..	5 025	6 245
Other non-life insurance	77	61	74	147	99	134	226	167
Treaty reinsurance	..	..	..	..	0	..	..	..
Total non-life insurance	14 496	16 727	20 828	23 645	28 249	35 246	39 735	47 628
1.2 Gross claims payments								
Life								
Domestic undertakings	1 935	2 037	2 355	2 085	2 557	2 957	3 293	3 609
Foreign controlled undertakings	582	483	1 128	760	1 194	1 485	1 757	2 061
Foreign companies (branches)	..	..	..	..	..	0	..	0
All undertakings	1 935	2 037	2 355	2 085	2 557	2 957	3 293	3 609
Non-life								
Domestic undertakings	7 968	9 163	9 440	11 314	13 322	15 041	18 341	23 049
Foreign controlled undertakings	4 786	5 327	6 301	7 496	8 700	-9 940	11 648	13 543
Foreign companies (branches)	2	3	11	10	34	128	77	121
All undertakings	7 969	9 166	9 451	11 325	13 356	15 168	18 417	23 170
Composite								
Domestic undertakings	..	..	619	592	664	572	617	771
Foreign controlled undertakings	..	..	..	..	..	..	1	5
Foreign companies (branches)	..	..	..	..	..	..	..	..
All undertakings	0	721	619	592	664	572	617	771
of which:								
Life	0	6	7	11	6	9	15	7
Domestic undertakings	..	..	7	11	6	9	15	7
Foreign controlled undertakings	..	..	..	..	..	..	0	0
Foreign companies (branches)	..	..	..	..	..	..	..	..
All undertakings	0	6	7	11	6	9	15	7
Non-life	0	715	612	581	657	564	602	764
Domestic undertakings	..	..	612	581	657	564	602	764
Foreign controlled undertakings	..	..	..	..	..	..	1	5
Foreign companies (branches)	..	..	..	..	..	..	..	..
All undertakings	0	715	612	581	657	564	602	764
Total								
Domestic undertakings	9 903	11 200	12 413	13 991	16 543	18 570	22 251	27 430
Foreign controlled undertakings	5 369	5 810	7 429	8 256	9 894	-8 455	13 406	15 609
Foreign companies (branches)	2	3	11	10	34	128	77	121
All undertakings	9 905	11 924	12 425	14 001	16 578	18 698	22 328	27 551

Table 1. Selected aggregates *(cont.)*

Million TRY

	2011	2012	2013	2014	2015	2016	2017	2018
1.3 Commissions								
Life								
Domestic undertakings	..	..	..	..	..	..	..	..
Foreign controlled undertakings	..	..	..	..	..	..	..	..
Foreign companies (branches)	..	..	..	..	..	..	..	..
All undertakings	..	..	..	..	..	..	..	..
Non-life								
Domestic undertakings	..	..	..	..	..	..	..	..
Foreign controlled undertakings	..	..	..	..	..	..	..	..
Foreign companies (branches)	..	..	..	..	..	..	..	..
All undertakings	..	..	..	..	..	..	..	..
Composite								
Domestic undertakings	..	..	..	..	..	..	..	..
Foreign controlled undertakings	..	..	..	..	..	..	..	..
Foreign companies (branches)	..	..	..	..	..	..	..	..
All undertakings	..	..	..	..	..	..	..	..
of which:								
Life	..	..	..	..	..	..	..	..
Domestic undertakings	..	..	..	..	..	..	..	..
Foreign controlled undertakings	..	..	..	..	..	..	..	..
Foreign companies (branches)	..	..	..	..	..	..	..	..
All undertakings	..	..	..	..	..	..	..	..
Non-life	..	..	..	..	..	..	..	..
Domestic undertakings	..	..	..	..	..	..	..	..
Foreign controlled undertakings	..	..	..	..	..	..	..	..
Foreign companies (branches)	..	..	..	..	..	..	..	..
All undertakings	..	..	..	..	..	..	..	..
Total								
Domestic undertakings	..	..	..	..	..	..	..	..
Foreign controlled undertakings	..	..	..	..	..	..	..	..
Foreign companies (branches)	..	..	..	..	..	..	..	..
All undertakings	..	..	..	..	..	..	..	..
1.4 Gross operating expenses								
Life								
Domestic undertakings	836	978	2 009	1 198	1 595	1 970	2 644	2 961
Foreign controlled undertakings	361	422	1 242	765	1 033	1 241	1 724	1 926
Foreign companies (branches)	..	..	..	..	..	..	..	..
All undertakings	836	978	2 009	1 198	1 595	1 970	2 644	2 961
Non-life								
Domestic undertakings	2 859	3 230	3 726	4 309	4 648	5 579	6 263	6 689
Foreign controlled undertakings	1 827	1 976	2 564	2 944	3 110	3 847	4 170	4 183
Foreign companies (branches)	8	12	19	20	24	26	30	44
All undertakings	2 867	3 242	3 745	4 329	4 672	5 604	6 293	6 733
Composite								
Domestic undertakings	..	..	..	..	309	316	333	436
Foreign controlled undertakings	..	..	..	..	..	5	2	3
Foreign companies (branches)	..	..	..	..	..	..	..	..
All undertakings	0	285	294	289	309	316	333	436
of which:								
Life	0	8	10	8	10	10	5	8
Domestic undertakings	..	..	..	..	10	10	5	8
Foreign controlled undertakings	..	..	..	..	..	..	0	0
Foreign companies (branches)	..	..	..	..	..	..	..	..
All undertakings	0	8	10	8	10	10	5	8
Non-life	0	277	284	281	299	306	328	429
Domestic undertakings	..	..	..	..	299	306	328	429
Foreign controlled undertakings	..	..	..	..	..	5	2	3
Foreign companies (branches)	..	..	..	..	..	..	..	..
All undertakings	0	277	284	281	299	306	328	429
Total								
Domestic undertakings	3 694	4 209	5 735	5 507	6 552	7 865	9 240	10 087
Foreign controlled undertakings	2 188	2 399	3 806	3 708	4 143	5 092	5 895	6 112
Foreign companies (branches)	8	12	19	20	24	26	30	44
All undertakings	3 702	4 506	6 048	5 816	6 576	7 890	9 270	10 130

Table 1. Selected aggregates *(cont.)*

Million TRY

	2011	2012	2013	2014	2015	2016	2017	2018
1.5 Insurance business written abroad by branches, gross premiums								
Life								
Branches and agencies	..	..	..	..	..	..	..	..
Subsidaries	..	..	..	..	..	..	..	..
Total	..	..	..	..	..	..	..	..
Non-life								
Branches and agencies	..	..	..	..	..	..	..	..
Subsidaries	..	..	..	..	..	..	..	..
Total	..	..	..	..	..	..	..	..
Composite								
Branches and agencies	..	..	..	..	..	..	..	..
Subsidaries	..	..	..	..	..	..	..	..
Total	..	..	..	..	..	..	..	..
of which:								
Life	..	..	..	..	..	..	..	..
Branches and agencies	..	..	..	..	..	..	..	..
Subsidaries	..	..	..	..	..	..	..	..
Total	..	..	..	..	..	..	..	..
Non-life	..	..	..	..	..	..	..	..
Branches and agencies	..	..	..	..	..	..	..	..
Subsidaries	..	..	..	..	..	..	..	..
Total	..	..	..	..	..	..	..	..
Total								
Branches and agencies	..	..	..	..	..	..	..	..
Subsidaries	..	..	..	..	..	..	..	..
Total	..	..	..	..	..	..	..	..

.. Not available

Note: Detailed metadata at: *http://metalinks.oecd.org/ins/20200312/42c7.*

Source: *OECD Insurance Statistics (database)*

Table 2. Number of companies and employees

	2011	2012	2013	2014	2015	2016	2017	2018
2.1 Number of companies								
Life								
Domestic undertakings	24	23	24	25	23	22	22	22
Foreign controlled undertakings	14	13	16	16	15	15	15	15
Foreign companies (branches)	..	0	..	0	..	0	0	..
All undertakings	24	23	24	25	23	22	22	22
Non-life								
Domestic undertakings	33	33	34	36	36	35	37	36
Foreign controlled undertakings	23	22	22	24	22	23	23	20
Foreign companies (branches)	2	2	2	2	2	2	2	2
All undertakings	35	35	36	38	38	37	39	38
Composite								
Domestic undertakings	..	0	..	0	..	0	0	0
Foreign controlled undertakings	..	0	..	0	..	0	0	0
Foreign companies (branches)	..	0	..	0	..	0	0	0
All undertakings	..	0	..	0	..	0	0	0
Reinsurance								
Domestic undertakings	2	1	1	1	1	2	2	2
Foreign controlled undertakings	..	0	..	0	..	1	1	1
Foreign companies (branches)	..	0	..	0	..	0	0	0
All undertakings	2	1	1	1	1	2	2	2
Total								
Domestic undertakings	59	57	59	62	60	59	61	62
Foreign controlled undertakings	37	35	38	40	37	39	39	38
Foreign companies (branches)	2	2	2	2	2	2	2	2
All undertakings	61	59	61	64	62	61	63	62
2.2 Number of employees								
Insurance undertakings	10 123	17 304	18 297	19 305	19 274	19 240	19 883	19 117
Intermediaries	16 706	16 994	15 603	15 587	18 931	35 992	40 231	20 605
Total	26 829	34 298	33 900	34 892	38 205	55 232	60 114	39 722

.. Not available

Note: Detailed metadata at: *http://metalinks.oecd.org/ins/20200312/42c7.*

Source: OECD Insurance Statistics (database)

UNITED KINGDOM

Table 1. Selected aggregates

Million GBP

	2011	2012	2013	2014	2015	2016	2017	2018
1.1 Insurance business written in the reporting country								
1.1.1 Insurance business, by ownership								
Gross premiums								
Domestic undertakings	208 608	230 559	215 494	219 832	217 673	298 817	305 746	352 480
Foreign controlled undertakings	60 570	75 289	69 361	57 959	58 471	..	..	..
Foreign companies (branches)	3 204	2 735	2 237	2 407	2 741	247	471	400
All undertakings	211 811	233 294	217 731	222 239	220 414	299 064	306 217	351 620
Premiums ceded								
Domestic undertakings	24 305	28 545	27 456	33 780	24 299	68 763	36 758	68 170
Foreign controlled undertakings	7 946	8 285	9 270	11 048	10 801	0	..	..
Foreign companies (branches)	356	179	53	47	52	115	199	113
All undertakings	24 661	28 724	27 509	33 827	24 351	68 878	36 957	68 283
Net written premiums								
Domestic undertakings	184 303	202 014	188 038	186 052	193 374	230 054	268 988	284 310
Foreign controlled undertakings	52 623	67 004	60 091	46 911	47 670	..	..	..
Foreign companies (branches)	2 847	2 555	2 184	2 361	2 689	132	272	287
All undertakings	187 150	204 570	190 222	188 412	196 062	230 186	269 260	283 337
1.1.2 Insurance business on foreign risks, gross premiums								
Life	..	..	..	..	..	..	..	..
Non-life	..	..	..	..	..	..	..	..
Composite	..	..	..	..	..	..	..	..
of which:								
Life	..	..	..	..	..	..	..	..
Non-life	..	..	..	..	..	..	..	..
Total	..	..	..	..	..	..	..	..
1.1.3 Life insurance payments, by class, gross premiums								
Annuities	31 964	..	20 899	22 295	17 278	..	..	..
Unit linked	98 203	..	112 727	114 296	117 452	..	..	..
Other life insurance	14 777	..	9 393	11 834	10 622	..	..	..
Total life insurance	144 943	163 481	143 018	148 425	145 353	121 964	187 390	204 870
***of which:** Pension contracts*	125 482	143 813	104 333	132 542	128 601	..	..	..
1.1.4 Non-life insurance payments, by class, gross premiums								
Motor vehicle insurance	12 786	12 643	12 133	12 069	12 883	18 956	16 564	15 520
Marine, aviation and other transport insurance	3 513	3 634	3 805	3 098	2 604	9 395	9 610	10 636
Freight insurance	718	778	942	885	808	..	..	..
Fire and other property damage insurance	15 413	16 087	16 500	15 969	15 544	30 491	32 392	33 815
Pecuniary loss insurance	5 498	5 707	5 717	5 966	5 791	5 064	5 921	6 018
General liability insurance	8 561	8 750	10 218	10 593	10 308	16 201	16 585	18 635
Accident and health	6 907	7 287	7 895	7 662	7 821	10 872	13 590	15 548
***of which:** Health*	..	..	..	..	..	8 287	7 817	11 055
Other non-life insurance	2 815	2 442	2 859	2 962	3 177	2 407	2 341	2 497
Treaty reinsurance	..	..	..	..	..	..	..	..
Total non-life insurance	56 212	57 328	60 070	59 206	58 936	93 387	97 003	102 669
1.2 Gross claims payments								
Life								
Domestic undertakings	162 040	166 655	166 084	161 503	172 514	131 443	227 698	263 732
Foreign controlled undertakings	36 240	51 269	42 535	26 653	29 078	..	..	..
Foreign companies (branches)	5	4	-1	4	5	..	..	..
All undertakings	162 044	166 658	166 083	161 507	172 518	131 443	227 698	263 732
Non-life								
Domestic undertakings	31 223	30 566	33 152	32 079	30 897	30 260	32 185	30 902
Foreign controlled undertakings	15 499	16 160	17 593	17 062	16 387	..	..	..
Foreign companies (branches)	2 082	1 785	1 405	1 469	1 871	43	..	280
All undertakings	33 305	32 351	34 557	33 548	32 768	30 303	32 185	31 182
Composite								
Domestic undertakings	19 413	20 735	21 625	22 527	23 077	50 234	64 884	65 265
Foreign controlled undertakings	1 006	615	754	2 170	2 734	..	..	..
Foreign companies (branches)	880	1 729	0	0	0	..	..	..
All undertakings	20 293	22 464	21 625	22 527	23 077	50 234	64 884	65 265
of which:								
Life	19 063	21 386	20 366	21 254	21 794	23 337	30 083	31 495
Domestic undertakings	18 219	19 657	20 366	21 254	21 794	23 337	30 083	31 495
Foreign controlled undertakings	721	342	326	1 876	2 413	..	..	..
Foreign companies (branches)	845	1 729	0	0	0	..	..	..
All undertakings	19 063	21 386	20 366	21 254	21 794	23 337	30 083	31 495
Non-life	1 229	1 077	1 259	1 273	1 283	26 897	34 801	33 770
Domestic undertakings	1 194	1 077	1 259	1 273	1 283	26 897	34 801	33 770
Foreign controlled undertakings	284	273	428	294	321	..	..	..
Foreign companies (branches)	35	0	0	0	0	..	..	..
All undertakings	1 229	1 077	1 259	1 273	1 283	26 897	34 801	33 770
Total								
Domestic undertakings	212 675	217 956	220 861	216 108	226 488	211 938	324 767	359 899
Foreign controlled undertakings	52 744	68 043	60 882	45 885	48 198	..	..	..
Foreign companies (branches)	2 967	3 517	1 404	1 474	1 875	43	..	280
All undertakings	215 642	221 473	222 265	217 582	228 363	211 981	324 767	360 179

Table 1. Selected aggregates *(cont.)*

Million GBP

	2011	2012	2013	2014	2015	2016	2017	2018
1.3 Commissions								
Life								
Domestic undertakings	..	..	..	..	..	..	..	..
Foreign controlled undertakings	..	..	..	..	..	..	..	..
Foreign companies (branches)	..	..	..	..	..	..	..	..
All undertakings	..	..	..	..	..	..	..	..
Non-life								
Domestic undertakings	..	..	..	..	..	..	..	..
Foreign controlled undertakings	..	..	..	..	..	..	..	..
Foreign companies (branches)	..	..	..	..	..	..	..	..
All undertakings	..	..	..	..	..	..	..	..
Composite								
Domestic undertakings	..	..	..	..	..	..	..	..
Foreign controlled undertakings	..	..	..	..	..	..	..	..
Foreign companies (branches)	..	..	..	..	..	..	..	..
All undertakings	..	..	..	..	..	..	..	..
of which:								
Life	..	..	..	..	..	..	..	..
Domestic undertakings	..	..	..	..	..	..	..	..
Foreign controlled undertakings	..	..	..	..	..	..	..	..
Foreign companies (branches)	..	..	..	..	..	..	..	..
All undertakings	..	..	..	..	..	..	..	..
Non-life	..	..	..	..	..	..	..	..
Domestic undertakings	..	..	..	..	..	..	..	..
Foreign controlled undertakings	..	..	..	..	..	..	..	..
Foreign companies (branches)	..	..	..	..	..	..	..	..
All undertakings	..	..	..	..	..	..	..	..
Total								
Domestic undertakings	..	..	..	..	..	..	..	..
Foreign controlled undertakings	..	..	..	..	..	..	..	..
Foreign companies (branches)	..	..	..	..	..	..	..	..
All undertakings	..	..	..	..	..	..	..	..
1.4 Gross operating expenses								
Life								
Domestic undertakings	6 488	6 511	6 453	6 694	6 794	8 085	3 332	8 978
Foreign controlled undertakings	989	961	976	929	850	..	..	..
Foreign companies (branches)	1	1	0	1	1	..	..	..
All undertakings	6 489	6 512	6 453	6 695	6 795	8 085	3 332	8 978
Non-life								
Domestic undertakings	6 110	6 843	7 125	6 782	6 639	15 414	15 040	16 657
Foreign controlled undertakings	2 921	3 168	3 589	3 549	3 562	..	..	..
Foreign companies (branches)	152	200	167	174	186	59	117	119
All undertakings	6 262	7 044	7 292	6 956	6 825	15 474	15 103	16 776
Composite								
Domestic undertakings	1 936	1 856	1 978	2 127	2 325	16 675	18 958	18 816
Foreign controlled undertakings	261	195	172	277	328	..	..	..
Foreign companies (branches)	79	22	0	0	0	..	..	..
All undertakings	2 015	1 877	1 978	2 127	2 325	16 675	18 958	18 816
of which:								
Life	1 751	1 637	1 736	1 874	2 038	3 140	2 574	2 916
Domestic undertakings	1 709	1 616	1 736	1 874	2 038	3 140	2 574	2 917
Foreign controlled undertakings	156	102	91	185	211	..	..	..
Foreign companies (branches)	42	22	0	0	0	..	..	..
All undertakings	1 751	1 637	1 736	1 874	2 038	3 140	2 574	2 916
Non-life	264	240	242	252	287	13 535	15 088	15 899
Domestic undertakings	227	240	242	252	287	13 535	15 088	15 899
Foreign controlled undertakings	105	94	82	92	117	..	..	..
Foreign companies (branches)	37	0	0	0	0	..	..	..
All undertakings	264	240	242	252	287	13 535	15 088	15 899
Total								
Domestic undertakings	14 534	15 209	15 556	15 602	15 759	40 174	37 330	44 451
Foreign controlled undertakings	4 171	4 324	4 737	4 754	4 740	..	..	..
Foreign companies (branches)	233	224	167	175	187	59	117	119
All undertakings	14 767	15 433	15 723	15 777	15 946	40 234	37 393	44 570

UNITED KINGDOM

Table 1. Selected aggregates *(cont.)*

Million GBP

	2011	2012	2013	2014	2015	2016	2017	2018
1.5 Insurance business written abroad by branches, gross premiums								
Life								
Branches and agencies	..	..	..	..	..	..	..	..
Subsidaries	..	..	..	..	..	..	..	..
Total	..	..	..	..	..	..	..	..
Non-life								
Branches and agencies	..	..	..	..	..	..	..	..
Subsidaries	..	..	..	..	..	..	..	..
Total	..	..	..	..	..	..	..	..
Composite								
Branches and agencies	..	..	..	..	..	..	..	..
Subsidaries	..	..	..	..	..	..	..	..
Total	..	..	..	..	..	..	..	..
of which:								
Life	..	..	..	..	..	..	..	..
Branches and agencies	..	..	..	..	..	..	..	..
Subsidaries	..	..	..	..	..	..	..	..
Total	..	..	..	..	..	..	..	..
Non-life	..	..	..	..	..	..	..	..
Branches and agencies	..	..	..	..	..	..	..	..
Subsidaries	..	..	..	..	..	..	..	..
Total	..	..	..	..	..	..	..	..
Total								
Branches and agencies	..	..	..	..	..	..	..	..
Subsidaries	..	..	..	..	..	..	..	..
Total	..	..	..	..	..	..	..	..

.. Not available

Note: Detailed metadata at: *http://metalinks.oecd.org/ins/20200312/aed0.*

Source: OECD Insurance Statistics (database)

Table 2. Number of companies and employees

	2011	2012	2013	2014	2015	2016	2017	2018
2.1 Number of companies								
Life								
Domestic undertakings	184	184	183	181	181	74	75	69
Foreign controlled undertakings	15	15	15	14	14	..	..	..
Foreign companies (branches)	1	1	1	1	1	1	1	0
All undertakings	185	185	184	182	182	75	76	69
Non-life								
Domestic undertakings	242	234	227	214	209	168	165	153
Foreign controlled undertakings	107	104	99	92	89	..	..	..
Foreign companies (branches)	16	15	10	12	7	13	11	12
All undertakings	258	249	237	226	216	181	176	165
Composite								
Domestic undertakings	21	21	21	25	25	21	22	19
Foreign controlled undertakings	7	7	7	8	8	..	..	..
Foreign companies (branches)	2	2	2	2	2	1	1	1
All undertakings	23	23	23	27	27	22	23	20
Reinsurance								
Domestic undertakings	31	31	30	29	26	16	19	17
Foreign controlled undertakings	20	19	18	16	13	..	..	..
Foreign companies (branches)	2	2	2	2	3	0	0	1
All undertakings	33	33	32	31	29	16	19	18
Total								
Domestic undertakings	478	470	461	449	441	279	281	258
Foreign controlled undertakings	149	145	139	130	124	..	..	..
Foreign companies (branches)	21	20	15	17	13	15	13	14
All undertakings	499	490	476	466	454	294	294	272
2.2 Number of employees								
Insurance undertakings	..	..	..	..	..	..	..	..
Intermediaries	..	..	..	..	..	..	..	..
Total	..	..	..	..	..	..	..	..

.. Not available

Note: Detailed metadata at: *http://metalinks.oecd.org/ins/20200312/aed0.*

Source: *OECD Insurance Statistics (database)*

UNITED STATES

Table 1. Selected aggregates

Million USD

	2011	2012	2013	2014	2015	2016	2017	2018
1.1 Insurance business written in the reporting country								
1.1.1 Insurance business, by ownership								
Gross premiums								
Domestic undertakings	2 154 120	2 278 908	2 289 259	2 430 627	2 619 954	2 702 786	2 835 259	2 631 364
Foreign controlled undertakings	349 856	317 074	321 246	330 660	324 083	393 449	401 025	273 750
Foreign companies (branches)	731	909	662	696	1 129	1 007	1 034	920
All undertakings	2 154 851	2 279 817	2 289 921	2 431 323	2 621 083	2 703 793	2 836 293	2 632 284
Premiums ceded								
Domestic undertakings	560 386	601 133	657 662	609 531	713 961	743 307	810 265	429 234
Foreign controlled undertakings	170 330	140 316	175 424	134 223	139 675	195 708	226 256	108 845
Foreign companies (branches)	254	298	275	287	252	260	274	307
All undertakings	560 640	601 431	657 937	609 818	714 213	743 567	810 539	429 541
Net written premiums								
Domestic undertakings	1 593 733	1 677 776	1 631 597	1 821 096	1 905 993	1 959 479	2 024 995	2 202 129
Foreign controlled undertakings	179 526	176 758	145 822	196 437	184 408	197 742	174 769	164 906
Foreign companies (branches)	478	611	387	409	877	747	760	613
All undertakings	1 594 211	1 678 387	1 631 984	1 821 505	1 906 870	1 960 226	2 025 755	2 202 742
1.1.2 Insurance business on foreign risks, gross premiums								
Life	..	38 347	22 113	..	..	..	..	..
Non-life	..	..	..	..	..	..	..	..
Composite total	..	..	..	..	..	..	..	..
Total	..	38 347	22 113	..	..	..	..	..
1.1.3 Life insurance payments, by class, gross premiums								
Annuities	255 059	272 564	248 568	261 327	264 944	254 313	247 002	277 044
Unit linked	..	..	..	..	..	..	..	..
Other life insurance	811 561	557 259	533 515	527 280	561 674	581 948	612 083	632 578
Total life insurance	1 066 620	829 823	782 083	788 607	826 618	836 261	859 085	909 623
***of which:** Pension contracts*	..	..	..	..	..	..	..	..
1.1.4 Non-life insurance payments, by class, gross premiums								
Motor vehicle insurance	315 167	329 520	342 548	379 889	393 897	422 808	459 200	297 284
Marine, aviation and other transport insurance	3 337	3 545	3 245	3 070	2 911	4 815	2 732	2 187
Freight insurance	28 836	31 107	33 819	36 319	39 175	41 305	43 059	30 091
Fire and other property damage insurance	215 618	224 336	232 328	243 389	248 174	250 765	258 294	174 853
Pecuniary loss insurance	34 165	34 967	35 133	33 690	36 271	38 699	41 003	36 874
General liability insurance	172 997	183 263	191 562	204 069	208 722	211 362	218 298	144 286
Accident and health	516 841	550 291	566 173	646 938	714 394	761 509	799 804	803 339
***of which:** Health*	..	..	..	..	..	..	..	..
Other non-life insurance	3 018	3 179	3 505	3 780	3 728	3 921	4 493	3 716
Treaty reinsurance	0	..	..	0	0	0	..	..
Total non-life insurance	1 289 979	1 360 207	1 408 312	1 551 144	1 647 272	1 735 184	1 826 883	1 492 630
1.2 Gross claims payments								
Life								
Domestic undertakings	345 963	356 040	369 618	357 201	376 240	396 611	416 664	436 219
Foreign controlled undertakings	61 430	66 275	66 267	69 748	68 967	79 082	86 000	92 293
Foreign companies (branches)	0	0	0	0	0	0	0	0
All undertakings	345 963	356 040	369 618	357 201	376 240	396 611	416 664	436 219
Non-life								
Domestic undertakings	3 355 889	920 214	917 856	980 750	1 077 317	1 145 423	1 228 757	1 055 839
Foreign controlled undertakings	539 753	80 801	84 201	76 540	79 309	84 878	95 499	71 727
Foreign companies (branches)	2 253	723	234	240	359	504	609	649
All undertakings	3 358 142	920 937	918 090	980 990	1 077 676	1 145 927	1 229 366	1 056 488
Composite, all undertakings	..	..	..	..	..	..	..	..
Total								
Domestic undertakings	3 701 852	1 276 254	1 287 474	1 337 951	1 453 557	1 542 034	1 645 421	1 492 058
Foreign controlled undertakings	601 184	147 076	150 468	146 288	148 276	163 960	181 499	164 020
Foreign companies (branches)	2 253	723	234	240	359	504	609	649
All undertakings	3 704 105	1 276 977	1 287 708	1 338 191	1 453 916	1 542 538	1 646 030	1 492 707
1.3 Commissions								
Life								
Domestic undertakings	..	..	..	53 082	56 784	67 963	59 387	..
Foreign controlled undertakings	..	..	..	11 165	10 339	10 639	10 700	..
Foreign companies (branches)	..	..	..	0	0	0	0	..
All undertakings	..	..	..	53 082	56 784	67 963	59 387	..
Non-life								
Domestic undertakings	..	..	..	..	..	..	..	..
Foreign controlled undertakings	..	..	..	..	..	..	..	..
Foreign companies (branches)	..	..	..	..	..	..	..	..
All undertakings	..	..	..	..	..	..	..	..
Composite, all undertakings	..	..	..	..	..	..	..	..
Total								
Domestic undertakings	..	..	..	53 082	56 784	67 963	59 387	..
Foreign controlled undertakings	..	..	..	11 165	10 339	10 639	10 700	..
Foreign companies (branches)	..	..	..	0	0	0	0	..
All undertakings	..	..	..	53 082	56 784	67 963	59 387	..

Table 1. Selected aggregates *(cont.)*

Million USD

	2011	2012	2013	2014	2015	2016	2017	2018
1.4 Gross operating expenses								
Life								
Domestic undertakings	66 258	67 534	65 424	67 225	68 488	69 722	75 161	75 904
Foreign controlled undertakings	9 782	9 962	9 814	10 285	9 952	11 175	11 838	12 374
Foreign companies (branches)	0	0	0	0	0	..	..	0
All undertakings	66 258	67 534	65 424	67 225	68 488	69 722	75 161	75 904
Non-life								
Domestic undertakings	239 829	250 270	261 844	281 766	298 911	308 839	310 003	343 131
Foreign controlled undertakings	28 759	22 153	23 185	23 274	23 035	26 711	26 891	31 608
Foreign companies (branches)	283	312	165	194	410	354	360	300
All undertakings	240 112	250 582	262 009	281 960	299 321	309 193	310 363	343 431
Composite, all undertakings	..	..	..	..	..	..	..	..
Total								
Domestic undertakings	306 087	317 804	327 268	348 991	367 399	378 561	385 164	419 035
Foreign controlled undertakings	38 542	32 115	32 999	33 559	32 987	37 886	38 729	43 982
Foreign companies (branches)	283	312	165	194	410	354	360	300
All undertakings	306 370	318 116	327 433	349 185	367 809	378 915	385 524	419 335
1.5 Insurance business written abroad by branches, gross premiums								
Life								
Branches and agencies	..	..	..	..	..	..	..	..
Subsidaries	..	..	..	..	..	..	..	..
Total	..	..	..	..	..	..	..	..
Non-life								
Branches and agencies	..	..	..	..	..	..	..	..
Subsidaries	..	..	..	..	..	..	..	..
Total	..	..	..	..	..	..	..	..
Composite total	..	..	..	..	..	..	..	..
Total								
Branches and agencies	..	..	..	..	..	..	..	..
Subsidaries	..	..	..	..	..	..	..	..
Total	..	..	..	..	..	..	..	..

.. Not available

Note: Detailed metadata at: *http://metalinks.oecd.org/ins/20200312/652f.*

Source: OECD Insurance Statistics (database)

UNITED STATES

Table 2. Number of companies and employees

	2011	2012	2013	2014	2015	2016	2017	2018
2.1 Number of companies								
Life								
Domestic undertakings	904	904	995	1 031	1 030	738	735	715
Foreign controlled undertakings	168	162	156	158	158	168	157	157
Foreign companies (branches)	..	..	..	..	..	..	..	0
All undertakings	904	904	995	1 031	1 030	738	735	715
Non-life								
Domestic undertakings	3 426	3 428	3 425	3 404	3 185	3 205	3 419	3 430
Foreign controlled undertakings	388	407	403	404	390	418	405	399
Foreign companies (branches)	8	9	11	9	13	19	13	14
All undertakings	3 434	3 437	3 436	3 413	3 198	3 224	3 432	3 444
Composite, all undertakings	**0**	**0**	**0**	**0**	**0**	**0**	..	..
Reinsurance								
Domestic undertakings	251	250	247	234	354	221	228	235
Foreign controlled undertakings	73	62	65	64	76	52	44	48
Foreign companies (branches)	1	1	1	1	4	2	1	1
All undertakings	252	251	248	235	358	223	229	283
Total								
Domestic undertakings	4 581	4 582	4 667	4 669	4 569	4 164	4 382	4 380
Foreign controlled undertakings	629	631	624	626	624	638	606	604
Foreign companies (branches)	9	10	12	10	17	21	14	15
All undertakings	4 590	4 592	4 679	4 679	4 586	4 185	4 396	4 442
2.2 Number of employees								
Insurance undertakings	..	..	..	..	..	..	..	..
Intermediaries	..	..	..	..	..	..	..	..
Total	..	..	..	..	..	..	..	..

.. Not available

Note: Detailed metadata at: *http://metalinks.oecd.org/ins/20200312/652f.*

Source: *OECD Insurance Statistics (database)*

www.ingramcontent.com/pod-product-compliance
Ingram Content Group UK Ltd.
Pitfield, Milton Keynes, MK11 3LW, UK
UKHW051502290926
15471UKWH00008B/1373

9 789264 313132